The China Society Yearbook,
Volume 5

The Chinese Academy of Social Sciences Yearbooks: Society

Volume 5

BEIJING
2011

The China Society Yearbook, Volume 5

Chief Editors

Ru Xin, Lu Xueyi, Li Peilin

Deputy Chief Editors

Chen Guangjin, Li Wei, Xu Xinxin

BRILL

LEIDEN • BOSTON

2011

This book is printed on acid-free paper.

This yearbook is the result of a co-publication agreement between Social Sciences Academic Press and Koninklijke Brill NV. These articles were translated into English from the original 《年中国社会形势分析与预测》 *The China Society Yearbook, Volume 5* with financial support from China Book International, supported by the General Administration of Press and Publication and the Information Office of the State Council of China.

ISSN 1872-7239
ISBN 978 90 04 18250 9

MIX
Paper from
responsible sources
FSC® C008919

PRINTED BY AD DRUK BV - ZEIST, THE NETHERLANDS

CONTENTS

LIST OF FIGURES

LIST OF TABLES

PREFACE

Compiled by the Chinese Academy of Social Sciences' subject research group for the 'Analysis and Forecast of the Social Situation', the publication of The China Society Yearbook, Volume 5 is under our more than ten years consistent academic principles of precise and solemnness.

During our compiling, we are studying the likely features of Chinese social situations in 2009–2010, as following:

1. China is gradually getting rid of global financial crisis

China celebrated her 60th anniversary in 2009 with a splendid pageant. In 2009, China›s economic and social development profoundly influenced by the global financial crisis. To guarantee economic growth, value people›s livelihood and maintain social stability, Chinese government adopted a series of countermeasures to cope with the influences. By investigating the key indices of economic recovery, new job opportunities, consumption growth, China will take lead in getting rid of the shadow of the financial crisis and start a new stage of growth.

2. China starts a new stage of growth

The new stage requires China entering medium term of industrialization and urbanization, transforming the dual structure of town and country, realizing urban-ruralinteraction. At this stage, China is entering a new growing stage of people live in the era of expenditure of mass, popularizing higher education, building social security system for all people. The new stage of growth means China's annual economic growth will recover to 8% and above. The stage also means the driving force for china›s development at this phase will rely on upgrading the industrial structures, transforming the social and economic structures and stimulating domestic consumption demand.

3. Except for economic reform, China's reform policy starts to aim at overall restructuring

China's reform and opening policy has been carrying on for 30 years. During the period, the main task is reforming the economic system. However, the various changes are coming forth with the establishment of the socialist market economy system, which requires more reforms to the systems. The overall restructuring will firstly aim at the major issues, such about employment, division of income, education, health and medical system, social security, urban-rural administration system, public institution administration, and the community and social organization reform.

The authors of The China Society Yearbook, Volume 5 are from professional research and survey organs, universities and related governmental sections. Apart from the General Report, the views and angles expressed in the articles are only for the related author only, neither for the subject group, nor for the author's employer.

As the different resources and spots of statistics and investigations results, please double check before quotation.

The research to the subject is supported by Chinese Academy of Social Science (CASS). The Institute of Sociology at CASS is the organizer and facilitator of the subject research, is also the compiler of the General Report.

The Editors
November 21, 2009

ACKNOWLEDGEMENTS

The publication of The China Society Yearbook, Volume 5 gained the complex contributions of all aspects. Ru Xin, Lu Xueyi, Li Peilin, Chen Guangjin, Li Wei and Xu Xinxin, are collecting and compiling the materials and Ru Xin and Lu Xueyi are general report managers. Our heartfelt gratitude also goes to Mr. Xie Shouguang, the president of the Social Sciences Academic Press, and Deng Yonghong, Zheng Yan, Qin Jinghua of Annual Report Publication Center at SSAP, and also Qiu Yang and Guo Rongrong of the International Publishing Center at SSAP. Additional thanks are also to Liu Baiju ,the academic secretary of Bureau for Scientific Research at CASS.

We especially would like to thank our innumerable friends all over the world for their earnest support of this book's publication, and their interest in China's social development. We thank the excellent work that was done by our precise and diligent translators, Liu Maomin. Further, the appreciations also go to Michelle Wan, the English polisher and reviewer of the book.

The Editors
December 20, 2010

LIST OF CONTRIBUTORS

CHEN Guangjin (陈光金) is Researcher and Assistant Chief of the Institute of Sociology, Chinese Academy of Social Sciences.

CHEN Lan (陈兰) is Assistant Researcher at the Institute of Labor Science, Ministry of Human Resources and Social Security.

DENG Dasheng (邓大胜) and Xue Shu (薛姝) are Associate Researchers of the Chinese Academy of Science and Technology for Development.

FAN Ping (樊平) is Associate Researcher at the Institute of Sociology, Chinese Academy of Social Sciences. His primary research area is sustainable development of rural areas. He obtained his MA from CASS in 1987.

FAN Zaiqin (樊在勤), SONG Erdong (宋尔东) and YAN Congbing (严从兵) are from the General Office of the Ministry of Public Security.

GU Xin (顾欣) is Professor of the School of Government, Peking University.

HUANG Yanfen (黄燕芬) is Professor of the School of Public Policy and Management, Renmin University of China.

LI Peilin (李培林) is Researcher and Chief of the Institute of Sociology, Chinese Academy of Social Sciences.

LI Yinhe (李银河) is Researcher at the Institute of Sociology, Chinese Academy of Social Sciences.

LI Yu (李宇) is Associate Professor of the Capital University of Economics and Business, and is mainly engaged in the research on the basic theory of social security, the social security fund management and the social insurance calculation.

Li Xiaozhuang (李晓壮) is doctoral student of the Beijing University of Technology.

Lin Fan (林帆) is doctoral student of the School of Public Policy and Management, Renmin University of China.

Lu Qingzhe (吕庆喆) is Director and Senior Statistician at the Research Office, the Institute of Statistical Science, National Bureau of Statistics of China.

Lu Xueyi (陆学艺) is Honorary Member of the Academic Division of Law, Social and Political Sciences, Chinese Academy of Social Sciences, and Researcher of the Institute of Sociology.

Ma Ying (马缨) and He Guangxi (何光喜) are Associate Researchers of the Chinese Academy of Science and Technology for Development.

Mo Rong (莫荣) is Assistant Chief and Researcher at the Institute of Labor Science, the Ministry of Human Resources and Social Security; Director of Academic Committee, Expert of Chinese employment issues; and President of Enterprise Human Resources Commission, China Association for Labor Studies.

Qian Yong (钱勇) is Director of the Research Office, the General Office of Ministry of Environmental Protection.

Qiao Jian (乔健) is Director and Associate Professor of the industrial relations department at the China Institute of Industrial Relations. His major research interests include: employee demographics, industrial relations and the theory of labor unions. He has lectured on several papers, including: "Generalities of Industrial Relations", "The Situation of Employees in China", "Labor Policy", and "The Psychology of Labor".

Song Guokai (宋国恺) and Hu Jianguo (胡建国) are Lecturers of Beijing University of Technology.

Wang Fayun (王发运) is from the Social Insurance Administration Center, Ministry of Human Resources and Social Security, and mainly studies the social security.

YAN Shihui (闫世辉) is Researcher of the Chinese Academy for Environmental Planning, Ministry of Environmental Protection.

YANG Dongping (杨东平) is Chief and Professor at the Institute for Educational Research, the Beijing Institute of Technology; Executive Vice-chairman of the Tao Xing-Zhi Research Association of China, and Chief of the 21st Century Education Research Academy, and is mainly engaged in the research on the educational theory, the educational public policy and the higher education.

ZHANG Liping (张丽萍) is Assistant Researcher at the Institute of Sociology, Chinese Academy of Social Sciences.

ZHANG Yi (张翼) is Researcher of the Institute of Population and Labor Economics, Chinese Academy of Social Sciences.

ZHAO Liwei (赵立卫) is Associate Researcher at the Institute of Labor Science, Ministry of Human Resources and Social Security.

ZHAO Yandong (赵延东) is Researcher of the Chinese Academy of Science and Technology for Development.

A NEW GROWTH STAGE OF DEVELOPMENT
—Analysis and Forecast of China's Social Development in 2009–2010

Li Peilin and Chen Guangjin

In 2009, China took great efforts to overcome the influences of the international financial crisis. They took progressive steps to restore the economy and enter a new growth stage of economic and social development, and during the later stage of the crisis achieved new development opportunities and power. The new China's 60th anniversary celebration and brilliant military parade in Tiananmen Square exhibited China's great achievements during its 60-year construction, reflected huge changes since reform and opening for more than 30 years, and also indicated a new starting point of development for next 30 years.

I. *General Situation of Social Development in 2009*

In 2009, China released a series of important measures to guarantee growth, livelihood of the people, and stability, which effectively resisted the impact of international financial crisis. Annual GDP growth was above 8%, and the economic structure was further optimized; the urban and rural residents' incomes were increasing stabilized, and the rate of increase in the overall price level of customer's expenses reached about 4%; more than 11 million people obtained employment in cities, and the tension of employment was under control.

A. *Economic Growth Returns to a Stable State*

In the first three quarters of 2009, China's GDP reached 21,781.7 billion yuan, calculated according to fixed prices. This was an increase of 7.7% from the previous year, the speed of growth continued to rise season by season, reaching 6.1% in the first quarter, 7.9% in the second quarter and 8.9% in the third quarter, the annual growth surpassing 8%. In September 2009, China's Purchasing Manager's Index

(PMI) rose to 54.3%. For seven continuous months, it had been above 50%, and in May 2008, reached its peak, which indicated a situation of expansion in the manufacturing industry. At the same time, the employee index for the manufacturing industry was 53.2% in September, and for four continuous months had been above the critical point. This indicates that labor demand further increased as the manufacturing industry returned to a state of stability.

In the first three quarters of 2009, overall investments reached 15,505.7 billion yuan, which was an 33.4% increase from the previous year. The national fiscal levy decreased the tax burden on enterprises, and under the backdrop of promoting growth the economic downturn was reversed. From May to September, for five continuous months, there was economic growth. For the first three quarter of 2009, the total national financial revenue was 5,151.887 billion yuan, which was a 5.3% increase from the previous year.

Agriculture and rural economy steady developed. In 2009, annual grain production reached a new record, a continuous 6-year production increase for the first time in nearly 40 years, and total output of summer grain crops amounted to 246.7 billion *jin* (1 *jin* = ½ kilogram). Through prompt and initiative market regulation, which implemented the lowest purchasing price for grain crops and increased national revenue and reserves and so on, farm prices after a plentiful harvest was effectively stabilized to guarantee farmers' increase in production and income.

B. *Sustained Increase of Urban and Rural Residents' Income and Expenses*

In the first three quarters of 2009, average disposable income per town resident was 12973 yuan, which was a 9.3% increase from the previous year, and without price factor actually increased 10.5%. Average money income per rural resident was 4307 yuan, which was an 8.5% increase from the previous year, and without price factor actually increased 9.2%. In the first three quarters, rural resident's income fell 11.1 percentage points from the previous year, and in recent 6 years, it was estimated that average net income per farmer would increase by about 6%.

In order to stabilize the increase in farmer's income, in 2009 the central financial institution budgeted 716.14 billion yuan in funds to support and benefit farmers, which was a 20.2% increase, and especially increased the subsidy strength for farmers, and four kinds of subsidies directly impacting grain, for agricultural materials, for improved variety and for the purchase of farm machinery and for implementation. This reached approximately 123.08 billion yuan.

With the increase of residents' income, personal savings and expenses all increased. In terms of personal savings, from January to September 2009, balance of personal deposits increased from 246,872.25 trillion yuan to 259,615.94 trillion yuan, which in nearly a 2.3 trillion yuan increase. The increase of expenses was more obvious. In the first three quarters of 2009, total volume of retail sales of social consumables reached 8,967.6 billion yuan, which was a 15.1% increase from the previous year, and without price factor, real growth was 17.0%, which was a 2.8 percentage point increase from the previous year. Among them, the urban retail turnover of consumables was 6,101.3 billion yuan, which was a 14.8% increase; the retail turnover of consumables at the county-level and below was 2,866.3 billion yuan, which was a 16.0% increase.

The expense increase played an influential role in economic growth and recovery. According to calculations, in the first three quarters of 2009, total consumption contributed 4 percentage points to the GDP growth rate.

C. *The Employment Situation is Stabilized and Better than Predicted*

In the first three quarters of 2009, overall, the employment situation in China is stabilized. The ratio between post vacancies and number of job-seekers continually rose in the labor market, employee demand increased, and the number of people who newly obtained employment increased to 8.51 million in cities; the unemployed registered in cities reached 9.15 million, registered unemployment rate was 4.3%, about 4.02 million laid-off workers obtained re-employment, and 1.20 million people who had difficulty obtaining employment found employment. It was anticipated that employment levels would be the same as the previous year throughout the whole country, that is, above 11 million persons.

In order to deal with the tensions that resulted from the financial crisis, from the end of September 2008 to the beginning of February 2009, the State Council and other related departments drafted and implemented a series of polices to stabilize the economy and expand employment, one being a policy to accelerate peasants and college graduates in finding employment. Statistics indicated that within the first half of 2009 two measures were implemented in the entire country that directly reduced the burden to enterprises by 16.6 billion yuan.

The employment status of peasant workers was obviously better than predicted in the beginning of the year. In February 2009, about 20 million peasant workers lost their job and returned to their native village earlier than anticipated, before the Spring Festival, because of the financial crisis. 80% of the 70 million peasant workers who returned to their native village before the Spring Festival returned to the cities after the Spring Festival, but 11 million of them only found temporary jobs after the Spring Festival. With the economic resurgence, peasant workers' employment status obvious changed for the better in comparison to June, and in some cities along the southeastern coast, even difficulties recruiting enough workers became a problem. In regards to peasant workers' work status, according to a direct report from the Ministry of Human Resources and Social Security detailing 250 administrative villages, compared to the number of peasant workers who went to other places for work from August to September 2008, until the end of October 2009, peasant workers who returned to cities reached about 97%. Up to the end of the third quarter in 2009, for the whole country, in total 151,980,000 rural laborers went to other place to work, which was 1.01 million more people than at the end of the second quarter, and increased 0.7%. The National Bureau of Statistics of China surveyed the situation, where nearly 200,000 rural workers from the 31 provinces across the country (autonomous regions, municipalities) go to other places for work. During the first three quarters of 2009, the influx of workers who went to western areas for work continually increased, by a margin of 4.7%. The increase rate of rural workers finding employment in this region was the quickest. Looking at income changes for peasant workers, labors who worked in the western area had an average income of 1382 yuan/month, which was a 57 yuan increase, a 4.3% growth, and the increase range was 1.1 percentage point higher in comparison to laborers who went to central regions, and 1.8 percentage points higher than the those who went to eastern areas.

Graduates' employment situation was basically stable, and through the implementation of a series of measures that promoted the employment of graduates, graduates' employment status was also better than predicted. According to statistics from the Ministry of Education, by September 1, 2009, graduates' employment rate reached 74%. But, according to investigations, under the influence of a sluggish market, average wage for entry-level jobs, and in many cases, graduates from popular fields of study had difficulty obtaining employment.

D. *Rapid Advancement in Establishment of Social Security System Covering Cities and Rural Areas*

The establishment of urban and rural medical insurance system has made prominent progress. During the middle of 2009, the Central Committee issued "Opinions of the CPC Central Committee and the State Council on Deepening the Reform of the Medical and Health Care System" (hereinafter referred to as the "Medical Reform Opinions").[1] Basic medical insurance system for city residents was promoted and the problem concerning medical insurance for retirees from closed and bankrupt enterprises made breakthrough progress. According to the requirements of "Medical Reform Opinions", in the next three years, all levels of governments will invest 850 billion yuan into the medical and health care system, and the central financial institution will invest 331.8 billion yuan. During the first half of 2009, the number of urban employees and residents who bought medical insurance reached 336 million, rural populations who participated in the new rural cooperative 6medical service reached 830 million, together surpassing 1.16 billion people. During the expansion of medical insurance coverage, the standard of medical insurance also gradually improved; city residents' medical insurance and the new rural cooperative medical insurance, in comparison to the current rates, increased in deductibles, and the reimbursement proportion for hospitalization also increased by above 5 percentage points from the previous year.

The establishment of retirement insurance has taken new steps. On September 1, 2009, the State Council officially promulgated "Guiding Opinions on Launching New Rural Social Endowment Insurance," and requested that by the end of 2009, experiments of new rural social endowment insurance must cover about 10% of counties (cities) across the country. The new rural social endowment insurance has changed, from insurance premium previously being paid mainly by farmers into a combination of individual payment, collective subsidy

---

[1] See Opinions of the China Insurance Regulatory Commission on the Insurance Industry's Further Implementation of the Medical Reform Opinions and Active Participation in the Establishment of a Multi-level Medical Security System, at http://www.lawinfochina.com/law/display.asp?ID=7872&DB=1.

and government subsidy, especially from the central financial institution, which gave funds to the local security system in order to directly subsidize farmers. This was a significant policy in benefiting farmer after the country had abolished the agricultural tax, and had implemented a series of policies to benefit farmers with direct subsidy and the new rural cooperative medical service. After the new rural endowment insurance system was built, farmers could enjoy individual account pensions and support by national funds through generalized preferences. In the construction of urban endowment insurance system, the state released provisional measures on basic endowment insurance for urban enterprise employees, which raised the integration level of countrywide urban endowment insurance system. So far, 25 provinces have implemented provincial-level planning of endowment insurance. The state also released measures concerning peasant workers, and it stipulated that peasant workers who work in cities and have established labor relations with employers should buy basic endowment insurance. This was also an important step to unify the national endowment insurance system.

The construction of urban and rural minimum social security system was unceasingly developing. By July 2009, a total of 22.328 million people from 11.205 million households from all cities obtained minimum social security; in rural areas, a total of 45.34 million people from 21.416 million households likewise obtained minimum social security.

E. *Improvement in Public Order Guarantees Harmony and Stability*

In 2009, China increased its crackdown on criminal activities, creating an environment of good social order for the new China's 60th anniversary. From January to October 2009, altogether, public security organs of the whole country registered 4,443,000 criminal offense cases, which was a 14.8% increase from the previous year. Meanwhile, public security organs further enlarged the crackdown on organized crime; from January to October 2009, a total of 45,000 criminal groups were ferreted out, which was a 3.1% decrease from the previous year. Organized crime was greatly reduced in scope, and the prominent tendency of organized crime has been obviously restrained.

During the 60th anniversary celebration for the new China, many volunteers participated in maintaining social order, creating a new dimension to mass prevention and mass treatment of organized crime, and raising the level of society's sense of security.

F. *Anti-Corruption and Crackdown on Gangs has Obtained Widespread Support*

In 2009, the state further increased its anti-corruption work strength, a new round of anti-corruption cases was undertaken, and a batch of major and serious cases was investigated and dealt with accordingly, which showed the determination and courage of the Central Committee on anti-corruption. The rectification strength of commercial bribery has increased; from January to June 2009, nationwide prosecutorial organizations altogether registered, investigated and dealt with 6277 cases of commercial bribery and 6842 people, and in total 918 million yuan was involved in these cases. 797 cadres at division chief level or above, who were suspects in serious cases, were investigated and dealt with accordingly (including 46 persons at the level of director-general of a department). According to the global corruption perception index issued by "Transparency International" in October 2009, China was ranked 72nd. This is the third year in which China's ranking has shown improvement.

Crackdown on organized crime was a serious matter in 2009. In July 2009, the state started a new round of special campaign for crackdown on gangs and criminals throughout the whole country; this was the third round of anti-criminal campaign since the nationwide anti-criminal movement first started in 2000. During the anti-criminal campaign in 2009, the crackdown on organized crime in the city of Chongqing had the greatest effect. In June 2009, Chongqing destroyed 14 large-scale criminal gangs, arrested 1544 suspects, 469 escaped criminals were pursued and captured within and beyond the boundaries, and a batch of business owner involved in gangs was caught. So far, Chongqing prosecutorial organizations has altogether registered to investigate and deal with 47 corruption cases of crime, 52 persons exposed in crackdown on gangs and criminal activities, 20 cadres at the prefectural division chief level and above, 10 cadres at department-level involved in serious cases, and 29 polices and 4 administrative law-enforcement officials involved in these cases. The anti-corruption and anti-criminal campaign was called "project of public aspiration," and has elicited great response in the whole country.

G. *Overall Stable and Positive Public Opinion and Public Attitude*

In 2009, China experienced the impact of the serious financial crisis, as well as had some large-scale events. These matters influenced public opinion as well as public attitude. However, overall, public opinion was rather positive, and public attitude remained relatively steady. With improvements in the economy and the 60th year anniversary celebration for the new China, positive influences to public opinion and attitude occurred.

Internet is the main emerging media to influence public opinion. According to investigations from the China Internet Network Information Center, by the end of June 2009, Chinese internet users reached 338 million, which is a 40 million people increase over 2008; the popularity index of the Internet reached 25.5%, which surpasses the average world level. The majority of comments from Internet users, regarding hot topics, have been rational and steady. The government also has sped up to respond to public opinion on the Internet, and from the Central government to local governments, they make feedback and accept public opinions on the Internet, a mechanism that the governments monitors.

According to findings from investigations, overall degree of satisfaction in living standards of urban and rural residents stabilized, almost obtaining a "quite satisfied" level; targets of some macroscopic factors such as the national economic position, the sense of pride for motherland, and the confidence in government management, etc. have widely risen; targets of the social security, and the carrying capacity of price fluctuation, etc. also increased. But confidence in future income increase and living standard improvement had a declining trend. The degree of satisfaction to personal economic position was still the most important factor in influencing city resident's attitude towards lifestyle.

II. *Obstacles to China's Social Development in 2009*

A. *Difficult Situation of Small and Medium-Sized Unemployment Pressure Still Severe*

Under the impact of international financial crisis, China's export trade sharply decreased, and development of small and medium-sized enterprises that can admit more employees was greatly affected. Although in 2009 the government has released a series of policies to help small and medium-sized enterprises escape difficulties, small and medium-sized enterprise still faced many difficulties, in areas such as financing, which greatly affected employment status. In the second quarter of

2009, data from research about labor markets of some cities showed that, for all job seekers, 50.4% were unemployed, 22.6% of total job seekers had never obtained employment, and the majority of others were 40–50 years old laborers. According to data, in the second quarter of 2009, the ratio between vacant posts and number of job-seekers for four age groups, 16–24, 25–34, 35–44 and 45 years old and above, was 0.8, 0.97, 0.90 and 0.85 respectively. It is evident the two groups that faced the biggest employment pressure was the young and the old. In 2009, there were 6.1 million college graduates. From the perspective of the supply-demand contrast in the labor market, the ratio between vacant posts and number of job-seekers reaching education level of junior middle school and below, at the senior high school, at the junior college, at the university, and at the master and above was 0.98, 0.89, 0.78, 0.71 and 0.71 respectively. This showed that the higher the educational level, the more difficult to obtain employment. Moreover, from the same set of data, 9.6% of the unemployed who sought employment were college graduates. Therefore, it is predicated that college graduates will face great pressure in finding employment in the future.

B. *Income Gap Remains an Issue, and Expanding Domestic Demand Faces Difficulties*

In looking at income, the situation in 2009 was different from the two previous years, namely the growing disparity between rate of increase for urban and rural residents' incomes. In 2009, a 4–5 percentage point difference existed between rate of increase in disposable income for urban and rural residents. The average disposable income per urban resident increased 8.4% in 2008, the average net income per rural resident increased 8.1%, the rate of urban and rural residents' income increase maintained balance, and the ratio between urban and rural residents' income dropped from 3.33:1 in 2007 to 3.31:1 in 2008, a drop which in the prior decade never occurred. But, in 2009, under the impact of the international financial crisis, farmers' income from their work or business in other places was greatly impacted. Increase in farmers' income was in general affected, therefore, the ratio between urban and rural residents' income and the gap between the rates of increase widened.

Although in the first three quarters of 2009, total volume of retail sales of the social consumables grew 17% over previous year, which was a 2.8 percentage points increase from the previous year, this was not yet applicable for the requirement of expanding domestic demands. According to investigations, the rule where income increases and decreases in Chinese families' consumption proportion, excessively low consumption rate of mid- and low-income families and excessively high savings tendency were due to restrictions on their incomes and influenced by large quantities of anticipated expense, such as for children's education, medical services and housing and so on, therefore adjusting the income distribution structure and consummating the social security system are important condition to expanding domestic demand. At present, China's economic growth mainly depends on investments, and in order to change the method of economic development, the issue of excessively low resident consumption rates must be addressed.

C. *Strained Labor Relations Lead to Frequent Labor Disputes*

Under the impact of international financial crisis, increased employment pressure also influenced labor relations. In the first half of 2009, in just the judicial sector of the whole country 170,000 cases of labor dispute were accepted, which was a 30% increase from the previous year. Moreover, cases of labor dispute have been the quickest to increase, touch upon the most extensive range, and have the deepest influence and receive the most social attention in civil cases accepted in the judicial sector of the whole country. The increase in cases was obvious especially in certain areas. In some southeast coastal provinces, the range of increase in cases of labor dispute arbitration and accepted in the courts was the lowest being above 40%, and the highest 1.5 times as much.

Peasant workers aroused the most labor disputes, and their rights consciousness strengthened day by day. Compared to the past, in 2009, the emphasis on peasant workers' rights changed from back pay to social security. The reality of the endowment insurance policy concerned them the greatest, and the proportion of labor dispute cases initiated as a result has rapidly increased all cases of labor dispute. Generally speaking, nationwide, the phenomenon of peasant workers' wages in arrears was greatly reduced. Therefore peasant workers' no longer sought for salary benefits but for long term security, and with the first generation of peasant workers, who entered the labor market in the 1980s, reaching retirement age soon, this problem will continue to be heightened.

D. Widespread *Group Incidents, and Short-Paid Environmental Protection Initiates More Events*

In 2009, appeal to higher officials and group incidents continue to increase, especially major events. For example, the Hubei Shishou group event occurred on June 17, 2009, the Jilin Tonghua Iron & Steel Group Co. Ltd. group event on July 24 and the Shanxi Luliang Coal Mine group event on October 12; they all have had widespread social influence. Some belonged to "the immediate interest group event" caused by infringing upon the benefits of employees and the mass, and some belonged to "non-immediate interest group event" caused by social dissatisfaction. The demands of most group events gave priority to the livelihood of the people and economic interests, such as the promotion of labor welfare treatment, the enhancement of immigration compensation standard, the objection of enterprise environmental pollution, the investigation of responsibilities of medical service, the pursuit of compensation, and so on.

It is especially noteworthy to point out, in recent years, group events initiated by environmental pollution have increased annually by the average speed of 29%, where the resistance degree was obviously higher than other group events as a whole. In the first three quarters of 2009, several events regarding environmental protection was brought to the attention of the entire country. Among them, some were quite prominent; for example, (1) in the Shanxi Fengxiang blood lead poisoning incident, 851 people had blood lead that exceeded the allowed figure. 174 children of moderate and serious lead poisoning had to be hospitalized for lead elimination treatment; (2) in the Inner Mongolian Chifeng water pollution incident, 4020 people needed to accept outpatient services because of the water pollution incident in the new city zone of the city. 88 people had to be hospitalized for examination; (3) in the Hunan Wugang children blood lead poisoning incident. More than 80 children had symptoms of blood lead exceeding the allowed figure, with 38 people having high lead blood symptom, 28 people with mild poisoning and 17 people with moderate poison. According to analysis from environmental protection departments, in ten serious events of environmental protection that occurred since the 21st century, six occurred unexpectedly in 2009. In addition, the group events that occurred in 2009 also assumed another important characteristic, namely collective action to achieve demands, such as "collective walking", "collective shopping", "collective drinking tea" and "collective resting," etc.

E. Frequent *Criminal Offense in the Economy, and Rampant Illegal Multi-Level Marketing*

In 2009, the aggregate of criminal offense was still high, new crimes increased unceasingly, and the intellectualization, violence and organization characteristics of crimes got increasingly prominent, especially crimes of gangs, serious violent offense,s network cheating crimes and frequent crimes of infringing upon wealth, etc. These have severely imperiled public safety and destroyed economic and social order. Moreover, under the impact of the international financial crisis and of the global economic depression, violent dunning, kidnapping and open plundering initiated by economic disputes got more prominent, and cases of crime infringing upon wealth and illegal financing increased obviously.

In addition, among topics greatly discussed in 2009 regarding problems of public security that involved economic and social order, illegal multi-level marketing was most prominent. Although it had existed for a long time, under current tensions in the employment situation, illegal multi-level marketing became increasingly widespread, and those impacted grew in numbers. Therefore it has been called "the economic cult" in society. In several southern county-level cities, the number of multi-level marketing personnel assembled surpassed one million, and heads of some multi-level marketing organizations also organized more than ten thousand multi-level marketing personnel to besiege law-enforcement officials and relevant governmental agencies.

F. *National Security Becomes Increasingly Complex, and Activities of Oversea Hostile Forces Intensified*

On the eve of new China's 60th anniversary celebration, separatist activity instigated by overseas hostile forces obviously intensified. On July 5, 2009, after the beating, smashing, looting and burning incident that occurred in Lhasa of Tibet, under planning and instigation from overseas racial separatist forces and the organization of "three

influences" in China, serious violent offense event of beating, smashing, looting and burning occurred in Urumqi, Xinjiang. The event
caused the death of 197 people and injured 1786 people, which badly
impacted social harmony and stability.

III. *China Enters New Growth Stage After the International Financial Crisis*

From key indicators of economic and social development, including economic resurgence, employment recovery, consumption growth
and price stability etc., China will take the lead in getting rid of the
shadow from the international financial crisis, and in entering a new
round of the growth cycle. But, from advancement in industrialization
and urbanization and the development phase of customer expenses,
China starts to enter a new growth stage after the international financial crisis. A new growth stage, on the one hand, means that China's
economic growth speed will increase by 8%. On the other hand, this
means that the driving force will be obviously different than the past,
and will rely more on upgrading the industrial structure, the transformation of economic and social structures and domestic consumption
growth. Some new characteristics assumed by this new growth stage
are very different than the characteristics in the past.

A. Industrialization *and* Urbanization *Advancement Enters Middle Period
of the New Growth Stage*

According to international experiences, if the value added of farm
drops 5% in GDP, the proportion of agricultural laborers drops 30%
in the employment structure, and urbanization level surpasses 50%,
it symbolizes significant transformation in economic and social structures. From the perspective of these structures, value of output structure, employment structure and town and country structure, they have
all entered the stage of structural transformation. In China's GDP, the
proportion of value added of farms will drop 10% in 2010 and about
6% in 2015; in the structure of employment, the proportion of agricultural laborers will drop 38% in 2010 and about 33% in 2015; in the
structure of town and country, the urbanization level represented by
the urban resident populations will reach about 48% in 2010, will surpass the critical point of structural transformation of 50% in 2012 or
in 2013 and will reach about 53% in 2015. These targets indicate that

China has entered the middle stage of industrialization and urbanization advancement as a whole, and the economic and social structure
will have profound transformation.

B. Changes in *Social Structure Breaks with the Dualistic Structure of Urban
and Rural Areas*

A long-term and prominent question of the non-balanced development in China is the dualistic structure of town and country and the
huge disparity between urban and rural development. Along with
industrialization and urbanization entering a new stage of structure
transformation, integration development of urban and rural areas
is required. Breaking with the dualistic structure of urban and rural
areas is to eliminate not only the barriers between modern industry
and traditional agriculture, but also gradually eliminate the barriers
between urban and rural areas in the social system, such as in employment, education, medical services, social security and household register. Breaking with the dualistic structure of urban and rural areas will
become a major feat, which will have profound influence in China's
development history.

C. *People's Lifestyle Enters a New Growth Stage of Mass Consumption*

In 2008, gross value of GDP was 30,067 billion Renminbi, total population was 1.328 billion, and average GDP per person 22640 Yuan.
Using the exchange rate between Renminbi and the US dollar on
December 31, 2008, this equates to 3313 US dollars; if GDP grows
8% in 2009, average GDP per person would amount to about 3500
US dollars. According to international practices, when per capita
income is more than 3000 US dollars, upgrading of resident expenses
becomes normality. Engel's coefficient of Chinese urban and rural
residents respectively reduced to about 37% and 43% in 2009. And
according to the standards of UN Food and Agriculture Organization,
it is observed that, as a whole the resident expense stage from comparatively well-off to ample was approaching. Large amount of household
consumption, such as housing and automobile purchases etc., became
increasingly popular; the expenditure proportion in the consumption of
education, medical services, communication, traveling and culture was
increasing rapidly. These characteristics indicate that China started to
enter the new growth stage of mass consumption as a whole.

D. *Higher Education Enters New Growth Stage of Mass Education*

China popularized 9-year compulsory education, and vocational education and degree education have also expanded rapidly; the gross enrollment rate of higher education reached about 24% in 2009. China's higher education has entered the popularization stage, and the educational level of the entire nation has obviously been enhanced. China is transforming from a big nation with the largest population and human resources into a powerful nation of human resources, and a new growth stage of mass education has come.

E. *Social Security Enters New Growth Stage of Extensive Coverage*

In recent years, expanding social security coverage has had fast progress. The minimum social security system covers urban and rural areas was established. The medical security system which gives priority to medical insurance for urban employees, medical insurance for urban residents and the new rural cooperative medical services, which essentially covers all people, was formed. And the retirement security system that covers urban and rural areas is rapidly advancing. In 2020, a social security system covering urban and rural areas based on three systems, basic endowment insurance, basic medical insurance, and minimum social security, will be formed. China has entered a new growth stage for social security system.

F. *From Economic Reform to Comprehensive Reform, Transition to a New Growth Stage*

In the 30 years of reform and opening up, although the reform was carried out in other domains along with economic system reform, economic reform was the focus. Presently, the socialist market economic system has essentially been established, but in order to keep up the economic reform, various other systems must also change. Thus, the reforms have expanded from the economic domain to cover other reforms. Currently, social reform concerning employment, income distribution, social security, urban and rural social construction, social management, institution operation, community and social organizations ought to be carried on first.

IV. *Development Trend and Primary Mission of the New Growth Stage*

In 2009, although social development was faced with many contradictions and problems, the economic situation obviously got better
because the international financial crisis was dealt with successfully,
and social development also made important progress in the direction
of coordinated development. In 2010, the Chinese economy and society will continue in the direction of economic and social coordinated
development.

A. *Transforming Development Pattern, and Further Restructuring of the Socio-Economic Structure*

The pattern of development must be transformed, first, from economic growth excessively depending on investments and exports to
depending on domestic consumption. The international financial crisis
tells us, a growth pattern that excessively depends on investments and
exports is not sustainable, and economic growth must be based on
the expansion of domestic consumption in the upcoming 30 years;
second, must be transformed from the quantitative expansion of low
cost economic growth to qualitative enhancement of increasing technical content, from "made in China" to "brand of China," and must
promote upgrading and renewing industries; third, from development
at the cost of resources and environment to development with resource
conservation and environmental protection in mind, and from the
impulse of mainly depending on the industry to depending more on
the modern service industry, and the low-carbon economy must be
vigorously developed.

In the execution of the 4 trillion yuan investment program, there
must be more emphasis placed on the livelihood of the people, especially in regards to employment, as well as urban, rural and regional
coordinated development, structural readjustment and independent
innovation, energy conservation, and discharge reduction and ecological construction. Mutual promotion between economic growth and
structural readjustment should be urged in order to bring about the
transformation of the national economy in dealing with the crisis.
The breaking of the dualistic structure of urban and rural areas must
be emphasized, and social development of urban and rural areas
must be strenuously promoted. The opportunity to expand domestic

demands should be utilized well so that policies and financial investments will have a disposition toward agriculture, farmers and the rural
areas, and thus bring about a huge market potential for rural areas.
Urbanization should be positively and safely promoted to form an
important impetus for economic growth.

B. *Readjustment of the Income Distribution Structure, and Unceasing
Improvement in Living Standards*

In the 30 years of reform and opening up, living standard has unceasingly been enhanced, but in recent years, the proportion of resident
income in the national income is decreasing, and in primary distribution, the proportion of labor income is decreasing, the resident family's consumption rate is decreasing, and the resident family's Engel's
coefficient is dropping slowly and fluctuates, which all have affected
the growth of domestic consumption. It is very important to unceasingly enhance residents' income and consumption level, not only for
the expansion of consumption and transformation of the pattern of
development, but also in order for the people to maintain a positive
social attitude and have a stable anticipated development.

Effective steps must be taken to reverse the trend in the widening income disparity; otherwise social conflicts will intensify and affect
social stability. Attention must be paid to the readjustment of the
income distribution structure to expand the medium-income group,
and to reduce the proportions of low-income earners and impoverished people. For the readjustment of income distribution structure,
not only does the proportional relationship between the payment for
labor and the capital income in primary distribution, and the proportional relationship among the income of country, enterprise and
resident in the national income need to be straightened out, but also
the leverage of finance, tax revenue, social security and social welfare,
etc. in the redistribution must be brought into play to vigorously push
the development of third distribution, such as philanthropy etc.

The readjustment of income distribution should be regarded as
a strategic measure for expanding domestic demand, for enhancing
living standards, for promoting common prosperity, and for maintaining social harmony and stability. We should further strengthen
people's livelihood, employment, social security, education, medical
service, housing in order to promote the equality of public service,

gradually eliminate people's worries, and stabilize residents' anticipated expenses.

C. *Small and Medium-Sized Enterprises Promoted, and Employment Expansion
and Freedom of the Labor Market Given Superiority*

Although China has entered a stage of industrial reform, China still
has a comparative advantage in labor in terms of the three essential
factors: capital, technology and labor, which promote economic and
social development. At present, small- and medium-sized enterprises
are the main channels in admitting laborers, and promoting development of small- and medium-sized enterprises is important in order
to solve the future employment problem. However, at the moment,
development of small- and medium-sized enterprises has not reached
its potential, where in developed countries, for every thousand people
there exist about 45 enterprises.

   In the future new growth stage, employment expansion, increase of
income, innovation encouragement, and social stability are important
responsibilities in the development strategy of promoting small- and
medium-sized enterprises. Therefore, there must be an increase support for small- and medium-sized enterprises, especially support their
innovative abilities, promote energy conservation and discharge reduction, enhance product quality, improve safety requirements in production, and drive employment. Policies concerning the market and the
legal system must be further consummated in order to alleviate the
financial difficulties of small- and medium-sized enterprises.

D. Speed Up *Development of the Social Security System and Comprehensive
Welfare Network*

Looking at the long run, in the next 10 years, the aging process will
change the downward trend of China's social dependency ratio and
the situation of full labor supply. Rapid changes to family structure will
also form become a serious challenge to China's tradition of younger
generation of a family providing for the older generation. The development of a social security system and welfare network covering all
the people are not only requirements to raise living standards and
expand domestic demands, but also to adapt to the changes of population and family structure and thus stabilize society.

In recent years, China's social security legal system has been rapidly advanced. In 2009, China issued "Plan on Recent Priorities in Carrying out the Reform of Health Care System (2009–2011)",[2] and requested that the basic medical security system cover all urban and rural residents within three years; promulgated "National Occupational Disease Control Program (2009–2015)", and planned that, by 2015, coverage of industrial injury insurance must reach 90% of workers who have labor relations; and also released "Guiding Opinions of the State Council on Launching New Rural Social Endowment Insurance," to push advancement of a new rural social endowment insurance. In 2010, "Measures on Transfer and Continuity of Endowment Insurance Relations" and "Measures on Peasant Workers Participating in Endowment Insurance," which have solicited the suggestions in public, should be released as quickly as possible, and "Law of Social Insurance" should especially be quickly released.

E. Vigorously *Pushing Equalization of Basic Public Services, and Quickening Integration Development of Urban and Rural Areas*

The imbalance of urban and rural development and the difficulties of developing rural consumption has always been a problem in expanding consumption and maintaining sustained economic growth. Currently, China has entered a new stage of eradicating the dualistic structure of urban and rural areas, and vigorously pushing for equalization of basic public services. Cultural awareness and skill of workers must be enhanced through investment increase to rural education; farmers' health status should be further improved through investment increase to rural medical and health services; the challenge of population aging and change in family structure should be dealt with through investment increase to the rural social security; farmers' cultural life should be improved through investment increase to rural cultural facilities; poverty should be further eliminated through support increase to rural low-income earners and the impoverished.

---

[2] See Notice of the State Council on Printing and Distributing the Plan on Recent Priorities in Carrying out the Reform of Health Care System (2009–2011), at http://www.lawinfochina.com/law/display.asp?ID=7414&DB=1.

F. *Establishing an Updated Social Operational, and Promoting Social Harmony and Stability*

In the present development phase, when institutional frictions and structural conflicts intermingle, and when unbalanced benefit and value conflicts coexist, besides rapidly raising the living standards of people, developing the livelihood of the people, readjusting the income distribution, consummating the social security system, etc., a social operational mechanism must be explored to meet the requirements of a new time and new stage.

The first is effective benefit coordinated mechanism. In some domains were conflicts of interest often occur, such as restructuring of enterprise, rural land-levying and urban and rural relocation, a mechanism of fair participation and just ruling, where many parties participate as well as a third party, must be established to avoid a one-man show of the government and to avoid control from other strong forces. The disadvantaged must not be infringed upon. This will reduce the possibility that hot spots of society cause conflicts of interest.

The second is elastic interest right-protection mechanism. Currently, people's rights consciousness has remarkable enhanced, but conflicts of interest always exist, therefore it is difficult to rely solely on basic-units of government to settle benefit contradictions and conflicts of interest. Various channels should be established for people to report interest demands. Trade union, the youth league, Women's Federation and all kinds of social organizations should be brought into play in serving people, in dealing with people's demands and in settling interest disputes, and an elastic right-protection mechanism should be constructed.

The third is reasonable interest compensation mechanism. Since the Reform, and in the past 30 years, development has been rapid, but the government, work units, enterprises and the collectives have also accumulated many historical problems. For these problems, we must, acting in a responsible manner, put forward certain funds to set up the compensation fund, and prominently settle a batch of prior debt problems in order to maintain social harmony and stability.

G. *Implementing Comprehensive Social Reform, and Strengthening Social Construction*

China's economic reform has provided strong social power for development. Social reform will also keep providing strong drive for development. Economic growth should depend more upon domestic demands through readjusting income distribution, reversing income disparity, and cultivating the ability of mass consumption. Through deepening social reform, strengthening social construction and consummating the social management system, the social systems that meet the requirements of a market economy and modern social mobility should be established to guarantee social harmony and stability. Through the reform of medical institution, educational systems and cultural organizations, the non-profit organization system that effectively runs and serves the public should be established. Through the development and consummation of social security systems, the welfare network should cover all people, and an insurance system must be built to avoid the risks brought by the market economy and social changes to the family. Grass-roots platform of public services should be built through the advancement of community development to settle social problems at the basic level. New channels that serve society, deal with demands, attract employment and control society should be established through the development of social organizations.

URBAN AND RURAL RESIDENTS' INCOME
AND CONSUMPTION IN 2009

Lu Qingzhe

I. *Urban and Rural Residents' Income Continue to Grow and Sources of Income Increase*

A. *Urban and Rural Residents' Income are Sustained and Rapidly Grow*

From January to September 2009, the disposable income per city resident was 12973 yuan, and without price factor, actually grew 10.5%; this was a 2.1 percentage points increase from the previous year. Average income per rural resident was 4306.5 yuan, and without price factor, actually grew 9.2%; this was a 1.8 percentage point drop from the previous year. Among urban and rural residents, wage income was 1493.0 yuan, which was a 9.9% increase from the previous year; household operation income was 2391.8 yuan, which was a 5.5% increase from the pervious year; property income was 112.9 yuan, which was a 11.8% increase from the previous year; and transfer income was 308.9 Yuan, which increased by 26.3% from the previous year.

B. *Urban and Rural Residents' Income Structure has Changed, and Sources of Income are Increasingly Diverse*

As urban and rural residents' income has rapidly grown, income structure has also changed. Wage income as the main body of urban residents' income accounted for 66.2% of gross wages in 2008, which was a 5.0 percentage point drop from 2000. Operational and property income increased, which became the majority of growth in urban residents' income, where the proportion of operational income was 8.5%, and property income was 2.3%, which increased 4.6 and 0.3 percentage points respectively from 2000.

Table 2.1: Changes of Urban Residents' Income Structure Unit: %

Items	In 2000	In 2001	In 2002	In 2003	In 2004	In 2005	In 2006	In 2007	In 2008
Total	100	100	100	100	100	100	100	100	100
Incomes from wages and salaries	71.2	69.9	70.2	70.7	70.6	68.9	68.9	68.7	66.2
Net operational income	3.9	4.0	4.1	4.5	4.9	6.0	6.4	6.3	8.5
Property income	2.0	1.9	1.2	1.5	1.6	1.7	1.9	2.3	2.3
Transfer income	22.9	23.6	24.5	23.3	22.9	23.4	22.8	22.7	23.0

Table 2.2: Changes of Rural Residents' Income Structure Unit: %

	In 2000	In 2001	In 2002	In 2003	In 2004	In 2005	In 2006	In 2007	In 2008
Net income	100	100	100	100	100	100	100	100	100
Wage income	31.2	32.6	33.9	35.0	34.0	36.1	38.3	38.6	38.9
Household operational income	63.3	61.7	60.0	58.8	59.5	56.7	53.8	53.0	51.2
Property income	2.0	2.0	2.0	2.5	2.6	2.7	2.8	3.1	3.1
Transfer income	3.5	3.7	4.0	3.7	3.9	4.5	5.0	5.4	6.8

As the crux of rural residents' income, the proportion of household operational income accounted for 51.2% of net income in 2008, which was a 12.1 percentage point drop from 2000; average wage income per rural resident was 1853.7 Yuan in 2008, which was 1.6 times that of 2000, and accounted for 38.9% of net incomes, which rose 7.7 percentage points from 2000. Wage income became an important source for farmers to increase their income. Rural residents' income amounted to 5737.0 yuan in 2008, which was 1.4 times 2381.6 yuan in 2000; cash income rate increased to 85.6%, which increased 9.9 percentage points over 75.7% in 2000. The increase of farmers' income, which strengthened the disposable ability of farmers, inevitably caused a change in income growth and expense growth for farmers. Farmer's production and life consumption further integrated into the cycle of the market economy cycle, which quickened income increase for farmers.

II. *Urban and Rural Residents' Consumption Level Distinctly Increased, and Consumption Pattern Obviously Optimized*

A. *Urban and Rural Residents' Consumption Level Distinctly Increased*

With rapid economic development, urban and rural residents' income greatly increased, average consumption expenditure per person grew largely, and consumption level increased. Average consumption level per resident was 8183 yuan in 2008, which was 1.25 times more than 3632 yuan in 2000, and without price factor, the average yearly increase was 7.8%. Among them, average consumption level per rural resident was 3756 yuan, which was 2 times more than 1860 Yuan in 2000, and without price factor, the average yearly increase was 5.6%; consumption level per urban resident was 13,526 yuan, which increased 97.5% over 6850 Yuan in 2000, and without price factor, increased about 6.4% yearly.

Through five groupings of income, we can observe rural residents' personal consumption level (without regard to price factor), from 2000 to 2008, rapidly increased as a whole, and the average personal consumption growth rate surpassed 10% per year, although resident consumption level of different income groups had differences. Among them, average personal consumption expenditure per person of the low-income group was 977 yuan in 2000, and increased to 2145 yuan by 2008, which was a 10.33% annual growth. The medium-income group's average personal consumption expenditure per person grew from 1501 Yuan to 3286 Yuan, which was a 10.29% annual growth. For the high-income group, average personal consumption expenditure per person grew from 3086 Yuan to 6854 Yuan, which was about a 10.49% annual growth.

Through five groupings of incomes, we can observe urban residents' consumption level (without regard to price factor). From 2000 to 2008, resident consumption level of different income groups had differences, but in each group, average personal consumption expenditure growth rate per year of each group gradually increased. Among them, average personal consumption expenditure per person of low-income families was 2899.1 yuan in 2000, and increased to 5374.6 yuan by 2008, which was about an 8.02% increase per year; average personal consumption expenditure per person of medium-income families increased from 4794.6 yuan to 10344.7 yuan, which was a 10.09% increase per year; and average personal consumption expenditure per person of high-income families increased from 8135.7 yuan to 22296.8 yuan, which was a 13.43% increase.

Looking at total volume of retail sales of social consumables, the sale of domestic market maintained swift growth, but growth speed slowed down. From January to September 2009, total volume of retail sales of social consumables was 8,967.61 billion yuan, which was a 15.1% increase from the previous year, but dropped 6.9 percentage points over 22.0% in the previous year. From the perspective of different regions, in urban areas, consumer goods turnover was 6,101.26 billion yuan, which was a 14.8% increase from the previous year, and the

Table 2.3: Personal Consumption Levels of Rural Household Incomes by Five Groupings
Unit: Yuan/Person

	Low-income families (20%)	Low- & medium-income families (20%)	Medium-income families (20%)	Medium- & high-income families (20%)	High-income families (20%)
In 2000	977	1233	1501	1877	3086
In 2003	1065	1378	1733	2189	3756
In 2005	1548	1913	2328	2879	4593
In 2008	2145	2653	3286	4191	6854
Annual increases in 2000–2008 (%)	10.33	10.05	10.29	10.56	10.49

Table 2.4: Personal Consumption Level of Urban Household Income by Five Groupings
Unit: Yuan/Person

	Low-income families (20%)	Low- & medium-income families (20%)	Medium-income families (20%)	Medium- & high-income families (20%)	High-income families (20%)
In 2000	2899.1	3947.9	4794.6	5894.9	8135.7
In 2003	3066.8	4557.8	5848.0	7547.3	12066.9
In 2005	3708.3	5574.3	7308.1	9410.8	15575.9
In 2008	5374.6	7993.7	10344.7	13316.6	22296.8
Annual increases from 2000–2008 (%)	8.02	9.22	10.09	10.72	13.43

increased range dropped 7.9 percentage points from the previous year. In the county level and below, turnover was 2,866.35 billion yuan, which was a 16% increase from the previous year, and the increased range dropped 4.6 percentage points from the previous year. From the perspective of different industries, total volume of retail sales of consumable in the wholesale and retail trade was 7,540.17 billion yuan, which was a 15.0% increase from the previous year, and the increased range dropped 7.0 percentage points from the previous year; total volume of retail sales of consumable in the lodging and food & beverage industry was 1,298.04 billion Yuan, which was a 17.4% increase from the previous year, and the increased range dropped 7.4 percentage points from the previous year.

B. *Personal Consumption Pattern of Urban and Rural Residents has Obviously Optimized*

(1) Engel's coefficient drops. In recent two years, as a result increases in food prices, Engel's coefficient of urban and rural families increased, but from the long-term trend, it still dropped. Engel's coefficient of urban residents dropped from 39.4% in 2000 to 37.9% in 2008, which was a 1.5 percentage point drop; Engel's coefficient of rural residents dropped from 49.1% in 2000 to 43.7% in 2008, which was a 5.4 percentage point drop.

(2) The proportion of consumption in development and enjoyment has increased. With the popularization of the TV set and high-speed development of network informatization, urban and rural residents become aware of the importance of knowledge and information, and investments in culture and education have increased. In 2008, the expenditure per urban residents in cultural entertainment and services was 736.1 yuan, which grew 1.79 times over that in 2000, and in average grew 13.67% yearly. For rural residents, expenditure in cultural entertainment and services was 314.5 yuan, which grew 68.45% over that in 2000, and in average grew 6.74% yearly.

With increase in income, urban and rural residents pay more attention to their physical and intellectual integrity. The past phenomenon, where serious illnesses were only slightly treated or not treated at all, greatly changed. Average expenditure per person for healthcare for rural family was 246.0 Yuan in 2008, which grew 1.81 times over that in 2000, and in average increased 13.78% yearly; urban family's expenditure for healthcare was 786.2 Yuan, which grew 1.47 times over that in 2000, and in average increased 11.98% yearly. Expenditure for healthcare products was 82 Yuan, which grew 22.6% from the previous year, and accounted for 10.4% of average expenditures per person for healthcare per year.

(3) The proportion of service expenditure increased. With the increase in residents' living standard, the socialization tendency of urban and rural residents' domestic services became increasingly obvious, the demands of service consumption rose unceasingly, and consumption expenditure gradually turn toward service consumption expenditure. In 2008, service consumption expenditure per urban resident was 2919 yuan, which accounted for 26.0% of consumption expenditures. In the rural residents' personal consumption expenditure, service expenditure increased from an average of 447 yuan per person in 2000 to 1042 yuan in 2008, where personal consumption expenditures increased from 26.7% to 28.5%, and increased 1.7 percentage points.

(4) Proportion of rural residents' consumption expenditure continuously increased. The increase in rural residents' income rate promoted the increase in rural residents' purchasing power. Cash disbursement of rural residents' personal consumption increased from 1284.7 yuan in 2000 to 3159.4 yuan in 2008, which in average was a 11.91% increase yearly; the proportion of cash consumption expenditure in gross personal consumption expenditures increased from 76.9% in 2000 to 86.3% in 2008, which was a 9.4 percentage point increase.

III. *Urban and Rural Residents' Quality of Life Evidently Improved*

A. *Quality of Food Expense Increased, Nutrition Structure Continuously Improved*

Food is important to people, and from changes to "food", the economic situation of a society is reflected, and the vicissitude of social history can be seen. In 2008, average expenditures for foods per rural resident was 1599 yuan, which grew 94.8% from that of 2000, and in average increased 8.7% yearly; urban residents' was 4260 Yuan, which grew 1.16 times of that in 2000, and in average increased 10.11% yearly. As food consumption expenditure grows, urban and rural residents pay more attention to the nutrition of diet, meal structure becomes more reasonable, and the quality of consumption is unceasingly enhanced. Looking at food consumption patterns, average grain consumption per rural resident fell from 250 kg in 2000 to 199 kg in 2008, and for urban residents, from 82.3 kg in 2000 to 77.6 kg in 2007. From the perspective of nutrition, the consumption of animal foods including meat, birds and beasts, eggs and milk etc. has obviously increased, and nutritional structure has improved. Average consumption per rural resident of meat, birds and beasts and its products rose from 18.3 kg in 2000 to 20.2 kg, and milk and its products from 1.1 kg in 2000 to 3.4 kilograms; The consumption of urban resident of pork rose from 16.7 kg in 2000 to 19.3 kilograms, and fresh milk from 9.9 kg in 2000 to 15.2 kg.

With the increase in urban and rural residents' income level and the changes in lifestyle, as well as the increase in pace of life, the number of times that residents dined out has obviously increased, the amount of consumption rapidly increased, and the proportion of food expenditure became increasingly large. In 2000, average expenditure per rural resident's dining out was 64 yuan, and increased to 209 yuan by 2008, which was a 145 yuan increase, and grew 2.3 times, and the proportion in food expenditure increased from 7.8% to 13.1%. In 2008, for urban residents, average expenditure from dining out was 878 Yuan, and the proportion was 20.6%, which increased 5.9 percentage points over that of 2000.

B. *Clothing Consumption Shifts to Ready-Made Clothing and Fashion*

In recent years, urban and rural residents' clothing demand experienced many changes; the quality of material, matching of design and colors became increasingly emphasized. Pursuit of famous brands, fashion and personalization of clothing, and ready-made clothes became the norm in clothing consumption. Average clothing expenditure per rural resident increased from 61.1 yuan in 2002 to 142 yuan in 2008, which grew 1.32 times, and in average purchased quantity increased from 1.4 pieces per person to 2.7 pieces. In 2008, clothing consumption expenditure per urban resident was 1166 yuan, which grew 1.33 times over 500.5 Yuan in 2000, where average expenditure for purchase of ready-made clothes per person was 839 Yuan, which accounted for 72.0% of clothing consumption expenditures, and in average, purchase quantity per person was 7.7 pieces of ready-made clothing. The changes of clothing reflected economic development, but simultaneously also reflected people's ideological changes. Along with the changing times, changes to clothing manifest an improvement to the quality of life.

C. *Household Consumer Durable Goods are Modernized and Upgraded*

The most remarkable change to urban and rural residents' living standard is manifested in the unceasing upgrade of consumer durable goods. During the initial stages of the reform, the "four new pieces," big-ticket items, the color television, the washer, the electric refrigerator and the tape recorder, were the main representatives of that era. However, these items have become the consumer durable goods which resident families generally posses. In 2008, for each hundred urban household, there was 133 color television sets, 94.7 washers, and 93.6 electric refrigerators, and the tape recorder was replaced by medium- & top-grade video and audio durable goods, such as the combination audio. For every hundred rural household, there were 99.2 color television sets, 49.1 washers and 30.2 electric refrigerators. With the increase in income, renewal and upgrading of home appliance for both urban and rural households became increasingly popular, and new modernized and electric consumables, such as air-conditioning, family computer, family car and mobile phone, etc., have entered many households, and continue to grow. For every thousand urban households in 1986, there were only 1.3 sets of air-conditioning, but in average, in 2008, every urban household had 1 set of air-conditioning. In 2008, for every hundred urban households there were 59.3 family computer, 8.8 family cars and 172 mobile phones, which respectively grew 21.8, 45.3 and 100.2 times over that in 1997. For every hundred rural households, in average there were 52 motorcycles at the end of 2008, which increased by 31 sets over that in 2000, and grew 1.4 times. There were 67 telephones, an increase of 41, and grew 1.5 times; 96 mobile phones, an increase of 92, and grew 21.3 times; 10 air conditioning sets, an increase of 9, and grew 6.4 times; 5.4 home computers, an increase of 4.9, and grew 10.4 times.

D. *Housing Conditions and Environment Improved Drastically*

Housing conditions and environment of rural residents drastically improved. In 2008, average housing expenditure per rural resident was 678.8 yuan, which increased 420.4 yuan over that in 2000, grew

1.63 times, and increased on average 12.8% yearly. The per-capita housing floorage increased from 24.8m^2 in 2000 to 32.4m^2 in 2008, which was a 7.6m^2 increase. Among them, housing of half timber construction and reinforced concrete structure accounted for 87.3%, which was a 7.7 percentage point increase over 79.6% in 2000. With increased rural residents' dwelling space, housing conditions had enormous improvements. In 2008, peasant households where water-flush sanitary privies were used accounted for 17.5%, which was a 10.5 percentage point increase from that of 2000. Peasant households without washroom accounted for 7.4%, which was a 6.3 percentage points decrease from that of 2000. Peasant households where clean fuel oil, fuel gas, electricity and methane etc. were never used accounted for 28.6%, which was a 21.2 percentage point increase from that of 2000. Peasant households with access of drinkable running water accounted for 43.2%, which was a 15.5 percentage point increase from that of 2000. Those which drank unhealthy shallow well water, rivers, streams and lake water etc. accounted for 24.4%, which was a 10.9 percentage point reduction from that of 2000. 42.4% of peasant households had cement or blacktop around their house, which was a 18.3 percentage point increase from that of 2004; and 34.5% of peasant households still had non-hard surfacing such as earth roads etc. around their house, which was a 15.9 percentage point decrease from that of 2004.

In recent years, as much new housing was completed, many urban families parted with their old, simple and crude facilities, and moved into bright furnished buildings, where housing conditions improved. In 2008, the housing floorage per urban resident increased to 23.0m^2, which grew 1.7 times over that of 8.6m^2 in 1985. Among them, 4.5% of urban families lived in unattached building, 83.0% of urban families in apartments, and only 12.5% still in tube-shaped apartments and one-story houses. The improvement of housing facility is more obvious. In 2008, 98.4% of families had running water in the house, 79.1% had restrooms and bathrooms, and 62.9% had air-conditioning or central heating. The kitchens of a majority of houses got rid of smokiness and used convenient clean fuel. In 2008, 87.3% of families used pipeline coal gas and liquefied petroleum gas, and the proportion of families in which the coal was main fuel fell to 8.3%.

E. *Transportation System Renewed, Journeys are Quicker*

Before the reform and opening up era, public means of transportion, such as buses, railroads and steamboats were main means of transportation for urban residents. After the reform, with fast economic development and the quickening in pace of life, exchange and communication became indispensable demands of urban residents' lives. Thus, transportation expenses began to occupy an important position in consumption expenditures. In 2008, transportation expenses per urban resident was 804 yuan, which grew 4.0 times from that of 2000, and accounted for 7.2% of consumption expenditures, which rose 4.0 percentage points over that of 2000. Traditional transportation and communication methods were unable to meet the urgent demands of urban residents in terms of traveling and communication, and thus more convenient and quicker modern transportation methods were sought. Public means of transportation are no longer the only choices in traveling; the family car, the motorcycle and the electric motor car have become part of ordinary families. In 2008, urban residents' expenditure for purchasing and using family vehicles was 466 yuan, which accounted for 58.0% of all transportation expenses; for every hundred urban households, 8.8 had a family car, which was a 16.7 times growth over that of 2000.

Before the reform, in the rural areas, main means of transportation were bicycles and manpower wooden handcarts, and there mainly existed only dirt roads. After the 30 years of development and construction, rural transportation infrastructure has drastically improved. In 2008, traffic mileage of rural road amounted to 3,125,000 km, which is nearly a 4 times growth since 1978; the rural road network has extended to plateau and mountainous areas, as well as to minority areas and impoverished old revolutionary base areas, and 88.7% of rural villages and towns had asphalt roads. With the expansion of rural residents' exchange with the outside, modern transportation and communication facilities rapidly entered the rural families, and expenditures in transportation and communication experienced swift growth. In 2008, every hundred rural households had 52.5 motorcycles, which grew 1.4 times from that of 2000; average expenditure per person in purchasing vehicles was 90 yuan, which increased 10 yuan from the previous year, and increased 12.7%; average expenditure of traffic passenger fares per person was 56 yuan, which was a 1 yuan increase from the previous year, and a 2.2% growth.

F. *Increasingly Enriched Cultural Life*

Tourism has become a new leisure activity for urban residents. With improvements to living standard and changes to lifestyle, especially since 1998, with the implementation of a five-day working week, as well as long holidays for "May 1" and "October 1" (National Day of PRC), sightseeing has become increasingly popular as a holiday time activity. From short-distance tours around the city and domestic tours during the weekend to domestic tours during the long holiday and traveling abroad, tourism gradually developed from simple group tourism to independent tourism. Urban and rural residents' expenditures for travel are growing year by year, and the number of tourists unceasingly increases. In 2008, the number of people who toured domestically reached 1.712 billion person-times, which grew 1.3 times from that of 2000; average expenditure per person for tour amounted to 511.0 yuan, which grew 19.8% from that of 2000. Increasingly numbers of residents enjoyed tourism, and it became an important way for people to cultivate sentiment and to increase experiences.

Cultural facilities unceasingly increased, and various entertainment options emerged. As material standard of living continued to increase, people started to seek out a more cultural lifestyle, and expenses for recreation classes increased. Leisure activities shifted from monotonous things, such as watching TV at home or going out to watch movies, to a variety of new options, such as going to teahouses, bars, coffee shops, bookstores and holiday villages, etc. In addition, with the increase of sporting arenas and community gyms, all kinds of big stadiums, natatoriums, gymnasiums and yoga centers became favored placed of exercise. People's educational investment idea also strengthened unceasingly. Whether with adult after work hours studies or children's extracurricular interest classes, educational expenses have largely grown. Statistics indicated that, in 2008, expenditure per urban residents for cultural and entertainment goods and services was 736.1 yuan, which was 1.79 times of that in 2000, and in average grew 13.67% yearly; per rural resident 314.5 yuan, which was a 68.45% increase from that of 2000, and in average grew 6.74% yearly.

IV. *Problems in Personal Consumption*

A. *Residents' Consumption Rate Unceasingly Dropped*

Although residents' consumption maintained quick growth since the reform, in reality, it is lower than the economic growth rate during that same period. Because residents' consumption is slower than economic growth, the trend in resident consumption rate (i.e. the proportion of residents' consumption in GDP) unceasingly dropped. The resident consumption rate was 48.8% in 1978 and about 50% in the 1980s, but after the 1990s, dropped year by year, and dropped to 35.3% in 2007, which was a 13.5 percentage point drop from that of 1978. During this period, urban and rural residents' consumption affected one another, where one dropped, the other increased. The influence of urban residents' consumption expanded gradually, and rural residents' reduced gradually; in 1990, the consumption scale of urban residents surpassed that of rural residents for the first time, to make up the majority of resident consumption. Afterward, this tendency continued to strengthen. In 2008, in resident consumption, the proportion of urban residents' consumption reached 74.8%, the proportion of rural residents' consumption was only 25.2%, and rural resident consumption rate also dropped to the lowest in history, 8.9%.

B. *Growing Disparity Between Resident Consumption*

While resident consumption continued to grow, the disparity between urban and rural areas and among regions in terms of resident consumption expanded.

Looking at the disparity between urban and rural areas, not only is the disparity among total amount of consumption expanding, but also among average consumption level per person. In 2008, the ratio between urban residents and rural residents in total amount of consumption (rural resident's total amount of consumption was 1) was 3.0, which rose 2.4 from that of 1978; the ratio of average consump-

Table 2.5: Resident Consumption Rate in 1978–2008 Unit: %

Year	Resident consumption	Rural residents	Urban residents
1978	48.8	30.3	18.5
1979	49.1	30.6	18.5
1980	50.8	30.7	20.0
1985	51.6	31.0	20.7
1990	48.8	24.2	24.6
1995	44.9	17.8	27.0
2000	46.4	15.3	31.1
2005	37.7	10.2	27.6
2006	36.3	9.5	26.8
2007	35.6	9.1	26.5
2008	35.3	8.9	26.4

tion level between per urban resident and per rural resident (average consumption level per rural resident was 1) was 3.6, which rose 0.7 from that of 1978. The disparity between urban and rural areas in total amount of consumption was relatively small, but the disparity increased rapidly; the disparity between urban and rural areas in average consumption level per person grew, but the disparity expanded slowly. Since 2000, the disparity in average consumption level per urban and rural resident has assumed a stable trend, about 3.6.

Looking at the disparity among regions, the disparity among regions of average consumption level per person was big, and continually increased. In 31 provinces, autonomous regions and municipalities, since 1993, Shanghai had the highest average consumption level per person of all residents, and the lowest was found mainly in Tibet, and also Guizhou or Gansu during some years. In 1993, the ratio between highest and lowest average consumption levels per person (the lowest average consumption level per person was 1) was 5.3, and increased to 7.8 in 2008, an increase of 2.5 from that of 1993. In terms of rural and urban residents respectively, the disparity among regions in average consumption level per rural resident was larger than that of urban residents among regions. The disparity among regions of rural residents continually increased, and for urban residents, disparity among regions was relatively stable; although in recent years there are increases.

C. *Average Propensity for Consumption Gradually Dropped*

Average resident propensity for consumption refers to the ratio between resident consumption expenditure and income, and it reflects how much of current income residents use for consumption. Urban residents' average propensity for consumption is equal to the ratio between consumption expenditure per urban resident and average disposable income per person, and rural residents' average propensity for consumption is equal to the ratio between average consumption expenditure per rural resident and average net income per person. Since the 1990s, resident's average propensity for consumption basically dropped year by year with the exception of a few years, and dropped from 0.85 in 1990 to 0.727 in 2008, a decrease of 0.123. Among them, urban residents' average propensity for consumption dropped from 0.847 in 1990 to 0.712 in 2008, a decrease of 0.135. The decreased scope was larger than that of residents. It indicated that urban residents' income used in immediate consumption was gradually decreasing, and amount towards savings was increasing. Changes of rural residents' average propensity for consumption can be divided into two stages. The first stage is from 1990 to 1999. Average propensity for consumption dropped year by year, and dropped from 0.852 in 1990 to 0.714 in 1999, a 0.138 decrease. During this stage, rural residents' propensity for consumption dropped, and propensity for savings increased. The second stage is after 2000. Average propensity for consumption increased year by year, and rose to 0.769 in 2008, a 0.027 increase. During this stage, rural residents' propensity for consumption increased, and propensity for savings decreased.

D. *Disproportion Between Consumption and Investment*

The speed of consumption growth was far lower than that of investment. The disparity between growth speed of consumption and investment increased, and consumption and investment were disproportional. Since 2001, for society as a whole, actual growth speed of fixed asset investment was quicker than that of total volume of retail sales of consumables (Figure 2.1).

Table 2.6: Residents' Average Propensity for Consumption from 1990 to 2008 Unit: %

Year	Resident consumption	Rural residents	Town dwellers	Year	Resident consumption	Rural residents	Town dwellers
1990	0.850	0.852	0.847	2001	0.760	0.736	0.774
1994	0.823	0.833	0.814	2002	0.769	0.741	0.783
1995	0.828	0.831	0.825	2003	0.760	0.741	0.769
1996	0.813	0.816	0.810	2004	0.757	0.744	0.762
1997	0.793	0.774	0.811	2005	0.765	0.785	0.757
1998	0.770	0.736	0.798	2006	0.754	0.789	0.740
1999	0.757	0.714	0.789	2007	0.740	0.779	0.725
2000	0.774	0.741	0.796	2008	0.727	0.769	0.712

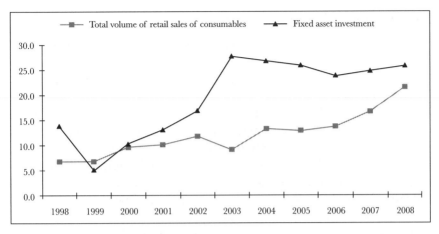

Figure 2.1: Growth Speed of Fixed Asset Investment of Entire Society and Growth Speed of Total Volume of Retail Sales of Consumables

Although growth of investment demand and consumer demand may drive economic growth in the short run, the significance of investment growth and of consumption growth to economic growth is different for the long run. Consumption is the final step in a production process, values and effectiveness of commodities are finally realized, and only when products enter the consumption step is the production process finished. But, investment is double sided. In the current period, enterprise investment in fixed assets increased and the government's capital construction investment not only can increase total demands in the current period, and will according to a certain proportion form capital stock, which expand the social productive capacity in next period, thus increase aggregate supply capability in next period. If growth of consumer demand and of investment demand is disproportional in economic growth, although excessive investments can be depended on to drive economic growth and achieve a balance between total demand and aggregate supply for the short run, it is difficult for the growth of total demand to catch up with the growth of aggregate supply in the long run, thus overproduction will become increasingly serious, and the macro-economy will be severely unbalanced. At present, the increasing disparity between speed of increase in consumption and investment has already brought about a surplus in consumables.

E. *Disproportion Between Consumption and Savings*

From 1991 to 2008, the proportion between total volume of retail sales of social consumables and personal savings had a gradual downward trend (Table 3.2), and dropped from 1.02 in 1991 to 0.50 in 2008, a 50% decrease.

To a certain extent, we can think that the proportion of total volume in retail sales of consumption in the saving deposits represents the proportion between consumption and accumulation. From the proportion between total volume of retail sales of social consumables and the saving deposits, which gradually decreased, we find that, at present, there exists a phenomenon where consumption grows slowly and there is a excessive accumulation. As saving deposits increased suddenly, the growth of resident consumption was actually relatively slow, and the growth rate of total volume of retail sales of social consumables was lower than that of the deposits in the corresponding period.

Accumulation comes from an expansion in reproduction. There must be certain accumulation in any society if expanded reproduction is needed; under the situation that accumulation effect does not change or unceasingly increases, growth of accumulation means the strengthening of society's material and technical foundation. But excessive accumulation will cause slow consumption growth, and further affect growth of accumulation in the future, which becomes disadvantageous in promoting production development and unceasing enhancement of material and cultural standards.

Table 2.7: Proportion Between Total Volume of Retail Sales of Social Consumables and Personal Savings from 1991 to 2008 Unit: %

Year	Total volume of retail sales of social consumables/ Personal savings	Year	Total volume of retail sales of social consumables/ Personal savings
1991	1.02	2000	0.61
1992	0.94	2001	0.58
1993	0.94	2002	0.55
1994	0.87	2003	0.51
1995	0.80	2004	0.50
1996	0.74	2005	0.48
1997	0.68	2006	0.47
1998	0.62	2007	0.52
1999	0.60	2008	0.50

V. *Suggestions on Enhancing Residents' Standard of Living and Consumption Level*

A. *Readjustment of Relationship Between Income and Distribution*

Income is the foundation of consumption, and has the most direct and important influence to resident consumption. Since the reform, China's GDP in average grew 9.8% per year, but disposable income per urban resident actually in average grew 7.2% per year, and average net income per rural resident actually in average grew 7.1% per year, where economic growth for the majority of years was quicker than the increase of resident income. In 2007, workers' salaries accounted for 39.7% of GDP, which was far lower than the level of developed countries. Urban and rural residents' average propensity for consumption both assumed a downward trend, and dropped to 0.727 in 2008, which indicated that raising the overall resident income level is the only way to increase consumer demand.

B. *Importance of Raising the Income of Rural Residents and Urban Low-Income Groups*

There is much space to promote rural residents' consumption. In looking at the possession of consumer durable goods, in 2008, every hundred urban households had 59.3 family computers, whereas rural residents only had 5.4 sets; every hundred urban households had 94.7 washers, and rural residents, 49.1 sets; every hundred urban households had 93.6 electric refrigerators, and rural residents, 30.2 sets; every hundred urban households had 39.1 cameras, and rural residents, 4.4 sets; every hundred urban households had 100.3 air conditionings, and rural residents, 9.8 sets. Rural residents' marginal propensity for consumption was higher than urban residents; in 2008, urban residents' marginal propensity for consumption was 0.56, and rural residents 0.65. Promoting rural resident's income increase to be used towards consumption is obviously important.

Average propensity for consumption of urban low-income groups was obviously higher than high-income groups; raising income of urban low-income groups would drive consumption capacity of this group greatly, thus push the entire society towards greater consumption. Most important, raising their income can help them improve their quality of life, and practically promote social harmony and stability.

C. *Promoting Upgrading of Consumption Patterns*

Medium-income groups have a higher marginal propensity for consumption. Experiences from developed countries also indicate that the medium-income group has stronger consumption capacity and desire for consumption, which is an important factor in driving consumption. It is important to cultivate a stable middle-income group, as they make up the crux of society, where social class structure has two small ends and a large middle section. We must research the income and consumption environment of urban residents, the consumer demand of the rural market, urban market and the different income groups in urban areas. We should subdivide the market according to the demands of different groups of income and consumption, integrate the market resources, carry on the distinctive operation of commodities and services, and gradually change the present situation where structural surplus and structural shortage of consumables in the market coexist.

D. *Raising Urban Residents' Propensity for Consumption*

Some findings indicate that the increase in consumption and income disparity reduces residents' propensity for consumption, because low-income earners' consumption capacity is insufficient, and high-income earners' marginal propensity for consumption progressively decreases. Therefore, the bigger the income differential is, the more residents' propensity for consumption suffers. From 1995 to 2008, the disparity between urban residents' highest and lowest incomes expanded nearly 5 times, the disparity between urban and rural incomes doubled, which was why resident propensity for consumption dropped 0.09.

Through the income distribution policy, as a matter of fact, increasing the income of residents will increase the scope of income increase for medium- and low-income groups. First, through the stipulation of a minimum wage standard, the labor insurance plan is strictly normalized, and the proportion of resident income in primary distribution is enhanced; Second, in the redistribution of income, high-income earners' income is readjusted through tax revenues, such as income tax and property tax. That income transfers from high-income earners to low-income earners through policies of encouraging capital transfer in order to raise the income level of medium- and low-income earners, especially of low-income earners; Third, through further consummation of the financial transfer payment system, the widening income disparity among different regions can be suppressed.

E. *Increasing Investments in Elementary Education, Basic Healthcare and Social Security*

While the government increases funds to public education, they need to emphasis readjustments to elementary education, as well as higher education, expenditure structures, strengthen the investments in elementary education, expand the beneficiary range of public education expenditure for residents, and raise all citizens' elementary educational level. In terms of public healthcare, the government needs to increase expenditures to public medical care and healthcare, expand the scope of social medical insurance, and gradually reduce the proportion of personal healthcare expenditures. In terms of social security, on one hand, sources of social security income must be jointly undertaken by the government, enterprises and individuals; on the other hand, expenditure projects of social security should be increased, and coverage of social security should be expanded. The government's functions in public education, medical and healthcare and social security should be strengthened to build a welfare protection system where "all people who thirst for learning can afford school education, patients can afford medical services, old people can be supported, and all people in difficulty can be helped." This is not only the premise to enhance residents' immediate propensity for consumption and to reduce the savings ratio, but also to slow down outside impacts and to enhance the guarantee of stable economic growth.

EMPLOYMENT AND POLICY UNDER INTERNATIONAL FINANCIAL CRISIS IN 2009

Mo Rong, Zhao Liwei and Chen Lan

I. *Analysis on the Employment Situation in 2009*

A. *8,510,000 People in Urban Areas Acquire New Employment, Reaching 94% of Annual Goal; Registered Urban Unemployment Rate is 4.3%, thus the Employment Situation Overall Remains Stable*

From January to September 2009, a total of 8,510,000 urban people became newly employed, achieving 94% of the annual goal of 9 million newly employed people;[1] a total of 4,020,000 laid-off workers got re-employed, achieving 80% of the annual goal of 5 million; a total of 1.2 million people who had difficulty obtaining employment became employed, achieving 120% of the annual goal of 1 million. At the end of the third quarter in 2009, a total of 9,150,000 urban people were registered as unemployed, and urban registered unemployment rate was 4.3%, which maintained the same from the previous year.

From July 2008 to the end of September 2009, the government organized suitable employment aid to earthquake disaster areas, a total of 652,000 people received organized labor service export, in which 475,000 population were from other provinces; a total of 1,357,000 workers from disaster areas got employment in their hometown, 219,000 people in welfare posts.

During the first three quarters of 2009, for the whole country, a variety of vocational training, more than 20 million man-hour, were launched in implementing special vocational training plan, a total of 9,569,000 people participated invocational skill appraisal (8,840,000 people in the corresponding period of 2008), 8,136,000 people gained occupational qualification certificate (7,510,000 people in 2008), where

---

[1] Data from the press conference of the Ministry of Human Resources and Social Security in the third quarter of 2009, at http://www.lm.gov.cn/gb/news/2009-10/23/content_330603.htm.

164,000 people newly became technicians and senior technicians (154,000 people in 2008).

B. *The Ratio Between Post Vacancy and Number of Job-Seekers Continuously Rises in the Labor Market, and Demand of Employees Increase 16.2% from the Previous Year*

The vocational supply-demand information in labor market collected by China Labor Market Information Network Monitoring Center for 102 urban public employment service organizations indicated[2] that, in the third quarter of 2009, employers recruited about 5,767,000 people through the labor market, and approximately 6,105,000 job-seekers entered the market; the ratio between post vacancy and number of job-seekers was about 0.94.

For different regions, the ratio between post vacancy and number of job-seekers for the eastern, middle and western regions were respectively 0.99, 0.89 and 0.87; in eastern regions, around Bohai Sea, the Changjiang Delta, the Zhujiang Delta and southeast Fujian, the ratio between post vacancy and number of job-seekers respectively was 1, 0.99, 0.84 and 0.98.

Compared with the previous quarter, in the third quarter of 2009, the demand for employees and the number of job-seekers increased by 572,000 people and 174,000 people respectively, which grew 11.3% and 3.0% respectively. By different regions, the demand of employees and the number of job-seekers in the eastern cities for the third quarter of 2009 increased by 504,000 people and 202,000 people respectively from the previous quarter, which grew 16.3% and 5.8% respectively; reduced by nearly 10,000 people and 37,000 people respectively for middle cities from the previous quarter, which dropped 0.8% and 2.7% respectively; and grew 10.7% and 1% respectively from the previous quarter in western cities. In the eastern regions, the Changjiang Delta and southeast Fujian, supply and demand population experienced big growth, and demand for employees increased to 333,000 people and 150,000 people respectively from the previous quarter, which grew 20.7% and 32.3% respectively; the number of job-seekers increased

---

[2] Data from Analysis on partial urban public employment service organizations market supply-demand situation in the third quarter of 2009 of China Labor Market Information Network Monitoring Center.

by 146,000 and 117,000 people respectively from the previous quarter, which grew 8% and 23.2% respectively; supply and demand population greatly decreased in the Zhujiang Delta area, the demand of employees and the number of job-seekers reduced by 41,000 and 59,000 respectively from the previous quarter, which dropped 32.8% and 36.9% respectively; the demand of employees around Bohai Sea area grew 5.7% from the previous quarter, and the number of job-seekers dropped 1.9% from the previous quarter.

In comparison with the corresponding period in 2008, in the third quarter of 2009, the demand of employees and the number of job-seekers increased by 660,000 and 774,000 people respectively, which grew 14.2% and 16.2% respectively. By different regions, in the eastern cities during the third quarter of 2009, the demand of employees and the number of job-seekers increased by 560,000 and 645,000 people respectively, which grew 18.9% and 22.1% respectively; increased 94,000 and 82,000 respectively in middle cities, which grew 8.7% and 6.7% respectively; and in the western cities during the third quarter of 2009, the demand of employees and the number of job-seekers grew 0.9% and 7.3% respectively. In the eastern regions, in the cities around Bohai Sea, the Changjiang Delta, Southeast Fujian, the demand of employee sincreased by 122,000, 345,000 and 122,000 people respectively, which grew 16%, 22% and 24.7% respectively; the number of job-seekers increased by 198,000, 311,000 and 155,000 people respectively, which grew 28.6%, 19.4% and 33.2% respectively; in the cities of the Zhujiang Delta area, the demand of employees and the number of job-seekers reduced by 35,000 and 33,000 people respectively, which dropped 29.7% and 24.6% respectively.

C. *For the Whole Structure, Demand for Employees in the Service Industry Makes Up the Bulk of Demand*

The demand for employees in the first, second and third industries accounted for 2.2%, 39.6% and 58.2% respectively. Compared with the corresponding period in 2008, during the third quarter of 2009, the demand proportion rose 1.6 percentage points in the second industry, and dropped 1 percentage point in the third industry.

From the perspective of industrial demand, the demand for employees in 81.6% of enterprises was concentrated in the manufacturing industry, wholesale and retail industry, lodging, food and beverage industry, resident services and other service industries, the leasing trade and commercial service industry and building industry, the demand for employees in the above various industries accounted for 33.6%, 15.8%, 11.9%, 9.9%, 6.3% and 4.1% respectively of the whole. Among them, the demand in the manufacturing industry and the building industry accounted for 85% and 10.5% of all demands in the second industry, combining to be 95.5%; the demands in the wholesale and retail industry, the lodging, food and beverage industry, resident services and other service industries, leasing trade and commercial service industry respectively occupies 27.1%, 20.4%, 17.1% and 10.9% of all demands in the third industry, and these four industries combined to equal 75.5%. (See Figure 3.1)

In the second industry, the demand proportion in the manufacturing industry during the third quarter of 2009 rose 1.7 and 2.6 percentage points respectively from the previous quarter and the corresponding period in 2008; in the building industry, it amounted to the same as the previous quarter, which dropped 0.4 percentage point from that in 2008. Compared with the previous quarter and the corresponding period in 2008, in the third industry, there were drops in the wholesale and retail industry, the lodging, food and beverage industry.

D. *From Employers' Perspective, 96.4% of Employee Demands Concentrate in Enterprises, and only 0.8% in Institutions, and 2.8% in Other Sectors*

In terms of employee demand of enterprises, domestically-funded enterprises accounted for 75.7%, where there were bigger demand for employees in private enterprises, limited liability companies and joint-stock companies limited, and accounted for 27%, 25.5% and 9% respectively, and only 5.1% in state-owned and collective enterprises; 6.2% in Hong Kong, Macao, and Taiwan business man-invested enterprises; 8.3% in foreign-funded enterprise; and 9.8% in individual ownership enterprises.

Compared with the corresponding period in 2008, in the third quarter of 2009, the proportion of employee demand in domestically-funded enterprise grew 3 percentage points, dropped 2.2 percentage points in Hong Kong, Macao, and Taiwan businessman-invested enterprises, and demand in foreign-funded enterprises dropped 1.3 percentage points from that of 2008. (See Figure 3.2)

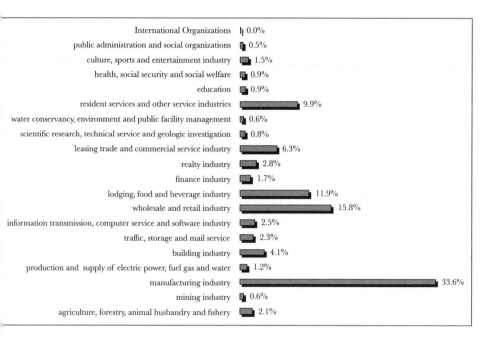

Figure 3.1: Demand Proportion by Grouping of Industry

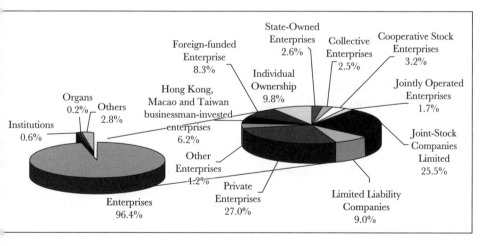

Figure 3.2: Demand Proportion by Grouping of Employer Property

E. *From the Perspective of Demands of Various Professions, Operators of Production and Transportation Equipment, Employees of Commerce and Service Industry Make Up the Biggest Group*

Operators of production and transportation equipment and employees of commerce and service industry are in largest demand, which accounted for 36.3% and 33.2% respectively, and in total accounted approximately for 69.5% of all demands. In addition, specialized technical personnel, clerks and other personnel concerned had bigger demand, which accounted for 11.6% and 10.1% respectively.

Compared with the corresponding period in 2008, in the third quarter of 2009, the demand proportion for commerce and service industry employees rose 0.1 percentage point; for operators of production and transportation equipment rose 3.5 percentage points.

In the job-seeking situation, job seekers were also mainly operators of production and transportation equipment and commerce and service industry people, and the proportion was 31.5% and 29.7% respectively. And in total accounted approximately for 61.2% of all job-seekers. The job-seeking proportion of clerks and other personnel concerned and of specialized technical personnel was 14% and 12.7% respectively.

Compared with the corresponding period in 2008, in the third quarter of 2009, the job-seeking proportion of commerce and service industry employees rose 0.3 percentage points, and operators of production and transportation equipment rose 1.7 percentage points.

In the supply-demand situation, the demand for commerce and service industry employees, operators of production and transportation equipment, farming and forestry industry employees, animal husbandry, fishery and water conservancy employees were bigger than the supply, and the ratio between post vacancy and the number of job-seekers was 1.02, 1.05 and 1.07 respectively (See Figure 3.3).

F. *For All Job Seekers, Unemployed Persons[3] Account for 51.8%*

Among them, the unemployed youth accounted for 23.7% (this year's graduates accounted for 42.2% in unemployed youth), people who had previous been employed but lost work accounted for 16.1%, and other

---

[3] Unemployed persons = newly unemployed youth + employed persons who become unemployed persons + other unemployed persons.

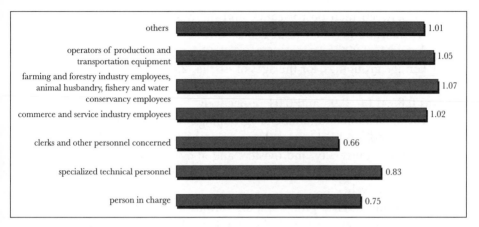

Figure 3.3: Supply-Demand Population by Profession Grouping

unemployed persons accounted for 12%; external workers accounted for 36.9%, migrant workers were composed of rural employees of the city and employees from other towns, and accounted for 15% and 21.9% respectively.

Compared with the previous quarter, in the third quarter of 2009, the job-seeking proportion of the unemployed person rose 1.4 percentage points, where that of unemployed youth rose 1.1 percentage points, people who had previous been employed but lost work dropped 0.4 percentage points, and other unemployed persons rose 0.7 percentage points; for migrant workers, the job-seeking proportion of rural employees of the city was similar to that of employees from other towns, dropped 1.4 percentage points.

Compared with the corresponding period in 2008, in the third quarter of 2009, the job-seeking proportion of unemployed person rose 3.3 percentage points, where that of unemployed youth rose 2.1 percentage points, people who had previous been employed but lost work rose 1.1 percentage points, and other unemployed persons rose 0.1 percentage point; for migrant workers, the job-seeking proportion of rural employees of the city rose 0.9 percentage points, and employees from other towns dropped 1.5 percentage points.

G. *The Structural Feature of the Labor Market is Still Obvious*

In sex groupings, there were more men job-seekers than women, 55.6% and 44.4% respectively. In terms of the supply-demand situation, the ratio between men post vacancy and the number of job-seekers was 0.91, the ratio between women post vacancy and the number of job-seekers was 0.99.

For age groupings, for the ages of 16–24, 25–34, 35–44, and 45 and above, the ratio between post vacancy and the number of job-seekers was 0.85, 1.06, 0.96 and 0.94 respectively.

For educational attainments groupings, for educational level of junior middle school and below, senior high school, junior college, college and university, and masters and above, the ratio between post vacancy and the number of job-seekers was 1.07, 0.96, 0.82, 0.78 and 0.76 respectively.

For technical class groupings, for various technical classes, the ratio between post vacancy and the number of job-seekers was bigger than 1, and labor demand was bigger than supply, where for senior engineers, senior technicians and technicians, the ratio between post vacancy and the number of job-seekers was bigger, 2.28, 2.24 and 1.95 respectively.

Employers demanding technical class employees accounted for 49.5% of total demand, and posts were mainly concentrated with primary skill personnel, medium skill personnel and technicians and engineers, and they occupied 42.6%.

II. *Impact and Challenge of Financial Crisis to Employment in China*

A. *The Impact from the Financial Crisis to Employment is Unprecedented*

(1) *Once the International Financial Crisis Hits China, the Economy and Employment are Heavily Impacted*

On one hand, the crisis first affected export-oriented enterprises and external investment and its employment. Because external demand plummeted, orders sharply fell, and the speed of export growth rapidly dropped; it dropped from a growth of 30.6% in March 2008 to −17.1% in March 2009, a 47.7 percentage point drop. If calculated according to 200,000 employment opportunities affected by export change of one percentage point, namely 9,500,000 employment opportunities were reduced. After this direct impact, many export processing enterprises and foreign-trade enterprises fell into difficult positions, partial small and medium-sized enterprise with bad anti-risk abilities went bankrupt, and large quantities of workers were out of work or given a long vacation. At the same time, as a result of the break of fund chain, foreign investments were largely reduced; in process and proposed foreign investment projects were impacted, and the adverse effect touched upon the economy and employment.

On the other hand, the crisis rapidly spread to the economy through the industrial chain. As producers of export products, while the export enterprises was heavily impacted, Chinese enterprises that provided energy, raw material, logistics and services for them also became impacted, where resource industries then suffered bigger losses because prices sharply fell in the international bulk commodity market as well as in domestic demands, and many enterprises fell into difficult positions. Then real estate, building industry, building materials, steel and iron, textile industry, equipment manufacture and tourist trade etc. were affected rapidly through ways of industrial chain and consumption etc., the impact was expanded to in land areas through coastal areas, thus greatly affecting China's economy and employment.

(2) *The Outburst of the Financial Crisis Impact Overlaps with the Inherent Contradicts in China's Economic Structure, and Employment Problem Becomes Increasingly Severe*
The impact of the financial crisis to China's economy and employment was sudden, and was concentrated during the second half of 2008, when China's economy was undergoing a downward trend. In addition China's economic system had inherent contradictions such as surplus capacity, excessive dependency on foreign demand, bad environment for small and medium-sized enterprises and weak anti-risk ability, and so on, which the financial crisis further intensified.

From the perspective of employment, supply and demand in the human resource market originally being under tension, unemployed people seeking employment, and new labor force in cities along with surplus agricultural laborers finding work in cities, formed the "overlapping of three peaks"; the third industry that could employ more workers had slow development, quality of workers could not meet requirements of enterprises, and it is difficult to relieve the middle and long term total contradictions and structural contradictions of employment. Under the sudden impact of financial crisis, originally prominent contradictions of employment were suddenly intensified and became exceptionally incisive.

(3) *The Financial Crisis Causes Existing Job Posts in Enterprises to Reduce by 8%, and the Urban Unemployment Rate Rises; a New Situation in the Recent 6 Years*

Under the impact of financial crisis, existing jobs have decreased. A sampling investigation by the Ministry of Human Resources and Social Security of some provinces and regions indicated that, from October 2008 to January 2009, an average of 40% of enterprises had reductions in posts, post fluctuation of all monitored enterprises off setled to a net reduction, decreasing by 8.1%.

In the impact of financial crisis to China's employment, peasant workers bore the brunt of impact. Peasant workers accounted for 58% of all workers in the second industry, 68% of workers in the processing and manufacturing industry, and many worked in coastal export processing enterprises. Therefore the situation of unemployment, of waiting for a job within an enterprise, or of returning to native villages was serious because of the financial crisis. According to investigations by the National Bureau of Statistics of China, before the Spring Festival in 2009, more than 12 million peasant workers lost their job and returned to their native village because of the effects of the financial crisis, which accounted for 8.5% of all peasant workers.

The urban unemployment rate rises, and it becomes increasingly difficult for those already experiencing problems finding employment to get employment. By the end of 2008, the urban registered unemployment rate rose 0.2 percentage points from the previous year, and increased by 560,000 people from the previous year, a high in the recent three years. The enterprises often decreased the number of flexible employees first, and many flexible employees lost their job, and the worsening of economic situation further worsen their situation in re-employment.

The reduction in urban employment demand caused more contradictions for graduates to find employment. In 2009, college and university graduates reached 6.1 million, which were 9% more than that of 2008, but enterprises that were main channels for employment reduced recruitment by 20%. In a sampling investigation during the first half of 2009, the unemployment rate of urban youth in the age group of 16–24 was above 11%, two times the average unemployment rate.

B. *Complete Effects of the Financial Crisis has Not Been Seen, and Impact to the Economy Especially to Employment will Continue for a Long Time*

(1) *The Financial Crisis from the USA has Evolved into a Global Economic Crisis with Cyclic Characteristics, Interconnected Relationship between Chinese Economy and Other Economies, thus China Cannot Ignore its Effects to Others When Fixing its Own Problems*

From historic experiences and economic theory, economic crises generally experience an integral cycle of "crisis—depression-recovery-prosperity," and the economy usually needs 2–3 years or longer to enter the recovery stage. In the present situation, the full downward trend of foreign economies, especially of the main economies, has not been seen, it is difficult for foreign demand to rise again in a short period, and it is more difficult for recovery to investment and consumption to occur during the inflation period before several years pass. Thus, recovery to China's export is a long-term process.

Overall, China's national economy was at a crucial stage where stability is maintained and it rises at times, but the partial economic indicators (such as growth rate of foreign trade, CPI and power consumption etc.) were still at a stage where the downslide or fluctuation was bigger than that of the previous year, and there were also uncertain and unstable factors in the rise process. In addition, foreign demands continued to lag, and domestic consumption was insufficient; the drive of financial investment lacked endurance, private investments had not started, and anticipation of inflation all add to the uncertainty of the future economic trend.

At the same time, the impact to central and western regions appeared, and some new problems were exposed. In provinces such as Hebei and Yunnan, the impact of the financial crisis had characteristics of "appearing late, deep impact, and leaving late," and large numbers of resource enterprises fell into a difficult position. For the whole country, the downslide of major sectors such as the steel and iron and the textile industry did not appear yet; only 30% of export processing enterprises have recovered to regular production level. Small- and medium-sized enterprises fell into difficult positions, and investigations by the Ministry of Industry and Information Technology indicated that, from January to March 2009, export order of partial small- and medium-sized enterprise reduced by 20–30% from the previous year, and some even reduced by 50%.

(2) *Whether Short-Term Recovery or Long-Term Sustainable Development, the Chinese Economy must Mainly Depend on Expanding Domestic Demand; Increase of Unemployed Persons and Reduction of Income not Only Directly Affect Production and Consumption, but also Affect the Strategy to Readjust Domestic Demands, which will have Negative Influence to the Growth of the Economy and Employment in the Short and Long Term*

The current employment has three characteristics: 1. New employment posts are counteracted by lost enterprise posts. From October 2008 to June 2009, the loss rate of enterprise posts was 8%; it was calculated that about 6.2 million persons lost their job, but newly-employed persons increased by 7.5 million. Thus there was only a 1.3 million posts increase after increase and reduction balanced out. 2. Reduction of income. For many peasant workers who returned to cities and found employment, the phenomenon of an unstable position and pay reduction was universal. 3. Unstable foundation although work status improved. For newly employed people, flexible employees occupied 30–40%; social security covered only half of this group, and those not guaranteed by the social security system had unstable work status.

Simultaneous reduction in employment posts and hours of operation caused the decrease of income, thus initiated decrease in consumption, and further affected employment and the level of confidence. On one hand, with the income reduction caused by decrease of employment and working hours, the decrease in consumption inevitably further caused economic depression and employment reduction. On the other hand, the existence of a mass of unemployed persons has formed huge pressure to employment, which directly influenced anticipated employment, consumption level was reduced, and affected the foundation of economic growth.

(3) *Implementation of Countermeasures and Effects of Such Take Time, and Influences of Economic Trend to Employment has Delays, Thus Recovery to Employment Situation will be Delayed*

First, from central policy to local implementation, the process takes time. New policies on economic development and employment formulated by the central government require each level of government to carry out; various regions must readjust and supplement and implement according to local circumstances. Objectively, a period of time is necessary to carry out various policies before full effects are achieved.

Second, the effect show of the economic policy to deal with the crisis has ductility. Generally speaking, besides the immediate impact investments have to the economy, they also have about one-year extendibility, and the results might not been since until after its completion. But monetary policy, as regulatory policy, must undergo a period of time before it has an effect.

Third, from historical experiences and theoretical research, influences from economic trend to employment are delayed. Employment usually lags about one quarter behind targets of economic growth and production capacity, and the impact from foreign investment lags behind 3–4 quarters.

(4) *Change to Unemployment Rate is the "Barometer" to Economic Change, Currently Main Economic Indicators of the Main Economies of the World and Unemployment Rate are in the Decline Period, and the Impact of Financial Crisis has not Fully Been Seen Yet*

The Federal Reserve estimated that the economic downward trend would be −1%– −1.5% in 2009, and the unemployment rate would reach 10.1%. The report from the EU Commission estimated that the EU economy would reduce to −4% in 2009, it was estimated that the European economy would contract −0.1% in 2010, and total unemployment of 27 EU countries would reach 10.9% in 2010.

It is estimated according to the recent ILO report that, global unemployment rate in 2009 would rise from 5.7% in 2007 to between 6.5% and 7.4% in 2009, and total unemployment worldwide would rise to between 210 and 239 million persons, a 29–59 million persons increase from 2007. At the same time, it is estimated that worldwide, half of operating posts were under serious impact, and impoverished people would increase by 200 million over that of 2007.

C. *Big Challenges for Employment in China Because of the Financial Crisis*

(1) *The Impact of Financial Crisis to China's Employment Highlights the Contradiction where Supply Exceeds Demand in Employment, and Sharpens the Structural Contradiction, where Policies are Urgently Needed to Resolve the Problems*

The impact of financial crisis to employment was manifested in four aspects. First, there was a huge decrease in enterprise jobs, and large quantities of peasant workers lost their original operating posts. Second, demand reduction blocked employment channels of newly increasing urban labors, and intensified the difficulties for graduates and other urban groups in finding employment. Third, flexible employees are greatly affected. The market demand for flexible employees dropped, 30–40% of new employment were flexible employment, and mainly benefited from subsidy and support of social security, but at present, only about half receive subsidies. Fourth, as the supply-demand contradiction of employment increased, the structural contradiction became even more prominent, and the difficulty in solving the problems became enlarged.

On the other hand, facing a severe and complicated employment situation, policy measures that solve unemployment problems under normal conditions are obviously insufficient, and therefore many kinds of macroscopic and microscopic, emergency and long-term, direct and indirect policy measures and channels are urgently needed to solve the employment problems.

To protect and increase employment, we not only deal with domestic demand, slow down the impact, and maintain steady growth from the macroeconomic angle, but we must also fully manifest the principle of employment first in various policies which guarantee growth to bring about stability and to promote employment through the guarantee of enterprise development, especially the support of small and medium-sized enterprises and the development of labor-intensive enterprises; we should not only draw up and take various temporary measures to meet current urgent demands according to actual demands, but also give further consideration, expand and deepen education and training, and improve educational level of workers to solve structural contradictions; we must not only pay attention to economic development, but al-so enhance the level of human resources and social security to strengthen the construction of services. It is important that all of the above be done well, especially combining policies and joining strong and weak points. This will be a great challenge in dealing with the crisis.

(2) An Economic Development Pattern that Depends on Foreign Demand and Investment is Difficult to Sustain, Speeding Up Adjustment to Domestic Demand is Imperative for the Economic Development Pattern, which will Bring Forth New Employment Demand

It is time to change the economic development pattern that highly depends on foreign demand and external investment. The main market of China's foreign trade processing industry is in Europe, the United States, Japan, and other developed countries and regions, and investments also stem from these regions. But these regions are severely afflicted areas of the financial crisis, the financial crisis has evolved into a global economic crisis, and economic stagnation and depression and sharp reduction of investment and consumption have become a universal problem.

Because the economic crisis follows its own laws, it is difficult for the economy to recover in a short period; therefore it must take time to return to a normal state. This means that it is difficult for China's foreign demand and external investment to recover to previous levels in a short time, and even difficult to obtain swift growth within a medium and long period.

A big part of exports for China is low-end processed products, but the comparative superiority of labor cost that supports this pattern will gradually diminish in the future. The industrialization process of developing countries is also the process where the whole social labor productivity is gradually enhanced. Economists tell us, under the existing condition of enterprise competition sand unrestricted flow of workers, wages inevitably reflect the labor productivity condition, and therefore labor cost inevitably rises. The low-end export processing industry, which is supported by the advantage of the labor cost, will gradually lose its competitive advantage, and the economic development pattern, which is supported by foreign demand, will change along with it, and therefore enhancing domestic demand will be the only choice for economic development.

Therefore, promoting structural readjustment of exports and pushing for industrial upgrade becomes the only choice. Under the background, where the global economy is becoming increasingly integrated, China's basic trend of participation in the international industrial division of labor does not change, and maintaining steady growth of foreign trade will be still the inevitable requirement of economic development. But under the tendency where labor cost continually rises, in order to maintain a comparative advantage in foreign trade, there must be a growth in labor productivity and wages as well. China needs to readjust its export products structure, to enhance the value of export products, and to increase the cost of labor. By adjusting the industrial structure, and promoting industrial upgrading, the quality of workers, and what is demanded from them will improve.

(3) *As New Employment is Affected, How to Stabilize Employment and Reduce the Loss of Job Affects the Overall Situation*

A severe employment situation fully indicates that stabilizing employment and increasing employment are equally important. First, under the impact of the financial crisis, net employment reduced by 8% at the end of 2008, and fluctuations in employment within enterprises counter balanced the net decrease. The majority of gains in new employment were counteracted by the decrease in capacity. Second, in an overall falling economy, it is very difficult to increase employment. Therefore, taking positive measures to stabilize existing employment posts is the key in stabilizing the employment situation. Third, employment is heavily related with economic development, economic growth propels employment, and employment is also an important sustaining force of economic development. Maintaining current employment and positions are important ways to maintain the capacity of social productive, to guarantee livelihood of the people and to promote consumption, and is also the foundation to guarantee social stability.

In the recent 10 years, under a background of economic growth, newly increased employment was to promote employment, but there was a lack of attention to stabilizing employment, and there was a shortage of related policies. To face the severe reality, stabilizing employment as well as focusing on newly increased employment are both important, and corresponding special operational policy measures should be proposed to strengthen capacity and employment positions. It is especially important that small- and medium-sized enterprises become main arenas to hire new people. However, in this crisis, many small and medium-sized enterprises have fallen into problematic situations. And if the development environment further shrinks, and not enough policies are implemented, the stability and expansion of employment will be affected.

(4) *The Impact of the Financial Crisis has Exposed that Human Resources and Social Security is Insufficient, Whether the New Situation and New Requirements can be Adopted, Strengthening Human Resources and Social Security Becomes a Big Challenge*

On one hand, the crisis has raised the standards for employment services and vocational training. First, at present, information on the employment market and monitoring of it are insufficient. For example, within regular employment departments, flexible employees and non-standard employees do not have stable positions, and they are the first to be at risk, but with the existing information, we are not able to fully understand this situation. Moreover, many small businesses or miniature enterprises are important parts of the employment situation, hiring many people. However, they are not included in the current normal statistics scope, and thus a complete picture of social employment cannot be grasped, and it becomes difficult to formulate related policies. Second, at the moment, China does not have a warning system of unemployment. Areas that do have such a system are flawed in technology, system and management, thus not allowing it to perform its proper role. When crisis occurs, it is difficult to make prompt judgment and to initiate the emergency plan. Third, peasant workers do not have sufficient vocational training. During the crisis, countless peasant workers and others with difficulty in employment lost their position or had fluctuating positions because they did not have enough vocational skill or high enough comprehensive quality.

On the other hand, the social security system has low coverage, where the degree of protection is insufficient. There is not enough security for the urban flexible employee group and unemployed group; the rural population has a low level of medical security; the rural endowment insurance system is not truly established yet, and it is difficult for the social security system to adapt to workers' migration and status changes. Under the impact of crisis, the above problems become more obvious.

III. *Employment Policies to Deal with the Financial Crisis*

A. *Prompt, Strong, Comprehensively Planned and Innovative Employment Policies*

(1) *Prompt and Strong Measures*
To deal with the serious impact of financial crisis brought to employment, the State Council and the Department concerned formulated and implemented a series of special operational policy measures to stabilize employment and expand the job market, which included a comprehensive document of policy measures released by the State Council, three documents released by the General Office of the State Council on peasant workers' jobs, graduate's employment and propelling employment. Three documents on the special training plan,

activities of employment services and reducing the enterprise burden and stabilizing the employment was issued jointly by the Ministry of Human Resources and Social Security, which composed of new employment policy to deal with the financial crisis. These seven documents were issued from the end of September 2008 to the beginning of February 2009, and various provinces and prefecture-level cities also released supporting policies from May to June 2009. From the Central Committee to all levels of local governments, it is rare to find in history such prompt reaction, and quick policy formation with such strength and quality.

These special operational policy measures involve the following contents and goals in six aspects. First, employment is driven by economic development. A large-scale investment program that drives employment is implemented; a 4 trillion program, where a total of 24.16 million employment posts will be created within two years. Second, in order to stabilize employment, enterprises are supported to overcome difficulties. Programs, such as "postponed payment of five kinds of social insurance premium, reduction of four kinds of social insurance premium rate, three subsidies, and two consultations,"[4] are implemented, to help enterprises and to stabilize. And it was planned to reduce enterprises' burden by 200 billion yuan in 2009, and to stabilize 20 million employment posts. Third, increased strength to policy support and business independency encouraged. A program to promote business establishment in order to drive employment was implemented, and 1.5 million urban and rural workers were to be supported to establish a business in 2009, which would drive employment

---

[4] ("五缓四减三补两协商" <Wu Huan, Si Jian, San Bu and Liang Xie Shang>. "Postponed payment of five kinds of social insurance premium" refers to the enterprises in difficulty that are incapable to pay the social insurance premium temporarily are allowed to postpone the payment of five social insurance premiums in retirement, medical service, unemployment, industrial injury and child-bearing under the certain conditions. "Reduction of four kinds of social insurance premium rate" refers to the reduction of four kinds of social insurance premium rate except the endowment insurance at specific stages. "Three subsidies" refers to pay the social insurance subsidy and the post subsidy using the unemployment insurance fund for the enterprises in difficulty in stabilizing posts, as well as to give the subsidy using special employment fund for the enterprises in difficulty to launch on-the-job training for employees. "Two consultations" refer to, when the enterprises in difficulty have to carry on reducing the staff because of economic hardship, for these which are truly incapable to only one time pay economic considerations, on basis of the legal equal consensus between the enterprise and the trade union or the staff, the agreement for payments by installments or payment of economic considerations by other ways may be signed.)

for 4.5 million persons. Fourth, aimed at key characteristics of groups, overall employment is planned. Employment of graduates is given priority in current employment work, and more than 5 million graduates should get employment in 2009; employment work of peasant workers should be planned well, and 8 million peasant workers should be helped to transfer their employment through the "Spring Wind Operation"; reemploying urban unemployed persons especially personnel with difficulty getting employment should be planned well, and 1 million such people should be re-employed through the employment aid action. Fifth, special vocational training plan are to be implemented to enhance the workers' employment ability. 15 million urban and rural workers are to participate in vocational training in 2009. Sixth, public employment services are strengthened to improve the employment environment. In 2009, free public employment services for 25 million urban and rural workers are to be provided.

(2) *Strong Unity, Comprehensive Planning and Integration of Strong and Weak Points*
The formulation and implementation of these policies reflect five integrations. First, positive employment policy is integrated with the macroeconomic policy. Second, expanding the job market is integrated with stabilizing employment. Third, short-term emergency countermeasures are integrated with the formation of long-acting mechanisms. Fourth, government guidance is integrated with market regulation. Fifth, central policy investments are integrated with local initiative.

(3) *Breakthrough in Policies on Stabilizing Employment, Unemployment Emergency and Establishing Independent Business*
It must be pointed out that, at present, new employment policies that are implemented have three initial breakthroughs.

– Policy measures to stabilize employment are introduced for the first time. Positive employment policies implemented since 2002 mainly gave priority to the expansion and promotion of employment in economic and social development, and made very good progress. Since the financial crisis, partial enterprises fell into difficult positions, employment pressure obviously increased, the employment situation became increasingly severe, and stabilizing existing posts became an urgent matter. The government promptly released a series of policy measures to lighten the burden on enterprises through postponed payments of five social insurance premiums and reduction of four social security premium rates. Polices to stabilize employment posts using unemployment insurance fund to pay social security subsidy and post subsidy, encouraged enterprises in difficulty and thus did not cut staff as far to a minimum. Since active employment policies were implemented, this was the first time an employment stabilization policy enacted, and filled the gap in such policies, employment stabilization and increase in job market has occurred simultaneously.

– For the first time, unemployment emergency policy measures under crisis at the national level began, which has provided good experiences for the establishment of a long-term unemployment early-warning mechanism. The "Employment Promotion Law," established in 2008, specifically requested the people's government, at county-levels and above, to establish an unemployment early-warning system to prevent, adjust and control possible large-scale unemployment. The unemployment early-warning system is different from conventional employment and unemployment policy measures, and non-conventional policy measures are taken when the employment situation is non-conventional. Because the law was only recently implemented, the unemployment early-warning system of various regions was not fully established, much less implemented. In dealing with the impact of the financial crisis, the government began for the first time emergency special operational policy measures at the national level to deal with unemployment, including 4 trillion government investments and large-scale construction projects, considered methods to drive employment, expanded credit support to the service industry and small- and medium-sized enterprises, started postponed levy and payment and reduction of social insurance premium, helped enterprises alleviate burdens and stabilize posts using unemployment insurance fund, implemented special training plans, and normalized enterprises' behavior on reducing staff, and so on. These measures are not only macroeconomic policies, but also employment and social security policies, which have provided good experiences to resolve sudden mass unemployment problems, and have also laid a good foundation for the establishment of a long-term unemployment emergency plan.

– Business establish promoting employment begins for the first time, which has become a new supporting point to deal with crisis. The job enlargement has four basic channels; first, enterprises and work units admit employment; second, the government develops the public posts to admit employment; third, workers get employment nimbly; fourth, independent business are established. China's employment situation is and will be severe at the moment and in the coming period, under the situation where the first three channels are limited in its function to expand the job market. Thus, establishing business that can admit employment has become an important action to implement a active employment policy, which is necessary in order to deal with the international financial crisis and to stabilize the employment situation. The government has improved the environment for establishing business through strengthening of services and training of business establishment, and has given support in market access, location arrangement, reduction and exemption of taxation, small secured loans, free employment services and vocational training etc., which has formed the "Trinity" working mechanism of policy support, training and services for small businesses to encourage more urban and rural workers to find employment through establishing their own business. Through establishing independent businesses, individuals not only depend on themselves for projects and finance, to manage their business on their own, to assume responsibility for its profits and losses, and to assume risks by itself, but also encourage and allow other individuals to get employment, thus creating more and more space for employment. Even if some entrepreneurs fail, their entrepreneurial spirit as well as government support, will compel them to try again. This method of facing the unemployment problem, encourage individuals to establish independent business, is the biggest difference in how the unemployment situation 10 years ago was faced.

B. *Positive Functions of the Current Employment Policy*

(1) *Additional Implementation of Positive Employment Policy has Stabilized the Employment Situation, and the Employment Market has Improved*
During the second quarter of 2009, the proportion between post vacancy and job seekers was 0.88 in the human resource market, which was 0.02 more than the first quarter; the urban registered unemployment rate was 4.3% during the second quarter, but unemployment reduced by 90,000 persons from the first quarter, becoming more stable. New employment also showed a trend of rise in its fluctuation; from

January to June 2009, newly increased urban employment increased 5.69 million persons, which achieved 63% of the annual goal of 9 million persons. New employment was 950,000 persons every month, a reversal from the downward trend (average 590,000 persons per month) during the fourth quarter of 2008.

At present, the overall employment situation is rather stable as a result of four factors. First, the years of implementation of positive employment policy has laid a certain foundation, and continues to have an influence. For instance, implementing employment aid to groups in difficulty was included in the "Employment Promotion Law", and local authority also did not loosen employment work to groups in difficulty; although the crisis brought bigger impact to employment, employment of these groups still maintained swift growth because of continued implementation of policy. Next, as a result of differences in local economic structures, central and western regions were less impacted during the first round of financial crisis. While employment decreased rapidly in coastal areas, central and western regions were less impacted, and newly increased employment was higher than previous years in these regions, therefore new employment also had continual growth, which was advantageous for the stability of overall employment. Third, domestic consumption demands continued to grow, which made up for the partial loss from reduction in foreign demand. The government quickly propelled domestic demand, and then pushed for the development of the service industry and employment increase. During the first half of 2009, social consumables increased by 15% from the previous year, and with no view of price, actually grew 16.6%, and increased 3.7 percentage points from the previous year. Fourth, the new employment policy has helped expand the job market and stabilize employment. In some regions, in light of the financial crisis, the new employment policy was carried out quickly and made preliminary progress. The government's large-scale investments to help spur employment also began to take effect, and strengthened the confidence and expectation of enterprises and workers.

(2) *Policies Aimed at Protecting Enterprises, and Stabilizing Employment Take Effect in Some Regions; Enterprises No Longer have Need to Reduce the Number of Staff*
According to a 15 key city, 5 province investigations by the Ministry of Human Resources and Social Security regarding unemployment, after a 7–8 month fluctuation in employment, enterprise posts have

stabilized and increased. In the monitored cities, 258,349 persons were terminated within enterprises in June 2009; the fluctuation balanced out to a net increase of 1510 posts, and the increased range was 0.23%. Overall, speed of job loss has decreased.

As part of the employment stabilization policy, the social security policy of "five kinds of postponed payment, four kinds of reduction and three subsidies" has lightened the burden of enterprises in difficulty, and has helped stabilize employment posts. By the end of June, two measures on postponed payment and reduction of premium rate were approved in the whole country, which immediately reduced enterprises' burdens by 16.6 billion yuan directly; more than 6,000 enterprises in difficulty were subsidized and supported using the surplus unemployment insurance fund of 1.79 billion yuan, and 3,180,000 posts were protected.

(3) *Special Vocational Training Program is Launched and Public Employment Services are Strengthened, Thus Enhancing the Educational Level of Workers, and Improving the Employment Environment*
Programs of special vocational training as well as support to enterprises' staff training using unemployment insurance, in the short term, have protected the jobs of staff in enterprises in difficulty, and have stabilized the emotions of worker who temporarily cannot find jobs; in the long term programs and support have enhanced workers' vocational skill and quality, and improved the supply-demand disproportion situation in the labor market, which have met the changes of future labor demands, and have revealed that vocational training helps stabilize employment and solve the structural employment contradiction. During the first half of 2009, vocational training of 12.14 million man-hours were carried out in the whole country, where 1.21 million man-hours of staff from enterprises in difficulty were trained, as well as 5.37 million man-hours of peasant workers, urban unemployed person of 2.39 million man-hours of urban unemployed, 1.49 million man-hours of new laborers, and 520,000 man-hours of those undertaking training.

(4) *The Combined Action of Employment Policy Measures Benefits Enterprises and Workers, Which Heightened Confidence and Stimulated Vigor*
After the employment policy was implemented, various regions have created different patterns and experiences, and corresponding service facilities, training methods and grade of services have improved;

workers have obtained actual benefits, and the employment situation improved.

- Entrepreneur environment improved, and services for business start-ups caught up. By the end of July, 2009, a total of 29 provinces released measures using business start-ups as a method to drive employment, and 82 cities began work to create an environment conducive to start-ups by exploring the "five systems" of establishing organization leaders, policy support, training and services to these businesses, and performance assessment, thus creating a better entrepreneurial environment. Some areas also encouraged peasant workers to return to their native village to establish a business and graduates to do so through measures of providing special funds and opening business parks. There was much progress for peasant workers establishing businesses. Some regions focused on aiding peasant workers who had returned to their native villages to set up businesses by attracting business investments. Any industry and domain not forbidden by law and regulation would be opened to all kinds of businesses, and the scope of petty secured loan and preferential taxation policy for existing laid-off workers to establish businesses would also be offered to peasant workers, who returned to their native villages, and other entrepreneurs.
- The employment situation of peasant workers was overall stable. During the three months around the Spring Festival of 2009, there were a total of 70 million floating peasant workers, but a large-scale phenomenon of peasant workers being detained in cities or blindly flowed between urban and rural areas did not occur. At present, employment of peasant workers is quite stable overall, and 95% of peasant workers have returned to cities and found jobs.
- Overall, graduates finding their first jobs was rather stable. In June 2009, graduates' first employment rate reached about 68%; the employment situation basically stable. This occurred not only because of enhancement of government departments to graduates' employment work, prompt measures, creation of four channels, the urban and rural basic units, the small- and medium-sized enterprises and non-public ownership enterprises, technological projects and independent business startups, as well as actions on employment services, and employment probation and employment aid. But most important, the government gave graduates priority in employment and strengthened college students' confidence of the future, which

stabilized the will of the people. Simultaneously college students' notion of employment began to change, and the expected value of work became more practical.

- Groups in difficulty have been well placed in employment. During the first half of 2009, a total of 790,000 persons who had difficulty finding employment were helped to obtain re-employment, 79% of the annual goal. Social security subsidies for flexible employees have stabilized the employment for half of groups in difficulty.

TOWARDS A SOCIETY WHERE EVERYBODY HAS SOCIAL SECURITY

Wang Fayun and Li Yu

Abstract

In 2009, the international financial crisis as well as the employment situation that came with it, had to be dealt with and stabilized. By the end of 2008, the financial crisis had engulfed the entire world, and the Chinese economy was under serious impact; export suddenly decreased, and production and operation of some enterprises faced countless difficulties, where the pressures to employment obviously increased. In order to lighten the burden of enterprises and to stabilize the employment situation, a policy of "five kinds of postponed payment and four kinds of reduction of premium rate" was implemented, enterprises in difficulty were allowed to postpone payment of social insurance premium within a certain deadline, and the insurance premium rate of medical, unemployment, industrial injury and child-bearing was reduced. In August 2009, to increase the support strength to small- and medium-sized enterprises, at a the State Council executive meeting, it was decided that small- and medium-sized enterprises in difficulty were allowed to postpone payment of social insurance premium or have rates reduced up until the end of 2010. By the end of September 2009, in total, various regions reduced the collection of insurance premium by more than 10 billion Yuan in medical services. Reductions of premium rates for industrial injury and child-bearing and the social insurance premium in total was nearly 7 billion Yuan. This is the first time that social security policy falls under the scope of macroeconomic policy.

2009 was a year that had great changes for social security policy. As early as October 14, 2008, ministries and commissions released Opinions on deepening the Medical and Health Care System Reform, in order to solicit opinions throughout the whole country. On December 28, the General Office of the Standing Committee of the National People's Congress promulgated the full text of the law of social insurance (draft) to the society to seek opinions. Since 2008, Measures on Peasant Workers Participating in Endowment Insurance, Measures on

Transfer and Continuation of Endowment Insurance Relations, Opinions on New Rural Endowment Insurance and Revision of Regulations on Industrial Injury Insurance were all issued to solicit opinions throughout society. Only regarding the Law of Social Insurance, the parties concerned of the Standing Committee of the National People's Congress received 47511 opinions, with 47324 opinions found on the website of National People's Congress, 21 published in the leading newspapers, and 166 seen in letters. On major websites, Netizens wrote more than 20,000 comments, and more than 200 related Blog articles. Initially problems of social security concerning the peoples' benefits was only spoken about among a few. However, the general public is now included in such dialogue, and it is part of the legislative procedure as well; this symbolizes that the Chinese government is transforming into a service government.

2009 was a year where social security had much development and leaned towards a goal of supplying everyone with social security. Past experiences prove that, when economic crisis erupts, it is also often when social security has the most development. The economic crisis from 1929 to 1933 caused the United States to approve the "Social Security Act" in 1935, and to establish the "OASDI" system, which has worked well to the present, and has laid the foundation for the beneficial cycle of American economic growth, and has borne the important task of paving the way for the States' social development. After the financial crisis in Asia in 1997, to promote the readjustment of economic structure and reform of state-owned enterprises, China implemented "two guarantees," established "three security lines," which have quickened the formation of a frame for the urban social security system. In 2009, China's social security development likewise manifested this kind of relationship between economic crisis and social security development. After fast growth for many years, Chinese economic development has entered a new stage, namely expanding domestic demand is regarded as the fundamental way to guarantee growth, quickening the transformation of development and structural readjustment is regarded as the main direction to guarantee growth. To expand domestic demand effectively, the social security system must be consummated rapidly, and problems regarding medical services and retirement, which obstruct resident consumption, must be solved as soon as possible, thus relieving extra worries of the common people. In this sense, the consummation of the social security system guarantees that a transformation of economic growth will be promoted, and may even be regarded as "the fourth driving force" of economic growth. Therefore, the Political Bureau of the Central Committee of the Communist Party of China launched collective learning to study the problems about social security, and quickened the construction process of the social security system covering urban and rural areas. This year, amount of policies concerning social security was dense, work impetus was powerful, and social response was intense, which was unusual. System construction had breakthrough progress, but simultaneously social security also faced many difficult problems.

I. *Towards Complete Coverage of Medical Insurance*

On April 6, 2009, the new medical reform plan was finally unveiled, a historical day in the advancement of China's medical and health care system reform. "Plan on Carrying out Reform of Health Care System (2009–2011)" marked a milestone, where medical reform will have comprehensive implementation.

Coincidentally, after 40 years of intense arguments, and several presidents' unremitting efforts and frustrations, on November 9, 2009, the US medical insurance reform plans passed the House of Representatives, huge progress on President Obama's medical insurance reform plans. Many people praised this effort. Pelosi, Speaker of the United States House of Representatives talked about the medical insurance reform plans in a similar manner to the Social Security Act approved by the House of Representatives in 1935. Reuter thought that the United States had taken an important step towards the biggest reformation of medical insurance policy in 40 years. The difficulty of the US's medical reform fully indicated that reform of the medical and health care system is a difficult problem worldwide. There are many similarities between China's and the US's medical reform plans, for example, both countries insisted on medical insurance, but not free medical services. They give priority to expanding coverage, China's medical insurance will cover 90% of urban and rural population by 2011, and the United States planned to expand coverage of medical insurance to 96% of its population. Both countries' governments provide subsidies for the low-income groups that participate in medical insurance; China provides subsidy for personnel who have difficulty gaining employment to participate in medical insurance for employees, for town dwellers to participate in medical insurance for town dwellers, and for farmers to participate in the new rural cooperative medical system; The United States will give subsidy for mid- and low-income earners to purchase medical insurance beginning in 2013. Both countries all invest large sums of money. All levels of Chinese governments will invest 850 billion yuan between 2009 and 2011, in which the central government will invest 331.8 billion yuan; The US estimated they will spend about 1 trillion US dollars within 10 years. Certainly, there are also many differences in both plans. For instance, the system design is different. China's basic medical insurance is divided into medical insurance for employees, medical insurance for town dwellers and the new rural cooperative medical system; the system in the United States is not as complex, and its big enterprise medical insurance for employees is mainly undertaken by private agency and so on.

Regarding the new medical reform, all circles gave positive appraisal, and believe that the direction the government is leading is clear, whether government's investment expansion, health insurance for all the people, key support to basic-unit health agencies or the practice of the basic drug system etc., all have manifested the government's sense of responsibility. Gradualness of reform is in accordance with national conditions, financial burden is in accordance with the reality of national condition, allowing all levels of government to be able to afford it, individuals can fully participate in it, and problems such as medical services being expensive can be alleviated. But different opinions appeared, renowned Chinese expert of liver and gall surgery, member of the National Committee of CPPCC (CPPCC is abbreviation for Chinese People's Political Consultative Conference) Huang Jiefu (黄洁夫) argued that "medical reform should give priority to system reform, and not only count investments." Some people argue it is not enough for the medical system reform to merely be heading in the right direction. In order for it to be successful, an accountability system must be implemented to support the new medical reform plan. It must define concrete jurisdictions and responsibilities of all levels of competent authorities with specific measures of surveillance and accountability, which guarantees that the reform does not lose focus, and can be thoroughly implemented. Some people pointed out that the new medical reform plan has many highlights, but regarding the National System for Basic Pharmaceuticals, there are actually some flaws. The list of national basic pharmaceuticals and the list of basic pharmaceuticals for medical insurance do things their own way, and are not integrated, and this has brought about many troubles for personnel of medical insurance and finance, and has badly influenced social justice.

Moreover, on March 1, 2009, Shenmu County in the northern Shanxi Province promulgated "Measures on the Implementation of Free Medical Services for All People (trial)," and immediately varying opinions emerged. Supporters believed that Shenmu is a pioneer of public welfare medical services, heading in the direction of new medical reform, and has earnestly solved the problem of medical services being expensive. Objectors argue that free medical service for all the people is too courageous and does not have enough practicality. It would be "utopia", and does not fully consider the consequences to citizens. The system design has many flaws, lacks a necessary monitoring mechanism, and there are many situations where people are hospitalized for a slight illness, and do not leave the hospital even when cured; this will lead to the destruction of the measure. After half a year, Shenmu County reported that by the end of September 2009, a total of 78.8 million yuan of medical expenses were reimbursed, and the real amount reimbursed for 7 months did not surpass the budget scope. Even so, most people still believe it is difficult for the measure to be promoted throughout the whole country.

In order to quicken the expansion of medical insurance coverage, three measures have been taken. First, the problem of medical insurance for retirees from bankrupt enterprises would be solved a year in advance. This problem has puzzled research on medical insurance for several years, but it cannot be solved without financial investment. At the beginning of 2009, the State Council requested that two years be taken to solve this problem, afterward, the State Council executive meeting decided that to shorten that goal by a year, and by the end of 2009, all retirees from bankrupt state-owned enterprises would be integrated in the local basic medical insurance for urban employees, and the central financial administration has arranged for a disposable subsidy fund of 42.9 billion yuan for this reason. Second, medical insurance for urban residents is comprehensively advanced. Medical insurance for urban residents was set to be implemented in 2010, but in 2009 the State Council requested that it be pushed forward, and all college students in school would be included. In April 2009, the Ministry of Human Resources and Social Security and the Ministry of Finance both requested that all cities launch plans for basic medical insurance for urban residents in 2009, 50% of the population should try and be insured, and for experimental cities, 80% of its population would be attempted to be covered by 2009. Third, related insurance policies need to be readjusted to meet insurance demands of flexible employees and peasant workers etc., to open up networks for the medical insurance system, and to guide local authorities in exploring various levels of subsidies and the corresponding levels of treatment, which enhance the flexibility and elasticity of system. The system made by man ought to be broken, and groups with difficultly obtaining employment would be allowed to have a choice of different medical insurance, which have brought into play a comprehensive role of medical insurance for urban and rural residents. The State Council requested that, at the end of 2009, total insured population of medical insurance for employees, medical insurance for urban residents and the new rural cooperative medical system reach 1.2 billion persons. The Ministry of Human Resources and Social Security determined that the annual plan of coverage expansion of medical insurance for employees and medical insurance for urban residents ought to reach 390 million persons by the end of 2009. During the first half of 2009, coverage expansion of many areas did not achieve half its goal, although half of the time specified had already passed because of the following three aspects. First, factual data was not clear. With a frequent floating population, many people separated from their household, and therefore medical insurance organizations could not find these people. Moreover, massive rural labors flowed into the cities, presenting duplicate participation. Second, local financial subsidies do not reach the desired position on time. Third, medical insurance organizations lack effective methods. Participation of medical insurance for urban residents is voluntary, and cannot resort to coercion. Thus coverage expansion mainly depends on propaganda. After the third quarter of 2009, various regions increased strength of coverage, and at the end of October, the insured population of medical insurance for employees and for urban residents reached 374.51 million.

Since the basic medical insurance system was established, medical insurance departments have made countless efforts to reduce individual medical expenses, but the mindset that medical services is expensive still rings highly in society. To alleviate the problem of medical services being expensive, five measures have been taken. First, the highest payment quota of medical insurance fund has been raised, it rose from being equivalent to 3–4 times of average local wages or average resident income at present to about 6 times or above, which has led to acting as a relief function for medical security system, and reduces the economic burden to seriously ill patients. To guide insured persons to low-rank hospitals to see a doctor, enhancing fund payment proportion of grass-roots medical institutions has been given priority. Second, unified planning of the outpatient expenses of basic medical insurance for urban residents has been positively carried out to expand the beneficiary scope of medical insurance for urban residents. Third, measures on individual account application of basic medical insurance for urban residents have been explored and readjusted, and unified planning of outpatient expenses of basic medical insurance for urban residents will be carried out at the right moment, and the reimbursement scope and proportion of outpatient expenses have been gradually expanded and enhanced, thus mutual aid and effectiveness of individual account funds can be increased. Fourth, management of medical insurance fund has been strengthened, and the surplus fund has been controlled, thus effectiveness of medical insurance fund can be raised. Fifth, negotiations mechanism of medical services and pharmaceutical price has been introduced, purchase by bulk is used by medical insurance in order to reduce the price of medical services and pharmaceuticals, and thus insured persons can enjoy quality services for a lower price.

Because current medical insurance has a lower unified planning level, it is not convenient for insured individuals to see a doctor or to make payments, and thus many complaints have appeared. As a result, the State Council requested that a unified planning level of medical insurance be rapidly enhanced, to reduce payment amount of trans-regional medical services, to realize municipal-level unified planning by 2011, and simultaneously to give priority to retirees', in order to solve the problem of seeing a doctor and payment. Each region positively explored good measures. In the Changjiang Delta area, Shanghai City took the lead to sign a cooperative agreement, with an agreed upon fixed number of years and payment, and for those who move out of urban areas, but already participate in urban medical insurance for employees, to have their medical insurance transfer with them.

II. *Experiments of New Rural Endowment Insurance*

In the recent ten years, the government has worked relentlessly in rural areas in terms of public finance, such as cancelling agricultural tax, implementing direct subsidy for agriculture, preventing miscellaneous

fees and school fees of rural compulsory education, and establishing
the new rural cooperative medical system, and so on. These policies
were favored by farmers, were known to them as, "no taxes for farming, no fees for school education, and reasonable cost to see a doctor." But, there was no policy on farmer's basic retirement security. At
the end of 2008, a nearly 70 year old Hunan farmer, Fu Daxin
(付达信), did not escape and calmly waited for police to arrest him
after he "robbed" at the Beijing Railway Station. He said that he
robbed to solve his difficult life, where he hadn't eaten meat for two
years, and wanted to live out his retimrent life in prison. He requested
earnestly that he be given a heavy sentence, and hoped to spend the
remainder of his life in the jail. Fu Daxin case explained that the
problem of endowment insurance for farmers, especially old farmers,
is very prominent. Families are unable to fully support their aging
members, and thus establishing a rural endowment insurance system
was very urgent. Especially after minimum social security system for
urban and rural residents was established throughout the whole country and completely coverage of medical insurance was also proposed
in 2009, the absence of an endowment insurance system for rural
residents became more prominent.

   In fact, as early as 1991, the Ministry of Civil Affairs started to carry
out experiments with rural endowment insurance in some areas. But
because these experiments focused on "individuals as main payment
subject, collective subsidy as auxiliary, suitably preferential policy," the
government basically did not invest, in fact farmers paid money to provide for their aged life, self-saving "old insurance for farmers," did not
excite farmers. Even if they had participated in the rural endowment
insurance, pension level was also low, and many people's monthly pension was less than 3 Yuan. In recent years, the central government paid
more attention to issues of agriculture, farmer and rural area, and proposed to build the new rural areas. Some areas started to explore new
rural endowment insurance. Government investment has increased,
and a total of 500 counties have developed experiments with new rural
endowment insurance, but various regions have various methods of
work, which are not standard. In September 2009, the State Council
printed and distributed "Guiding Opinions of the State Council on
the Trial New Rural Endowment Insurance" and started to establish
a new rural endowment insurance system, which integrates individual
payment, collective subsidy and government subsidy. This was done
to promote social fairness and justice, to eradicate the dualistic struc-

ture of urban and rural areas, to realize basic equalization of public services, for farmers to not have to worry about retirement life, to approach extra worries step-by-step, and also simultaneously to deal with the international financial crisis, to expand domestic consumption demand, to quicken the consummation of the social security system covering urban and rural areas, and to promote harmonious social construction and long period of order and stability of the state. The institutional innovations of new rural endowment insurance are mainly manifested in two aspects. First, it puts into practice integrated financial means. Individual payment, collective subsidy and government subsidy, and local financial institutions give subsidies for the farmer's payment. Insured rural residents pay the endowment insurance premium according to stipulations; payment standards are 100 yuan, 200 yuan, 300 yuan, 400 yuan and 500 yuan. Each region may also practically increase the payment scale, the insured person chooses his or her own payment scale, and the state readjusts the payment scale based on average net income increase per rural resident. Village collectives that have met the conditions offer subsidies for insurance, and the villagers' committee democratically decides the subsidy standard. The state encourages other economic organizations, social benefit organizations and individuals to provide economic funding for the subsidies. Local authorities that provide subsidies must not provide less than 30 yuan a year per person; for these who choose the highest standard, suitable encouragements may be given, and the concrete standard and methods are determined at the provincial-level people's government. For the groups in rural areas who have difficulty with payment, including the serious disabled person etc., the local authority subsidies their retirement insurance premium at the lowest standard. The state establishes an lifelong individual account of endowment insurance for every insured person of the new rural endowment insurance, individual payment, collective subsidy, and subsidies from other economic organizations, social benefit organizations and individuals, as well as subsidy from local authority. This information is all recorded into an individual's account. At present, the saving amount for individual accounts is calculated according in Renminbi of the one-year deposit interest rate of financial organs promulgated by the People's Bank of China every year. Second, it implements the union of foundational pension and individual account pension, and the national financial administration pays the sum of lowest standard foundational pension, 55 yuan per person per month. The local authority may raise the foundational pension standard according to situation. For rural residents with a long-term payment plan, the foundational pension may be suitably increased, and the local financial administration increases funds. The monthly drawing standard for individual account pension is the total savings amount of individual account divided by 139 (same as the computing coefficient of the individual account pension of current basic endowment insurance for urban employees). If the insured person dies, the fund balance in the individual account, minus government subsidy, may be inherited legally; the balance from government subsidy is used to pay the pension of other insured persons. The central financial administration subsidizes completely foundational pension of lowest standard in central and western areas, and subsidizes 50% in the eastern area. 60 year old and above rural people, who do not have basic endowment insurance for urban employees, receive pensions month by month. These two outstanding features of the new rural endowment insurance system have emphasized the important responsibility borne by the state for providing for elderly farmers, and have determined the principle requirement of government financial investment. This is different from the old rural endowment insurance where farmers could only depend on their own savings. The State Council decided that experiment coverage of new rural endowment insurance would reach 10% of counties (cities, and regions) in 2009. Regions of implementation would gradually expand, and would eventually be implemented throughout the entire country, and cover all rural residents within an age range before 2020.

The new rural endowment insurance system has been commended. In the experimental areas, with the implementation of the new rural endowment insurance system, farmers' idea of retirement support has tremendously changed, and this new idea has gradually taken root in people's minds. Rural old people can have a fixed income, and regain self-confidence in life. In general, farmers favor the new rural endowment insurance; they are enthusiastic about it, and some say, "a pension is equal to several sons!" Most people believe that this is an important reform, which benefits millions of farmers, and promotes social justice; they are full of expectation for concrete implementation and consummation of this system. Establishing a new rural endowment insurance system is the first step in solving the difficult problem in history of farmers' social retirement life. It also establishes unified planning of urban and rural social security system, and not only does it help solve the problems in agriculture, for farmers and within the rural area, but it also helps drive rural domestic demand effectively. In regards to the responses from various social aspects, the following must be done well in carrying out the new rural endowment insurance. First, at present the work of experiment site must be done well, and then the system can be implemented throughout the whole country, based on the work of the experiment sites, to allow all rural old people a chance to enjoy the material benefit of the policy as soon as possible; rules and regulations must be established, management strengthened, and services should be done well, thus forming a complete set of rules and regulations. Next, benefits to farmers must be given priority throughout implementation; flexibility and elasticity of the system should be enhanced, and government subsidy ought to obtain its goal promptly, because the subsidy the government assumes will have a direct impact on the results of the policy. The people hope that the amount of government subsidy for new rural endowment insurance will be readjusted continuously along with the enhancement of economic development level, thus allowing farmers' insurance compensation to meet the real standard of living. Third, the new rural endowment insurance allows for the voluntary participation of farmers and does not resort to coercion, and also does not unilaterally seek an insured rate. However, it must also insist on bringing into play the positive role of traditional rural retirement security means, and children must undertake the responsibility to support old people. Finally, supervision to the new rural endowment insurance fund must be strengthened, and the security of the fund must be guaranteed to maximize benefit to insured farmers.

Regarding the experiment site of new rural endowment insurance, local authorities are optimistic, and requested to increase experiment sites. Some areas carry out certain provincial-level pilot programs with provincial-level financial investments. Some local authorities argue that the goal of having the whole country covered by 2020 is too slow, and requested to speed up the progress. Through analysis on the enthusiasm of local authorities, on one hand, an explanation is central financing subsidizes the experiment site of new rural endowment insurance, moreover unlike differences of subsidies to the fund of endowment insurance for employees, this time the central financial administration not only gives subsidy to central and western areas, but also suitable subsidy to eastern areas; On the other hand, another explanation is that this policy is a common aspiration of the people, and people will bring pressure to those cities and counties which lag in implementing such a system. Beijing, Tianjin and Zhengzhou etc. also released measures on endowment insurance for urban and rural residents based on the new rural endowment insurance system, which established a complete coverage retirement security system.

Of course, pilot programs of new rural endowment insurance just started up, many major issues need to be explored and further implemented. First, the individual account pension level of new rural endowment insurance is tied up with the investment yield of individual account fund, and before finding safe investment means, it must be determined whether it is appropriate for the individual account fund of new rural endowment insurance to calculate the interests according to the deposit interest rate of bank. Another issue is whether millions of peasant workers need simultaneously to participate in endowment insurance for employees and the new rural endowment insurance, and how both link up. Third, the foundational pension level of 55 yuan per month is possibly low. But it is still an achievement because it started, and as the system grows it will get better, and Chinese farmers will certainly obtain material benefits.

III. *Perplexity of Peasant Workers Endowment Insurance*

Since 2007, the state has increased its attack strength, and therefore the phenomenon of arrears of wages of peasant workers has greatly decreased, peasant workers' demand has shifted from salary benefit toward lifelong benefits and social security. On October 13, 2009, CCTV's Half-Hour Economy column reported that, 54-year-old Yi Chengfang (易承芳) from Hengyang of Hunan worked in a cosmetics factory of Guangzhou with her husband since 1987. Originally she thought she would retire in 2010, but she suddenly discovered that she was actually unable to retire in Guangzhou at that time and draw from the pension although she has participated in the endowment insurance, because her time limit of insurance premium payment was less than 15 years in Guangzhou. However, she could not continue to pay the insurance premium up to 15 years, thus she had to withdraw from the endowment insurance, and draw from her individual payment amount and interests in her individual account. Yi Chengfang's 11 years of payment for endowment insurance premium was just the bank's current deposits for 11 years, therefore "providing for the elderly" was still far for her. With the first generation of floating workers gradually meeting retirement age, Yi Chengfang's example is not the norm, but has universality, which reflected the dilemma of current endowment insurance system prominently.

The state unified the system of endowment insurance for enterprise employees in 1997, and expanded the coverage of endowment insurance; henceforth the first generation of floating workers fulfilled payment duty, and received individual account. As a result of peasant workers' constant mobility, and because endowment insurance relations are non-transferable, before returning to their hometown every year, the overwhelming majority of peasant workers chose to withdraw the endowment insurance at the end of the year, and those who do not withdraw the endowment insurance are more or less facing with same problem that Yi Chengfang faced.

Yi Chengfang's puzzle firstly indicated that the endowment insurance policy is rigid and lacks human-oriented operation in some areas. The appearance of the phenomenon where people are unable to retire is because the policy design lacks elasticity, as well as units concerned did not strictly check when verifying the employees' personal information for the payment of endowment insurance premium. Since the policy stipulated that the employee must pay endowment insurance premium for 15 years or more before retirement, and then those whose age does not fit the conditions are not allowed to pay, otherwise paying for less than 15 years is regarded as a reason to refuse providing pension. Permit first and then reject like this, which it is obviously not the responsibility of peasant workers. It is unfair to let individual peasant workers bear the consequence of policy error. As for peasant workers, when they paid the premium for more than ten years, and discovered that their payment was actually done in vain, the credibility of the government is weakened, especially the endowment insurance system. Certainly, because the policy startup of peasant workers participation in endowment insurance is late, and imperfect, it is inevitable to present the flaws in the policy, therefore it is necessary to treat it quickly, especially the problem of being unable to retire. According to the principle that special cases should be handled with special methods, they should be allowed to make up the lacking number of year through a method of individual payment, and they should be allowed to retire in their working places of more than ten years, and furthermore simply let them withdraw their individual payment and interests and terminate endowment insurance relations. In this way, the system can be more human-oriented, and the "dead angle" of the system can be ceased.

Yi Chengfang's puzzle also explained that the task of carrying out the national treatment to off-farm workers is arduous. Social security should not be bond by one's region, and any citizen who participates in social security, regardless of where he moves to in the country should enjoy the corresponding social security for one's premium payment, which is not only the starting point for the formulation of a social security policy, but also the responsibility of the social security system. Social security of "administering affairs within own boundary" violates the original intention of this system. At present the unified planning level of endowment insurance is low, and the fund of endowment insurance restricts people's activities to a designated area, which have taken shape to form local benefits. Facing local benefit, rights and interests of people from other areas are often repelled. In recent years, in an attempt to solve some residual problems from history, some areas have formulated flexible policies one after another, for example, insured persons who have been at their retiring age but have not met their number of payment years are allowed to continuously participate in the endowment insurance and pay the premium until the treatment conditions can be met. But, for peasant workers, the policy is always somewhat evasive in this aspect. It looks as if the task that carries out the national treatment especially "provincial treatment" or "urban resident's treatment" to peasant workers is also very arduous.

Yi Chengfang's puzzle also explained that it is necessary to speed up national unified planning of endowment insurance. Endowment insurance must be found throughout the whole country. In recent years, provincial-level unified planning work of endowment insurance advancement made big process, and before the end of 2009, it would be realized in the whole country. Thus, the gap of benefit between cities and counties in the province should be polished down to solve the problem of transfer and continuation of endowment insurance relations in the province. But provincial-level unified planning can only alleviate the difficultly of endowment insurance relations transfer, and cannot fundamentally solve the difficultly of transfer. This becomes increasingly problematic because peasant workers have strong inter-provincial mobility. Without a unified endowment, peasant workers are left aimlessly drifting on the road, without support from anyone.

IV. State Run Institutions' Endowment Insurance Reform is in a Dilemma

At the beginning of 2009, the State Council decided to first carry out the pilot endowment insurance system reform in institutions in Shanxi Province, Shanghai, Zhejiang Province, Guangdong Province and Chongqing City, and to push the pilot classified reform of institutions, and those areas, which were not experiment sites, would still carry out the original institution retirement system. After the State Council promulgated the implementation of experiment site in five provinces and cities, a large response was stirred in society, especially among the academia in the pilot areas. Because there are fears that integration of unified planning and individual account and implementation of computing method of new retired treatment will bring about a large reduction in treatment for retirees, and under the influence of the understanding that "more changes equals less treatment," the tide of retirement in advance also appeared in some pilot areas. Some deputies to the National People's Congress suggested that the State Council and the Ministry of Human Resources and Social Security suspend this pilot reform, and begin to formulate the joint endowment insurance system reform plan of state organs, institutions and enterprises. Although five provinces and cities carried out for about one year "pilot reform of endowment insurance system of institutions," in general, polices were difficult to advance and most provinces and cities are still carrying out survey and argumentation of the plan.

State run institutions is a unique phenomenon in China and is the important component of political, economic, cultural and social system in China. They undertake functions, which provide massive public services and social management for the society, at present it employs about 30 million people, especially large quantities of high-quality talents concentrated in departments of education, science, culture and health. Endowment insurance system in institutions have encountered resistance and been in difficult positions in the past. As early as 1992, the personnel departments launched pilot programs in Yunnan, Jiangsu, Fujian, Shandong, Liaoning and Shanxi provinces etc., but because there were differences in implementation among regions, a countrywide unified comprehensive reform plan was not formed. This time, the pilot reform plan has five main aspects. First, it implements the union of social unified planning and individual account, much like endowment insurance for enterprise employees. The work unit pays about 20% of total wages, individual pays about 8% of their own wages, and the individual account is established; Second, it is consistent with the methods of basic pension of enterprise employees, but joins with the system, and adopts old measures for old persons, and new measures for new persons; Third, it gradually implements provincial-level unified planning; Fourth, it establishes a normal regulation mechanism of pension; Fifth, it establishes vocation annuity system. The system design has already taken into consideration the rationality of the changing and integrating system, but it still caused great disturbance at the beginning. The reasons are mainly as follows. First, policy propaganda did fulfill its goal; many people did not understand the true intention of reform, and they misunderstood the reform and thought it would reduce treatment level to lighten the national burden. Second, the institution has a complex structure. Some undertake social management functions and participate in public management, and some are engaged in production and operation, and so on, but the reform did not completely reach its desired goal, thus confusion was unavoidable. Third, the practical situation of institutions was underestimated. For a long time, the institution mainly carried on the management according to the pattern of the Party and government organs; they were not separated. In terms of social security, it likewise followed suit. The retirement treatment did not line up with premium payment even thought the endowment insurance system of institutions was implemented in some areas, and the system reform still remained at initial stages of collection and payment in cash, the work unit management and balanced retirement pension. Especially since many outstanding people are found within institutions, thus these social influences cannot be neglected.

If reform of endowment insurance of institutions were not carried out, it is unable to establish a personnel administration system that is beneficial for mobile personnel, and personnel management is unable to achieve "personnel mobility." Reform of institution is also a type of system engineering, and endowment insurance reform is only a supporting measure. If that were individually hastily advanced, it is unavoidable that many handicaps would appear. Reform of social security system follows a trend of "first easy, then hard" in terms of implementation. It starts with the small resistance and gradually pushes into the "depth zone." Without a doubt, endowment insurance reform of institutions has involved many personnel, has a large scope and strong policy, has penetrated into the "depth zone" of reform, and various profitable notions collide, thus creating many difficulties.

Fundamentally, endowment insurance reform of institutions is first facing the challenge to fairness. For a long time, personnel of institutions and civil servants enjoyed "unbreakable security" (铁保障 *Tie-BaoZhang*). Now the reform is carried out only in institutions, which is obviously unfair. Institution personnel are faced with complex struggle between benefits, and they have intense feelings of being deprived, therefore they faced trials in terms of the economy, politics and social psychology.

Fundamentally speaking, the endowment insurance reform of Institutions should be pushed along with wage reform in institutions. In fact, after civil servant's wages were reformed, the wage level has been higher than within institutions; if the wage system of Institutions is not reformed, the advancement of endowment insurance reform will be untimely. Moreover, after the current pilot plan is implemented, many professors and senior engineers may remain in the mentality that "having enough food and clothing" is enough. It is delightful that, the wage reform of Institutions has been started. Performance salary was implemented in public health and grass-roots medical and health institutions starting October 1 2009, and will be implemented in other institutions after January 1, 2010.

The dilemma of endowment insurance reform of institutions also indicated that the social security reform must have top design, unified consideration and comprehensive advancement. It is also unreasonable to list every group and to make a respective set of retirement system, which cannot win understanding and approval. Different groups have different benefits and different demands, our society has developed to the stage where social justice and fairness are emphasized; policies must analyzed the consequences before they are released, otherwise unfairness may appear, which breaches the original intention of reform.

In brief, in 2009, the social security work made big progress towards everybody having social security, and the frame of the social security system with minimum social security for urban and rural residents, endowment insurance for all people and medical insurance for all people, and covered urban and rural areas was formed, but it also faced some prominent problems, such as difficulty transferring social security relations, and reform of the endowment insurance of institutions, and so on. Looking into 2010, quickening to achieve complete coverage of social security, normalizing transfer and continuation of social security relations in different areas, enhancing a unified planning level of social security, achieving national unified planning as soon as possible, and raising the security level etc. will be the emphasis of the work. This is not only what is expected from all different circles in regards to social security work, but is also the main direction that social security work will head towards in the next period.

REPORT ON CHINA'S EDUCATIONAL DEVELOPMENT IN 2009

Yang Dongping

Abstract

In 2009, in terms of China's education, on one hand, all kinds deep-seated contradictions and problems in education were still evident, dealing with the civil service examinations; Meanwhile, from the central government to the local governments, the educational reformation from top to bottom and from bottom to top was also intense. China's education was on the eve of big reformation.

I. *Education in 2008*

According to "2008 National Statistical Bulletin of the Educational Development" of the Ministry of Education, by the end of 2008, in total 3038 counties (cities and regions) accepted the "popularizing of nine-year compulsory education and clearing young-adults analphabet" ("两基" Liang Ji). This was 99.1% of all counties, and the population covered reached 99.3%.

In 2008, there were 133,700 kindergartens in the whole country, which increased by 4600 from the previous years, 24,749,600 infants in kindergarten (including preschool), which increased by 1,261,300 from previous years.

Also, the school-age population and schools at the elementary school and junior middle school level reduced year by year; school-run conditions of middle and elementary schools further improved, thus the supply demand relations for compulsory education became obviously more relaxed. From Table 5.1, we see that, compared with the situation in 2000, the number of elementary schools dropped 45.6% in the whole country in 2008, and the number of enrolled students dropped 20.6%; the number of junior middle schools dropped 9.4%, and the number of enrolled students dropped 10.7%.

Table 5.1: Basic Education from 2000–2008

		2000	2005	2008
Elementary schools	Number of schools (Ten thousand)	55.36	36.62	30.09
	Enrolled students (Ten thousand)	13013.25	10864.07	10331.51
Junior middle schools	Number of schools (Ten thousand)	6.39	6.25	5.79
	Enrolled students (Ten thousand)	6256.29	6214.94	5584.97
	Gross enrollment rate (%)	88.6	95	98.5
	Proportion of students entering schools of a higher grade (%)	51.1	69.68	83.4
Senior high school	Number of schools (Ten thousand)	3.62	3.15	3.08
	Enrolled students (Ten thousand)	2517.68	4030.95	4576.07
	Gross enrollment rate (%)	42.8	52.7	74.0

Note: the statistics at the stage of junior middle school and high school include vocational education.

It is predicted that, if 12.8 years of education is taken as the average anticipated education years, by 2020, the goal is that total enrolled students at the stage of compulsory education will reduce by more than 18 million from that of 2008.

Enrolled students at the senior high school level are still increasing. In 2008, the gross enrollment rate at the senior high school level was 74%, an 8 percentage points rise from the previous year. Among them, enrolled students of regular senior high schools accounted for 54.1%, and enrolled students of secondary vocational education accounted for 45.9%.

In 2008, the overall scope of higher education reached 29.07 million persons, where the gross enrollment rate of higher education reached 23.3%. There were 2,263 general colleges and universities in the whole country, with 1,079 colleges and universities with undergraduate courses, and 1,184 higher vocational schools (college). The student recruitment number and the enrolled student scale of higher education increased continually. Teachers and administrative staff of

Table 5.2: Student Recruitment of General Colleges and Universities in Recent Years

	2003	2005	2006	2007	2008	2009
Recruitment number of general college and undergraduate course (Ten thousand)	382.17	504.46	546.05	565.92	607.66	629
Growth over previous year (%)	19.24	12.77	8.24	3.64	7.38	4
Recruitment number of graduate students (Ten thousand)	26.89	36.48	39.79	41.86	44.64	50
Growth over previous year (%)	32.72	11.8	9.07	5.20	6.64	5
Among them: master students (Ten thousand)	22.02	31	34.2	36.06	38.67	–
Doctoral students (Ten thousand)	4.87	5.48	5.6	5.80	5.98	–

Note: Data is planned number at the beginning of 2009.

general colleges and universities were 2,051,000 persons, in which full-time teachers were 1,237,500, and the ratio between students and teachers was 17.23:1 (See Table 5.2).

In 2009, general colleges and universities planned to recruit 6.29 million students, a 4% growth from the previous year; it is estimated that average enrollment rate would be close to 62%, almost a 5 percentage points increase from that of 2008. Statistics indicated that in 2009 the applicants for general colleges and universities reached approximately 10.2 million, in which holders of high school diplomas reached 7,500,000 persons, which accounted for 73.5%; applicants reduced 3.8% from that of 2008, reached more than 800,000 persons, which initiated fervent discussion in society. In 2009, in total 10 provinces and regions, Liaoning, Tianjin, Zhejiang, Anhui, Fujian, Guangdong, Shandong, Hainan, Ningxia and Jiangsu, implemented a new plan of college entrance examination after the new curriculum in senior high schools were implemented.

Non-governmental education continued to grow. In 2008, all levels of and all kinds of non-governmental schools (educational institutions) reached 100,900, which increased 5,700 from the previous years; enrolled students for all kinds of educational degrees reached

90   YANG DONGPING

Table 5.3: Proportion of Enrolled Students in Non-Governmental
Education from 2006 to 2008 (%)

	2006	2007	2008
Number of infants in kindergarten	34.26	36.99	39.68
Enrolled students of general elementary schools	3.85	4.25	4.65
Enrolled students of general junior middle schools	6.61	7.19	7.67
Enrolled students of general senior high school	9.85	9.75	9.70
Enrolled students of secondary vocational schools	11.20	12.96	13.98
Non-governmental colleges and universities	16.13	18.55	19.86

Data from the national statistical bulletin of development in 2006, 2007 and 2008

28,244,000 persons, which increased by 2,409,000 persons from the previous years. The proportion of enrolled students of all kinds of non-governmental schools is showed in Table 5.3.

The non-governmental education has grown rapidly at the preschool education level, but actually encounters a "cold current" in the domain of higher education. In 2009, in recruitment of non-governmental colleges, the source of students fell about 40%–50%; the college city in Langfang of Hebei and Xi'an's ten thousand-person college had few students. According to analysis, it is because state-run colleges and universities increased the enrollment of students, some students went into secondary vocational education, the number of students who study abroad increased, graduates faced difficulties obtaining employment, and non-governmental colleges and universities were not as advanced.

In 2008, total educational funds were 1,450.074 billion yuan, a 19.37% increase from previous year; national financial educational funds were 1,044.963 billion yuan, a 26.20% increase from previous year.[1]

[1] The Ministry of Education, the National Bureau of Statistics and the Ministry of Finance: "2008 National Statistical Bulletin on the Execution of Educational Appropriations" in "*China Education Daily*" (《中国教育报》) on November 20, 2009.

II. *Significant Situations and Central Issues of Education*

A. *The "Program" is Formulated, and Minister of Education is Changed*

In August 2008, formulation work of the "National Program for Medium- and Long-Term Educational Reform and Development" was officially started, the State Council leaders decided to publicize the policy, asking the people for political advice and suggestions on social problems, and trying harder to take practical measures to tackle public difficulties. This was regarded as a significant action in changing the educational policy-making method.

In January 2009, the Ministry of Education issued the proclamation to openly solicit opinions for the research and formulation of the "Program," and promulgated the detailed list of 11 special topics and 36 sub-subjects, which caused an intense reaction in society. By February 6, opinions and suggestions collected reached more than 1.1 million pieces. On February 6, the office for the "Program" issued a proclamation and raised 20 questions in 4 aspects to unceasingly solicit public suggestions. By February 28, 2009, the public gave more than 2,125,000 pieces of opinions. Among them, the departments of education received more than 14,000 e-mails and letters, Netizen sent more than 11,000 pieces of comments through the websites of departments of education; in social websites and campus websites, more than 2.1 million comments on educational reform were issued.

This was a very good beginning but hereafter decision making on the "Program" returned to old policy of internal decision-making. Although internal expert symposiums was held many times to carry on rounds of internal opinion solicitation and revision in the text, public discussion was no longer pursued, and therefore public opinions and public's enthusiasm faded away, a striking contrast to the beginning of the year when hundreds of millions people expected and positively participated.

On the eve of Teachers' day, Premier Wen Jiabao (温家宝总理) attended 5 classes in Beijing No. 35 Middle School, and gave a speech. He thought that China's education could not yet meet demands of economic and social development, and demands of the state talent cultivation, which sent out the signal to quicken the educational reform. On October 31, renowned scientist Qian Xuesen (钱学森) died. His theory about why the Chinese universities could not cultivate outstanding innovation talents is called "Qian Xuesen's Question," which initiated people's strong response to request reform of education. On October 31, the 11th Session of the National People's Congress democratically to relieve Zhou Ji (周济) of his post of Minister of Education, and to appoint Yuan Guiren (袁贵仁) as Minister of Education, which aroused enthusiasm amongst the entire society again.

B. *The Impact of Financial Crisis to Employment of College Students and Education*

In 2009, an important situation was the influences to China's education and employment of college students of the global financial crisis, which occurred at the end of 2008. At the beginning of the year, various national sectors took many measures to guarantee the employment of college students.

According to investigations from the School of Pedagogy at Peking University, the financial crisis caused the problem about graduates' employment, which had already been severe to become even more prominent. Only 34.6% of graduates have settled with a work unit at graduation, which fell to 40% below for the first time in the recent 8 years. "First realization rate" ("初次落实率" Chu Ci Luo Shi Lu) (including a signed contract, decision on a work unit, and waiting for a contract, attending graduate schools, study abroad, liberal profession and flexible employment etc.) dropped from 71.1% in 2007 to 65.0% in 2009, with 69.6% male graduates, and 60.1% female graduates. Master degree graduates decreased the greatest, and dropped 18.7 percentage points; doctorial graduates dropped 13.2 percentage points; graduates of junior college dropped 5.8 percentage points; graduates of undergraduate course had the smallest range of fall, and dropped 4.4 percentage points. But starting salary was improved because the structure of employment had sweeping changes, and the proportion of employment in state-owned enterprises and institutions had obvious developments.[2]

Meanwhile, the education training market and the continuing education market rise against the market trend, thus many people chose to pursue higher education. In 2007 the scope of the education training market was approximately 370 billion yuan, and it is estimated that by 2010 it will reach more than 500 billion yuan. A batch of education

---

[2] Yuan Chunlin (原春琳): *"Financial Crisis Brings Biggest Impact to the Employment of Master Graduates"* in *"China Youth Daily"* (《中国青年报》) on November 10, 2009.

training organizations was favored by international risk investment, and obtained a large amount of funds. The West's economic recession, the reduction of tuition fee and the increases of overseas student recruitment have had positive driving influence for the education of Chinese student abroad. According to the notifications of News & Cultural Office and Consul Section of the American Embassy, the data of 2009 annual "Open Doors Report" indicated that, from 2008 to 2009, in total 98,235 Chinese students went to the US to study, a 21.1% increase from the previous year. From January 1 to November 15, 2009, the American diplomatic corps in China issued 90,000 student visas and visas of exchange and visiting scholars, which increased 23% from that of 2008. Another change which is worth paying attention is, formerly, Chinese students favored going to the US for advanced studies after graduation from undergraduate courses, but the 2009 report showed that, from 2008 to 2009, more and more Chinese students chose to go to the US for bachelor's degrees.[3]

C. *Frequent Occurrence of Corrupt Events in College Entrance Examination and the Academic World*

In 2009, all sort of corrupt events occurred in education, including corruption in college entrance examination, academic corruption and corruption of college cadres etc.

In recent years, the order of college entrance examination was under control, and the overall situation has had improvement. But in Songyuan City of Liaoning Province there appeared large amounts of corruption. Teachers participated in the market of tools for cheating, which indicated that cheating in the college entrance examination has assumed new characteristics, collectivization and use of technology in some areas. There are other representative corrupt cases in the college entrance examination; for example, the event that Luo Caixia (罗彩霞) from Guizhou Province took the test for someone else reflected the violation from the basic-unit local administration to the system of college entrance examination. Some students from Chongqing pretend to be minority students to obtain awarded marks;[4] the test of sports

---

[3] "US Embassy in China: 2009 Chinese students in the US increase 23% sharply in the first school year" at http://goabroad.sohu.com/ 20091119/n268337775.shtml/

[4] Chongqing City cancelled the enrollment qualifications of 31 students with false minority statuses finally, and gave the inner-party warning for 15 cadres; see *"China Youth Daily"* on July 8, 2009.

awarded-marks projects "three models and three electricity" (model airplane and ship, ship model, vehicle model and radio direction finding, radio communication and electronic manufacturing) increased in Zhejiang and it was thought that most students were from families of power and influence. These all indicated that the present system of awarding marks in the college entrance examination is being abused to seek private interests for a small number of people because of the absence of a standard and fair procedure. According to investigations, in total 196,000 examinees of Chongqing in 2009, as high as 70,000 examinees obtained awarded marks unexpectedly, and accounted for more than 35% of all examinees.[5] Awarding marks in the college entrance examination have 14 items according to the provisions of the Ministry of Education, but accumulative total preferential policies have reached 192 items in various regions.[6] Another famous scandal is that, a 70-year-old well-known tutor of a doctoral student from the Central Conservatory of Music had sex with a woman student who had registered herself for the examination for doctoral student of this school. He received a 100,000 yuan bribery. Afterward the Central Conservatory of Music severely punished the party professor. It exposed "the hidden rule" in student recruitment of art academies.

Academic corruption occurred frequently in colleges and universities, and many have involved top-level schools and scholars. Original associate professor He Haibo (贺海波) of Zhejiang University embezzled the findings of other people to publish many papers, and the name of Li Lianda (李连达), post-doctoral tutor, academician of the Chinese Academy of Engineering and dean of the School of pharmacy of Zhejiang University was also involved with the "questionable paper." The Zhejiang University decided to dismiss He Haibo from teaching, and no longer appoint Li Lianda. Chen Zhanyun (陈湛匀), professor and tutor of doctoral student of Shanghai University was relieved the qualifications of Academic committee member of this school because of plagiarism, and was dismissed from the related administrative post. Jia Shiqiu (贾士秋) from the School of Journalism and Communication of the Zhengzhou University was relieved his administrative post and dismissed from teaching because he made

---

[5] The editorial of "*Beijing News*" (《新京报》), "*How does 'High School Headmaster Recommendation System' Dodge Cheating*" on July 14, 2009.
[6] Cheng Mo and Luo Man (程墨、罗曼): "*Public Announcement of Awarded Marks: Antiseptic of Sunshine College Entrance Examination*" in "*China Education Daily*" on July 8, 2009.

false claims of academic achievement, and provided false materials. Vice-President Huang Qing (黄庆) of the Southwest Jiaotong University had his doctorate revoked and qualifications to tutor graduate students because of doctorate paper plagiarism. In 2009, academic candidate Zhou Zude (周祖德), President of the Wuhan University of Technology was revealed to have plagiarized, and lost an election for academician. The paper was signed also by Lu Jierong (陆杰荣), Vice-president of Liaoning University, and Doctor in school Yang Lun (杨伦) who confirmed the plagiarism, the school authority said Lu Jierong was not directly responsible for the event, and plagiarism was done by the doctoral student alone. It was also disclosed that the doctorate paper of Xu Zhiwei (徐志伟), President of the Guangzhou University of Traditional Chinese Medicine, was suspected of plagiarism. Xu Yan (许燕), Associate Professor of the School of Journalism, Fudan University was also suspected of plagiarism, and the situation was handed over to the school. Six professors from Xi'an Jiaotong University sued "Changjiang Scholars" for counterfeiting academic achievement.

According to investigations from Jiusan Society on the academic atmosphere of the colleges and universities and the scientific and technological circles, as high as 86% of the people believe that the phenomenon of bad academic atmosphere existed partially or universally, which indicated that this problem is serious in China, and questioned intensely China's system of technological prize. For example, the leader steals other people's achievements in scientific research, the scientific and technological achievements are counterfeited to obtain a prize, and the official standard was dominant in the assignment of scientific research subjects, and so on. These showed that administrative authority is oversized and lacks a supervision mechanism to combat academic corruption.[7]

In September, 2009, Chen Zhaofang (陈昭方), original Standing Vice-president of Wuhan University, and Long Xiaole (龙小乐), original Standing Assistant Secretary of school party committee, were authorized to be arrested by the Hubei Provincial People's Procuratorate because they were suspected of bribery crimes, causing an "earthquake" among higher educational circles in China. But this was still only the tip of the iceberg. In recent years, only colleges and universities

---

[7] Ye Tieqiao (叶铁桥): "*Challenge to the Confidence of Technological Prize*" in "*China Youth Daily*" on September 9, 2009.

of Wuhan Area had similar cases take place. Li Haiying (李海婴), original Vice-president of Wuhan University of Technology, Li Hanchang (李汉昌), original Vice-president of Zhongnan University of Economics and Law, Liu Guanglin (刘光临), original President of Wuhan University of Science and Technology, Wu Guomin (吴国民), original Party Committee Secretary of Wuhan University of Science and Technology, Yang Yongcai (杨永才), Original Party Committee Assistant Secretary of Wuhan University of Science and Technology, Li Jinhe (李金和), original Vice-president of Hubei University, Chen Shaolan (陈少岚), original Secretary of China Three Gorges University, Ding Jie (丁杰), original Party Committee Secretary of Hubei Normal University, Gao Yong (高勇), original President of Hubei College of Chinese Traditional Medicine, and Peng Zhenkun (彭振坤), original Secretary of Hubei University for Nationalities, and so on, were on trial and condemned because of embezzlement, bribery, etc.

D. *Independent Reform Within Colleges and Universities Begin*

Under formidable social pressures, independent reform starts to sprout in colleges and universities, and it is first manifested in the reform of the enrollment system for college entrance examinations.

In November, after five universities, Tsinghua University, Shanghai Jiaotong University, University of Science and Technology of China, Xi'an Jiaotong University and Nanjing University, announced that they would recruit students independently, Peking University, University of Hong Kong and Beijing University of Aeronautics and Astronautics also announced that they would recruit students independently. Five universities, Beijing Jiaotong University, Beijing University of Posts and Telecommunications, University of Science and Technology Beijing, Beijing Forestry University and Beijing University of Chemical Technology would also implement joint examinations for the five schools. The national college entrance examination and student recruitment are transforming from a uniform system into more diversified methods.

The nine universities in the first group of "985-Engineering" (Peking University, Tsinghua University, Zhejiang University, Harbin Institute of Technology, Fudan University, Shanghai Jiao Tong University, Nanjing University, China University of Technology and Xi'an Jiaotong University) built up China's first alliance of well-known colleges and universities, and signed the "Agreement on Cooperation and Exchange of Talent Training of First-class Universities." According to the agreement, both sides would send "exchange students" to one another, mutually recognize credit hours of undergraduate course, and jointly train graduate students, mutually cultivate the best talents.

The University of South Science and Technology that Shenzhen City prepares to construct is most compelling. It is reported that this university constructed according to brand-new ideas and standards of international first-class universities will start to recruit students in 2010. Nearly half of the professors will be recruited from foreign countries; technology, commercial science and management science will become three big disciplines of the University, and the proportions are; 30% for technology, 20% for commercial science and 15% for management science. Shenzhen Municipal Party Committee and the Municipal Government decided to promulgate "Regulations of Shenzhen University" as the basis of independent schools to establish modern university system where "party committee leaders take charge and school presidents take responsibility, professors do scholarly research, have democratic management, and run the school legally," thereby to further expand the decision-making power, and to advance the administrative reform. The University of South Science and Technology appointed retired Professor Zhu Qingshi (朱清时) from the China University of Technology as president through democratic selection, and has declared a "non-administrative" policy. It is possible that this education innovative practice, from bottom to top, can become the startup and growing point to break the unified administrative system.

Some educational policies are also readjusted by the state. The state reforms the training system for graduate students, and will largely increase the proportion of graduate students. The prominent problem in postgraduate education is that the training scope for practical personnel is too small and cannot meet social demands. It is reported that, for more than 400,000 graduate students recruited every year at present, graduate students of specialty degree only account for 10%. The Ministry of Education requested that the units authorized to recruit students for specialty degree reduce academic recruitment by proportions of 5%–10%, based on the number of recruitment in 2009, and increase the recruitment of specialty-degree graduate students.

Pilot programs for undergraduate university started, big transformation will be implemented, universities at different levels will no longer be weighed according to the same standards, assessment standards will be changed from "criticism" to "appraisal," and students, parents and the public are encouraged to participate in the program and supervise.

E. *Conflict in the Balanced Development of Compulsory Education*

People are unsatisfied with education because of the intensity of the entrance examinations and competition for school selection during elementary and middle school. They argue that it enormously impaired students' physical and intellectual integrity, reduced education quality, is alienated from the function of education, and has increased parents' burden. Revolving round scholars' denouncements of "hot mathematics contest", hot examination for certificates and hot school selection, various local governments reiterated that elementary and middle schools need to be normalized, to promote balanced development of compulsory education, and formulated some measures and targets, which initiated hot discussion.

Shandong Province looked into education quality in 2008 and severely began to rectify all kinds of illegal acts in terms of running schools; Jiangsu Province stipulated that students' schoolwork burden could not be increased through legislation in 2009. Guangdong Province promulgated "Opinions of Guangdong Province on the Implementation of Advancing Balanced Development of Compulsory Education," and would make every effort to take 3–4 years to comprehensively realize equal opportunity for all school-age children and youth at the stage of compulsory education in the entire province, and simultaneously it would forbid the act of "school selection" of public elementary and middle schools and selected student recruitment for entering middle schools. Schools are not allowed to use public resources to construct or support minority schools. The general office of Henan provincial government issued "Opinions on Normalizing the Actions of Elementary and Middle School Administration to Advance the Education for Comprehensive Development," it strictly stipulated the homework workload and the guarantee of sleep time for students in elementary and middle schools, and it firmly stops the phenomena where students are organized to optionally participate in all kinds of nationwide examinations, joint examinations or other competitions, grade exams and so on; it also stipulate that the administrative departments of education and schools cannot issue targets in any form for the entrance examination for colleges and higher schools, cannot carry out place disposal and rewards and punishment by standard of enrollment quotas and test scores in the entrance examination for college and higher education; effective measures have been taken to solve the problem of large class sizes. Beijing implemented the provisions of

"Law on Compulsory Education;" school-age children and youth at the stage of compulsory education are exempt from examination to enter a nearby school, various schools cannot select students through examinations or tests, and the Municipal Education Committee would increase reform against the unfair phenomenon in entrance from elementary school to middle school in 2009.

Chengdu Bureau of Education strictly ordered that training for mathematics contest end and that reform of these contests would be done in the administrative aspect. It specified that teachers who have extracurricular concurrent jobs of teaching for these contest or run private classes will be punished severely and even dismissed; non-governmental schools cannot set the contents about mathematics contest in the test questions for their selection from elementary school to middle school or middle school to senior high school; if the public schools select students by the test scores of mathematics contest, president of the schools will possibly be dismissed from his post; service training schools for teachers and the children's palace, these "semi-official" training organizations, must close down classes of mathematics contest training. Besides ending training of mathematics contest, clean up of awarding marks system in entrance examination for high schools need to occur, making up a missed lesson illicitly needs to be strictly, and normalizing student recruitment procedures need to occur.

With the "Regulations on Compulsory Education (Draft)" where Shandong and Zhejiang provinces are soliciting opinions, heated debate has occurred about whether paid private tutors ought to be forbidden. "Regulation (Draft)" of Shandong Province stipulated that in-service teachers of public schools are not to be engaged in paid lessons. "Regulation (Draft)" of Zhejiang Province stipulated that school teachers are not to be engaged in paid family education during working days, are not to hold concurrent jobs and teach in addition to extracurricular training organizations; and are not to organize students to accept paid family education during holidays.

Chengdu extinguished mathematics training, Shandong and Zhejiang forbad paid family education, and so on. These all have caused intense social disputes, especially since considerable amount of parents approve of mathematics training and paid family education, which indicated the diversification of actual benefits behind the educational policy and the public's confusion in some core value. It also indicated that the disorderly elementary education must have radical treatment, and some prohibitions with temporary solutions are difficult to be truly effective before normalization among schools is realized. But, in order to promote a balance among schools in compulsory education, there must be standard legal governmental action.

F. *New Problems in Rural Education*

Starting in Fall of 2009, in central and western areas, average educational fund per student in rural compulsory education has enhanced to 300 yuan/year for elementary schools and 500 yuan/year for junior middle schools, which achieved the quota standard stipulated by the Central Government. This will enable improvement to school-running conditions of rural elementary and middle schools, and enhancement of rural compulsory education quality will be promoted. Rural education is facing new situations, and it needs to change from quantity growth to quality promotion; improving rural education quality and simultaneously guaranteeing rural students' educational opportunity can promote educational fairness.

Since the beginning of the year, reduction of rural students and rural education crisis in universities have been reported frequently. According to data from the Ministry of Education, from 1989 to 2008, the proportion of rural freshman in colleges and universities was gradually rising overall, from 43.4% in 1989 to in proportion with urban students in 2003, and reached 53% in 2005. But, at the same time, data from some key universities indicated that the proportion of rural students was dropping. For example, the proportion of rural freshman in China Agricultural University was in average about 39% from 1999 to 2001 every year; but, after 2002, it started to drop, and dropped to a record low in 2007, only 31.2%. According to data from Nankai University for 3 years, the proportion of rural freshman was 30% in 2006, 25% in 2007 and 24% in 2008, where a downhill trend is also obvious. In recent years, in Peking University and Tsinghua University, the proportion of rural freshman was less than 20%.[8] Namely, reduction of rural students mainly occurred in research universities.

This is mainly because of the disparity between urban and rural areas and the disparity among social strata at the senior high school level. The changed school system and the school selection system of "school

---

[8] Yuan Xinwen (袁新文): "Rural Student are getting fewer and fewer in Key Universities" in "*People's Daily*" (《人民日报》) on January 15, 2009.

selection by money" and "school selection by power" have greatly intensified injustice in education, causing the the key school system of elementary and middle schools to expand the disparity among social strata. For example, when the key high schools of Rushan County of Shandong recruited students in 2009, the matriculated score line was different in urban and rural areas, the line for rural student was 678 points, and 601 points for urban students. Rural students who have more deficient educational resources and more difficult study conditions must reach an enrollment score of 77 more points than urban students! This is obvious a discriminating policy.

The removal and combination of rural schools caused new problems. School education was expensive, drop out rate of rural students increased, which is compelling and disquieting. Guangdong Province started to readjust the layout of rural elementary and middle schools starting from 2000. Take Huazhou City as an example; in 2007, it removed and combined 105 teaching sites, in 2008, 207 elementary schools and 9 junior middle schools, in total 321 schools were removed and combined within two years, 37.5% of total schools. In Dapu County, elementary schools were reduced from 254 in 2002 to 142 at present, 112 elementary schools were removed and combined within seven years, 42.3%. Because school expenses rose sharply, and travel was often far, many students had to stop attending school.[9] While schools are neglected and continuously reduced, town elementary schools are huge, with a tremendous school and class quota. According to findings, the drop-out rate has obvious increased during the adjustment process in layout to rural elementary and middle schools because rural home education expenses increase suddenly, and is difficult to support. Next, the journey is far, and has hidden dangers, teaching quality of new schools is not high, the school conditions are limited, and so on.[10]

Meanwhile, boarding schools are massively constructed in rural areas as a means to solve the problem of far schools and to improve the education quality. But, many rural areas throng to construct boarding schools, lack operating funds and teacher organization, and the lodging

---

[9] Wang Hongwang (王宏旺): "Pains in the School Combination of Rural Elementary and Middle Schools for Eight Years" in *"Nanfang Country Daily"* (《南方农村报》) on April 1, 2009.
[10] Yu Haibo (于海波): "Vigilance of Drop-out Rate Bounce in the Rural School Layout Readjustment" in *"Seeking Truth"* (《求是》) on August 16, 2009.

and meal conditions are bad, thus creating new problems. Through one-year tracking investigations to 144 schools in three areas: North Shanxi, Central Shanxi Plain and South Shanxi, the Project Group of "Rural Education Action Program" (REAP) composed of scholars from Northwest Socio-economic Development Research Center and the Agricultural Policy Research Center of the Chinese Academy of Sciences discovered that, because of long-term malnutrition, the physical growth of many children lagged in the investigated regions. Stature of non-boarders is 5cm less than the average stature of contemporaries in the World Health Organization, and stature of boarders is 9cm less than the average. Because integrated home-based education is lacking, boarders not only have lagged physical growth, but also they may have abnormal psychological development. The psychological test result of 2000 sampled students indicated that boarders' psychological health degree is obviously worse than that of non-boarders.[11]

III. *Reconsiderations and Forecast*

Facing the problem is the premise to solving the problem, and of further reform and opening of education. These are people's expectation, not only to the Minister of Education, but also to the "National Program for Medium- and Long-term Educational Reform and Development" (hereinafter referred to as "Program") that is in process.

A. *Completing the Formulation of "Program" through Public Participation*

Draft "Program" will publicly solicit opinions in the society. How to transform formidable social pressures into actual powers of education reform and to cause "Program" to become the high-level programmatic document which can guide the vigorous development of China's education in the 21st century through public participation and open discussions, are the most important education issues for 2010, and also the great challenges. The formulation of educational reform is not only a matter of the Ministry of Education, and should not unilaterally be decided by the administrative department of education. It needs to be

---

[11] Ke Jin (柯进): "Rural Boarding School Students' Normal Growth Is blocked" in "*China Education Daily*" on April 5, 2009

further opened, and should be more public and transparent, thus "the formulation process of "Program" can become such a process that carries forward the, draws on the wisdom of the masses, unifies the thoughts, and condenses common understanding." Regarding open decision-making and asking the people for political advice and suggestions on social problems, the government and concerned departments of education need to study, and need to have open psychology. China's education is on the eve of big reformation, and we must make great efforts to achieve material educational transformation.

To break the unilaterally leading pattern of the Ministry of Education at present, we suggest to establish interagency cross-domain appraisal group or appraisal meeting participated in by and composed of people from all circles, especially virtuous and talented persons from the economic world, scientific and technological circles, public administration, the National People's Congress and the democratic parties etc. They participate in the revision of "Program," and cause this organization to grow into a standing educational consultation and review organ, which forms into a scientific and democratic system for educational decision-making.

B. *Government's Administration According to Law and Governing Education Legally are Key to Promoting Balanced Development of Compulsory Education*

The change to the Minister of Education has aroused the public's strong aspiration to reform of education. In the column "I Talk with the New Minister of Education" set at www.people.com.cn, netizens' comments reached around a thousand. Nearly 170,000 Netizens participated in on-line investigations of "expectations of the new Minister of Education," where "improving the quality of teachers," "lightening students' schoolwork burden, and realizing education for all-around development," "enhancing the treatment of teachers," "governing the corruption of 'school officers'," "achieving educational fairness, and breaking the disparity among different regions in education" became Netizens' "five main expectations" to the new Minister of Education.

To solve the people's intense discontentment with education, and to suppress the severe education for entrance examination, school selection competition, hot mathematics contest and hot examination for certificates, government's administration according to the law and governing education legally are the key points. Many investigations showed that, in some areas, cadres' seeking achievement (enrollment quotas and campus school etc.) is the main reason that there is still disorder in elementary education. Therefore, acts of government must be first normalized, school-running acts of elementary and middle schools can then be normalized; In addition, investigation and prosecution of various illegal school-running acts must be actually implemented, and not simply through documents. Finally, real recovery to the normal order of elementary education involves cutting off the benefit chain which seeks profits from school and which makes profit from students, and breaking the benefit alliance between administrative departments of education and the key schools, in order to recover the commonality and commonweal of public education.

C. *Paying Great Attention to New Situation and New Problems in Rural Education*

After the free nine-year compulsory education has been realized basically in urban and rural areas, education of ten million off-farm worker children in cities, as well as of left-behind children in rural areas, becomes the biggest weak link and main sphere of educational unfairness. Meanwhile, during the fast urbanization process, "schools entering town" become the administration goal of some areas, to cancel and combine the rural schools massively; not only do high schools enter the city, but also junior middle schools enter the county town, thus "rural schools are moving towards collective disappearance." This stern reality, which eliminates rural education, indicates the advancement and price where rural areas and farmers are "urbanized" ("被城市化" Bei Cheng Shi Hua); it not only deprived of the wish of farmers and their participation, but also large numbers of floating children and boarding schools cause parent-child separation or situation where the parents accompany the children into the city, and so on, which will change the cultural and educational ecology in rural areas profoundly, the relations between education and life, and the family pattern, even the parent-child relations, in rural society. Its influence to rural development is very profound and complex, which should be paid great attention to.

OFFICIAL START OF MEDICAL AND HEALTH CARE SYSTEM REFORM IN CHINA

Gu Xin

Abstract

In 2009, new rounds of medical and health care system reform (here-after referred to as "New Medical Reform") officially began. This was one of the most significant events in the China's social and economic development. On April 6, "Opinions of the CPC Central Committee and the State Council on Deepening the Reform of the Medical and Health Care System" (No. 6 [2009] of the CPC Central Committee, hereinafter referred to as "New Medical Reform Plan") was promul-gated, and the next day "Plan on Recent Priorities in Carrying Out the Reform of the Medical and Health Care System (2009–2011)" (No. 12 [2009] of the State Council, hereinafter referred to as "Implementa-tion Plan") was also promulgated.[1] "New Medical Reform Plan" pro-posed some new strategic conception, which pointed out new direction for the reform and development of medical and health care. However, at the same time, because the medical and health care system reform is complex, and new problems arise while old problems remain unsolved, therefore the new medical reform will certainly face a series of brand-new challenges. To deal with these challenges, the central authority and local authority must implement more supporting polices for every link of the new medical reform. How the new medical reform will be carried out will depend on the various provincial-level governments and their implementation plans. By mid-November 2009, about 20 provinces, one after another, promulgated respective implementation plans for New Medical Reform. The final version of the implementa-tion plan for new medical reform of various provinces will depend on approval by the National People's Congress and the Chinese People's Political Consultative Congress and the budget situation for 2010.

---

[1] See the website: of the Ministry of Health, at http://www.moh.gov.cn/publicfiles/business/htmlfiles/mohzcfgs/s7846/200904/39847.htm. Hereinafter the contents on "new medical reform plan" quoted in this paper no longer give their source.

The central government version of "New Medical Reform Plan" as well as of "Implementation Plan" explicitly points to a new aspect in medical reform, namely "establish basic medical security system covering urban and rural residents," and "medical insurance for all the people" in short. This is precisely what the former medical reform plan failed to highlight. Before 2003, the medical security system was mainly restricted to urban areas, and was composed of free medical service and basic medical insurance for urban residents. Coverage of free medical service is becoming more and more narrow, but coverage of medical insurance for urban employees is becoming more and more extensive. It is noteworthy that, although at present it has become one of the main force of the basic medical security system, but the establishment of medical insurance for urban employees at the beginning was to help the state-owned enterprise reform and economic restructuring This is a rather narrow thought. At least before 2000, social development was not independently pursued in China's public policy, but was subject to and attached to the intrinsic requirement of economic development.

Since 2003, the economy-oriented development concept has broken down slowly. "Promoting the livelihood of the people" has become the Chinese government's new administrative program; construction of social security system has become a core to "promoting the livelihood of the people." Thus, development has two tracks, namely social development and economic development are simultaneously pursued. In the aspect of medical security, on account of government subsidy, public voluntary medical insurance, the new rural cooperative medical system and basic medical insurance for urban residents are established one after another. The principle of medical security for all people determined in "New Medical Reform Plan" is a new principle, which not only promotes new medical reform, but also promotes entire social and economic development. Precisely then, the "New Medical Reform Plan" has profound meaning, which exceeds medical and health care system reform.

From drafting to soliciting opinions and then revising and publicizing, the new medical reform plan has taken two and a half years. Policy decisions have been pursued cautiously. The medical and health care system reform is involved in broad coverage and has strong specialization. A public policy launches open discussions and opinion solicitation all over the country, which it is unprecedented in China, therefore its progressive significance is worth affirming. Moreover, in the finalization process for the "New Medical Reform Plan," the decision-making department admitted good opinions from all circles of society, thus breathing new live into the new medical reform. According to preliminary investigations, from finalization to draft for opinion solicitation, the "New Medical Reform Plan" had more than 130 revisions, and many revised spots go beyond revision to style, which has substantial meaning.

I. *New Exploration of Medical Security for All People*

The clearest part of the "New Medical Reform Plan" is the discussion on the medical security system. Speaking of the consummation of medical security system, the "New Medical Reform Plan" has made material breakthrough in abstract ideas and in concrete measures. In fact, medical security for all people is not simply a plan on paper, but is being realized. The path towards medical security for all people has been built, and the next challenge is to maintain that path and at the right moments to update it; at the same time, the services for medical security must also improve in quality. According to the "New Medical Reform Plan," we need to carry on positive exploration in the following aspects to consummate the medical security system.

First, expand coverage of medical security. The "Implementation Plan" of the new medical reform has states that, by 2011, the basic medical security system will comprehensively cover urban and rural residents; specifically speaking, the insured rate of medical insurance for urban employees, medical insurance for urban residents and the new rural cooperative medical system must be enhanced to 90% above.

With the consolidation of medical insurance for urban employees and start of medical insurance for urban residents, by the end of 2008, coverage of urban basic medical security system had achieved 52.2%. Moreover, in urban area, a few people (including civil servants, administrative department staff and some retirees) still enjoy free medical services; some people have participated in various commercial medical insurances, and it is estimated the total for both accounted for about 10% of urban population. Therefore, in 2008, coverage of medical security for urban residents reached more than 60% for the first time.[2] By the end of 2008, in total 815 million people participated

---

[2] See Pages 348 and 353 of "2009 China Health Statistical Yearbook" compiled by the Ministry of Health of the People's Republic of China, published by the Peking

in the new rural cooperative medical system, which surpassed total rural residents, 721 million, of that year, and approaches to reach the gross population of agricultural household registration, 882 million.[3]

To reach coverage of medical security for all people within 3 years is not difficult in terms of rural areas. The difficulty lies in urban areas. With the unceasing advancement of urbanization, urban residents will exceed 600 million in the next 3 years, and possibly reach 700 million by 2011. Employed populations in urban area were 290 million in 2007, and will possibly reach 350 million–410 million in the future. Therefore, medical insurance for urban employees and for urban residents which are geared to the needs of the employed populations and non- employed in urban areas will face intense challenges to expand coverage. Medical insurance for urban residents must have a breakthrough in voluntary medical insurance, and medical insurance for urban employees must resolve the problem which the private enterprise escapes its employer liability of payment for social security. To achieve the goal of coverage of urban basic medical security system to reach 90% within 3 years, all levels of governments must make enormous effort. If the central government and party's organization departments regard coverage of basic medical security system as one of the important targets of local government achievements assessment, coverage of basic medical security system is guaranteed to expand.

Second, increase the funding level. Besides expansion of coverage, another important aspect in consummating the basic medical security system is to enhance the funding level. Only with high funding levels can the goal, where the medical security organization pays the majority of expenses when accepting medical services, and the insured person pays a small part of expenses, be achieved. To enhance the funding level, the key lies in subsidy from the public financial administration, namely the government provides subsidy to help people participate in public medical insurance.[4] The "New Medical Reform Plan" stated that "the central government and the local governments must increase investment to medical security, and give attention to both supply and demand." "Subsidizing demander" was neglected in the past, and

Union Medical College Press in Beijing (中国协和医科大学出版社) in 2009.

[3] See Pages 347 and 353 of "2009 China Health Statistical Yearbook" compiled by the Ministry of Health of the People's Republic of China, published by the Peking Union Medical College Press in Beijing in 2009.

[4] Gu Xin (顾昕), Gao Mengtao (高梦滔) and Yao Yang (姚洋), "Diagnosis and Prescriptions: Directly Facing China Medical System Reform" published by Social Sciences Academic Press (社会科学文献出版社) in Beijing in 2006.

therefore the establishment of such a principle is new for the "New Medical Reform Plan."

What is more valuable, "subsidizing demander" is not something only found on paper; it will be implemented concretely. Wang Jun (王军), Vice-minister of the Ministry of Finance announced in the press conference on new medical reform that in the next three years, all levels of governments will increase the budget to 850 billion yuan to use in advancing five new medical reforms, where 2/3 are used to subsidize the demander.[5] This is an unprecedented for the public financial administration. Regardless of what angle it is looked at from, it has extraordinary significance. 2/3s of 850 billion yuan amount to 566.6 billion yuan. This is enormous amounts of money, and will be invested mainly in two domains: first is the public health service system; second is the medical security system. Specifically speaking, "New Medical Reform Plan" proposed that,

(1) From 2009, according to the standard of 15 yuan per person, the disbursement of public health service is increased, and it will be increased to 20 yuan per person to use in disease prevention and control, mother and child health care, environmental sanitation, health promotion, and so on.

(2) "The system of basic medical insurance for urban residents should be further consummated, the employed populations should be quickly covered, and the problem regarding basic medical insurance for employees and retirees from closed, bankrupt and difficult state-owned enterprises, as well as for jobholders from private economic organizations and flexible employed persons should be solve emphatically." A large amount of the 566.6 billion yuan will be used to pay the premium of medical security for employees and retirees from closed, bankrupt and difficult state-owned enterprises in the next ten years to at one time solve the issues left over from history.

(3) The government subsidy level of basic medical insurance for urban residents and the new rural cooperative medical system is enhanced from the lowest being 80 yuan per person to 120 yuan. In many

---

[5] See Li Yusi (李雨思)'s "Wang Jun, Vice-minister of the Ministry of Finance in detail Explained How to Spend 850 billion Yuan Investments for Medical Reform" published at http://www.ce.cn/cysc/newmain/s/zyy/200904/08/t20090408_18739568.shtml.

areas, the government subsidy level has surpassed 80 yuan, has even surpassed 120 Yuan, and it will be further enhanced from now on.

(4) Urban and rural medical assistance system is consolidated and developed to pay premium for low-income earners to participate in all kinds of public medical insurance, and simultaneously provide aid for medical expenses that they should pay themselves but are unable to do so.

All these will give people direct benefits.

Third, increase the security level. With the enhancement of medical security funding, how to guarantee insured persons obtain suitable medical security, namely how to spend the money of medical security fund on those in need is very important. At present, the basic medical security system has not obtained a high level. Total payment of all kinds of medical security fund has not yet reached high proportion in business income of medical institutions, and was less than 40% in 2008 (See Table 6.1). That is to say, when insured persons accept medical services, less than 40% of medical expenses are paid by the basic medical security system. This should reach 70% at least, in order for the basic medical security system to properly carry out its role.

The basic medical security system has not reached a high level because of low funding. But, at present a ubiquitous problem is that

Table 6.1: Payment Level of Basic Medical Security System from 2004 to 2008

Unit: Hundred million yuan, percentage

	Expenditures of medical insurance fund for urban employees	Expenditures of medical insurance fund for urban residents	Expenditures of new rural cooperative medical system	Expenditures of free medical services	Total expenditures of basic medical security system	Business income of medical institutions	Proportion paid by medical security fund
2004	862.2		26.4	323.5	1212.0	4194.7	28.9%
2005	1078.7		61.8	374.3	1514.8	4694.9	32.3%
2006	1276.7		155.8	374.6	1807.1	5196.9	34.8%
2007	1561.8	10.1	346.6	376.0	2294.5	7016.3	32.7%
2008	2019.7	63.9	662.3	378.0	3123.9	8181.4	38.2%

Data from Pages 941 and 945 of "China Statistical Yearbook" in 2009; Page 516 of "China Labor Statistical Yearbook" in 2008; Pages 98 and 100 of "China Health Statistical Yearbook" in 2005, and Pages 100 and 102 in 2006, Pages 98 and 100 in 2007, Pages 92–93 and 335–336 in 2008 and Pages 347–348 in 2009.

many areas have excessively high balance of urban and rural medical security fund, which causes insured persons to be unable to enjoy expected medical security with the existing funding. Thus, the "Implementation Plan" proposed the following specific reform measures, "all medical insurance expenditure determined by revenue. Annual surplus and accumulative total surplus in the medical insurance fund for urban employees and the medical insurance fund for urban residents should be reasonably controlled, and those areas with excess surplus should take measure to enhance security level etc., thus lowering the surplus to a reasonable level. The current surplus of the unified planning fund of the new rural cooperative medical system should be controlled, in principle, at less than 15% in, and the accumulative total surplus should not surpass 25% of the unified planning fund in the same year."

For the whole country, the fund of new rural cooperative medical system has some surplus every year, and the surplus rate is also very high. But what is heartening, in the past years, current surplus in the fund of new rural cooperative medical system dropped year by year, it was 40.3% in 2004, and dropped to 15.6% by 2008 (See Table 6.2), and the accumulative total surplus was equivalent to 25.4% of the funds raised during the same year, which were very close to the targets set in the "Implementation Plan" of new medical reform.

In 2007, the fund revenue of medical insurance for urban residents was 4.3 billion yuan, but expenditure merely 1.01 billion yuan, not

Table 6.2: Revenues and Expenditures of New Rural Cooperative
Medical System Fund from 2004–2008

Unit: Hundred million yuan, percentage

	Fund revenue	Fund expenditure	Current surplus	Current surplus rate	Accumulative total surplus	Proportion of accumulative total surplus in current funds raised
2004	44.2	26.4	17.8	40.3%	17.8	40.3%
2005	82.5	61.8	20.7	25.1%	38.5	46.7%
2006	211.1	155.8	55.3	26.2%	76.0	36.0%
2007	423.3	346.6	76.6	18.1%	131.9	31.2%
2008	784.6	662.3	122.3	15.6%	198.9	25.4%

Data from Page 347 of "China Health Statistical Yearbook" in 2009; Pages 13 and 26 of "2008 Report on the Research of Total Expenditure for Public Health in China" compiled by the Institute of Health Economics of the Ministry of Health in December 2008.

even a quarter, and the proportion of current surplus reached as high as 76.5% of current revenues. In the same year, half of the provinces did not have expenditures, and only the current surplus rate of Guangdong Province is less than 15%. Because medical insurance for urban residents only started since the second half of 2007, it is unavoidable to have some problems with fund surplus control. In 2008, the surplus level of the medical insurance fund for urban resdients dropped largely, and was 39.9%.[6] Its surplus rate was still quite high, and not only higher than the surplus rate of the fund of new rural cooperative medical system, but also higher than of medical insurance for urban employees. In brief, surplus control of medical insurance fund for urban residents should be improved.

The medical insurance fund for urban employees has a generally high surplus rate. By the end of 2008, accumulative total surplus of the medical insurance fund for urban employees reached as high as 330.36 billion yuan. This is an enormous amount of money. During the same year, the expenditure of medical insurance fund for urban employees was only 201.97 billion yuan, namely average expenditure was 16.83 billion yuan every month.[7] According to this expenditure level, even if payment of medical insurance for urban employees were postponed, accumulative total surplus of this insurance fund could be used to pay for 19.6 months.

Money of the public medical insurance fund is from the people, and therefore it should be used for the people. A lot of medical security funds are deposited, which is an enormous waste. Whether in terms of short-term demand of expanding domestic demand, guaranteeing growth, readjusting the structure and paying attention to the livelihood of the people, or long-range objectives of consummating the medical security system, reducing the surplus rate of urban and rural medical security fund is crucial for current medical security reform, and demands immediate action. The "New Medical Reform Plan" proposed the opinions on reform—positively exploring reasonable surplus levels, and properly readjusting the surplus rate. This is one of new bright spots of the new medical reform.

---

[6] Data from the Ministry of Human Resources and Social Security; it will be soon issued in "China Labor Statistics Yearbook".

[7] See Page 945 of "2009 China Statistical Yearbook" compiled by the National Bureau of Statistics of China, published by China Statistics Press in Beijing in 2009.

Fourth, clearly define the position of the medical security organization. With enhancement to funding and payment level of the medical security fund, the medical security organization has strong capacity for group purchase, and theoretically it is capable to purchase medicine services in the name of group purchasers for the insured persons in order to benefit those insured. But, how does the medical security organization purchase better medicine service? Simply, it is a question of how to "spend" money. This is a future challenge to the medical security reform for all people.

The medical security organization acting the part of medicine service buyer has indeed been written down in the "New Medical Reform Plan." But, regarding this role, the "New Medical Reform Plan" does not elaborate in detail. Rather it is dispersed in the elaborations about other subjects, which appears very scattered. To explain how the medical security organization acts the part of medicine service buyer, the following matters must be explained in turn.

First, purchase contents. About this point, Article 6 of the "New Medical Reform Plan" states: "begins with providing security for serious illness, and then extends gradually to outpatient services of slight illness." This means that, in the next three years, the payment of basic medical security system will cover all kinds of medical services. Exploring the coverage of clinic services will be one development priority of the basic medical security system in the next three years.

Second, negotiation mechanism of seller and buyer. About this point, Article 11 of the "New Medical Reform Plan" states: "positively explore the establishment of negotiations mechanism between the medical insurance operating organization and the medical institution, and to bring into play medical security and restrictions on costs for medical services and medicine expenses."

Third, choice of payment mode. About this point, Article 12 of "New Medical Reform Plan" states: "strengthen the supervisory function of medical security to medical services, consummate the payment system, explore positively and implement payment per capita, payment by disease class and payment of total amount in advance etc., and establish an active constraint mechanism which pays equal attention to encouragement and punishment."

Thus it can be seen, the "New Medical Reform Plan" touches upon important links of the medical security organization purchasing medicine services, but its fragmented discussion weakens its impact.

Among them, the most important reform is how expenses are paid for. The person paying may guide the person collecting the money, therefore as a group purchaser, the medical security organization should be capable of enabling the medical institution to become the main part of the normal market, namely has strong consciousness of performance-to-price ratio to make reasonable diagnosis and treatment, and reasonable medication in view of patient's concrete conditions of disease. Under the situation of medical security for all the people, if the medical institution makes unreasonable diagnosis and treatment of the patient's condition, then the main problem is caused from the payment segment of the medical security organization.

Payment for medical security is not simple, as the insured person's agent, the medical security organization is responsible to utilize these specialized payment ways to control the actions of medical institutions. The different payment methods have different advantages and disadvantages, and apply to different types of medicine services. Therefore, there should not be solely one medical security payment method, but a combination of many payment methods. How these methods will be combined should be decided by medical service contents and price in various areas, and is the result of negotiations between the medical security organization and the medical institution in various areas, and is impossible for the higher government to impose uniformity.

In China, how operations regarding medical security get professionalized, how the medical security organization carries on negotiations with the medical institution, and how the medical security organization realizes good management, are the challenges to the new medical reform, and urgently need various areas to positively explore.

II. *Public Medical Institution, Corporatizing or Administration?*

If medical security reform is the key to solve the problem of medical services being expensive, then the key to alleviate the problem of medical services being difficult to accept is reform of medical system. Because the public hospital has dominant position in China's medical system, the core of medical reform is the reform of public hospital. However, compared with the clear direction and measures of medical security reform, regarding reform of public hospitals, the "New Medical Reform Plan" actually has two trains of thoughts. One is public hospital becoming corporatized; the other is public hospital returning to administration.

First, "the guiding principle" part of the "New Medical Reform Plan" (Article 1) has reiterated the principle of "four separations" brought forward by General Secretary Hu Jintao in the Report to the Seventeenth National Congress of the Communist Party of China, namely "separate government administration from medical institutions, management from operation, medical care from pharmaceuticals, and for-profit from nonprofit operations." Among them, "separating management from operation" is the core of public hospital reform. Namely let the public hospital separate from the administrative subordination relationship from all levels of health administrative departments, and carries out independent judicial status of public hospital (Article 8 of "New Medical Reform Plan"). After implementing the administration disconnect, the public medical and health care organization only has division of size, famous and non-famous, and specialty and comprehensibility, but no longer has administrative rank. After the administration disconnect, it is most important to "establish and consummate the structure of hospital legal person management" (Article 9 of "New Medical Reform Plan"). The council is the core of legal person management structure, and is composed of representatives of key interest groups of the hospital (including investor, medical care personnel, consumer or community representatives etc.). Because the government invests in the establishment of public hospital, the government may certainly send directors into the council. Hospital's administrative officers, especially chief of hospital, are selected by the council, and are responsible for the council. Regarding medical care personnel, the public hospital corporate body system has the greatest advantage, which enables them to become high-income earners legitimately. The medical care personnel (especially doctor) are freelance, once they are hired, and then they full-time or part-time staff of the hospital; part-time staff may select to work in several units. Under the frame of the corporate body system, the chief of hospital and administrative officers become professional managers. Doctors depend on medical skill and chiefs depend on management ability for income, and matters including "medical services supported by dealing with medicines" ("以药养医" Yi Yao Yang Yi), "receiving bribes" ("收红包" Shou Hong Bao), "taking return commission," ("拿回扣" Na Hui Kou), etc., will be reduce.

After public hospitals are corporatized, how they will develop and whether they need to expand or not, all are important contents of its strategic management, which will be decided by the council independently. Among them, whether they need to introduce social capital and how much capital, from what channels, and how it should be used, all are the responsibility of the public hospital council. Certainly, because the government can send directors into the public hospital council, policies regarding social capital that concern the government will be heavily influenced.

Without a doubt, corporatizing public hospitals will bring immense changes for the public medical institution, which liberates not only the hospital, but also doctors. Certainly, as a result of the inheritance of the old system as well as restrictions of the current system, the reform road of corporatizing public hospital is exceptionally difficult. How a system of administration + commercial institution turns towards becoming a corporate body + general adoption of the market principle, is still unclear. Originally, the "New Medical Reform Plan" defined the principle of public hospital reform, namely impel the public hospital towards becoming a corporate body. But, just like many reforms in China, the principle "is clear," but measures are absent. Regarding reform of public hospitals, the keynote of "Implementation Plan" for new medical reform is to encourage local governments to carry on pilot programs, and then determine concrete ways of public hospital reform 3 years later based on the experiences. Because the central government version of the "New Medical Reform Plan" is skims over this point, the implementation plan of new medical reform released by many provinces does not give explicit direction and concrete method of public hospital reform.

III. *Functions of Government and Market in the Pharmaceutical Supply Security System*

A big challenge to the new medical reform is how to set pharmaceutical policy. According to Article 7 of the "New Medical Reform Plan", "establishing and consummating pharmaceutical supply security system" is one of important targets of the new medical reform, and the consummation of the national basic pharmaceutical system is the foundation of pharmaceutical supply security system. How to define the functions of government and market in the pharmaceutical supply security system is the core of this big challenge. How to deal with this challenge not only will affect the development of medical service industry, but will also have very important influences to the development of the medicine industry.

In reality, China is a big power of pharmaceutical production, thousands upon thousands of pharmaceuticals are produced in China and go on the market, and therefore the pharmaceutical supply security should not be the issue. The issue rather is that a handful of weak enterprises con their way into the domain of medicine production and circulation, and those enterprises with actual strength repeatedly. As a result, a great deal of pharmaceuticals of poor quality, but are expensive, floods into the market. China's pharmaceutical market's circulation and consumption is highly distorted, and a policy of survival of the fittest is unable to take shape. Even more significant, in public hospitals, which occupy 70–80% shares in the pharmaceutical consumption market, there is a situation of "unrealistic high medicine prices;" public hospital purchase medicine at a high price, and sell at a high price, which cause medicine prices in the public hospital pharmacy to be far higher than retail pharmacies around. Without a doubt, this absurd situation has initiated consumers' anger. Common people do not know whether the medical expenses are reasonable or not; but, for the same medicine, obviously the cheaper medicine is extremely easy to obtain, but medicine price at public hospitals still remain expensive.

All this stems from the public hospital's need for "medicine as income," namely one main income source of public hospital is through selling medicine, and accounts for 40% (See Table 6.3). Because the public hospital does not earnestly pay attention to the performance-to-price ratio of medicines, instead it purchases medicines with general curative effects, but the price is still expensive. Some weak medicine manufacturers may sell their low quality medicines at a generally expensive price through various commercial briberies; those enterprises are also able to introduce their medicine into hospitals because hospitals do not care excessively about circulation channels in any case. Because the public hospital has a monopolistic position, even if its medicine price is expensive, the patient also has no alternative.

Confronting this issue, regardless of whether it is the public, the media or the government, the blame is put on bad medical ethics of medical care personnel; many people also put blame on the weak sense of social responsibility in the medicine industry; in brief, all resort to moral criticism. Furthermore, some people blame the chaotic phenomena of the medicine market on the adoption of the market principle, and hope to solve the problem through abolishing the market principle and implementing government control.

Table 6.3: Income Source of Public Hospitals from 2003–2008

Unit: Hundred million yuan, percentage

	Gross income	Medical income		Medicine income		Other income		Government allocations	
		Amount	Proportion	Amount	Proportion	Amount	Proportion	Amount	Proportion
2003	2549.22	1149.01	45.1%	1107.19	43.4%	68.72	2.7%	224.30	8.8%
2004	3339.78	1490.47	44.6%	1347.28	40.3%	74.62	2.2%	427.40	12.8%
2005	3700.64	1758.09	47.5%	1591.82	43.0%	77.73	2.1%	272.99	7.4%
2006	4029.58	1949.88	48.4%	1664.17	41.3%	77.50	1.9%	338.03	8.4%
2007	4902.23	2378.42	48.5%	2023.47	41.3%	83.54	1.7%	416.81	8.5%
2008	6090.22	2914.20	47.9%	2563.98	42.1%	101.81	1.7%	510.24	8.4%

Data from Page 85 of "China Health Statistical Yearbook" in 2004, Page 100 in 2005, Page 102 in 2006, Page 100 in 2007, Page 93 in 2008 and Page 93 in 2009.

Actually, in the final analysis, the occurrence of public hospital purchasing and selling at a high price appears in the medicine market because the government is unable to implement appropriate control in two ways. First, because it inherits characteristics of a planned economy, the government's strict low-price control to medical services has caused the pattern where doctors' income is less than that of a barber, which has forced doctors to become professional medicine salesmen. Second, the government stipulated the ceiling of medicine sales profit rate, namely 15%; as the matter stands, when purchasing medicine, the public hospital cannot consider naturally performance-to-price ratio of medicines, but as much as possible they purchase high-price medicines.

Simply the two improper controls of the government has caused "unrealistically high medicine price" of public hospitals. In order to deal with "unrealistically high medicine prices," as a result of government's diagnosis that there were too many circulation links, temporary solution was taken, but a permanent cure was not implemented, there was intervention in medicine circulation links, and in various areas, a medicine bid system was implemented. It is to be noted that so-called "medicine bid" is not medicine purchase. The intermediary organs of various regions that invite bids carry on secondary screening to medicines circulated in the market, which has set up "secondary market access" for medicine purchase of public hospital. The concrete medicine purchasers are still various hospitals; under selected medicine varieties and bidding price, various hospitals are actual deciders of concrete quantity purchased and purchasing price. Because government's control to the medical service price and to medicine sale profit rate still remains unchanged, the public hospitals mostly favor purchasing high-price medicines on bids, and low-price medicines on bids are relatively less purchased. For the production enterprises of low-price medicines, the price has been very low, but quantity purchased does not increase, therefore they may naturally reduce production or even lose enthusiasm to keep production of these medicines going. Therefore, rationally, these enterprises have two options. First, they withdraw from the high-end market of medicines (namely the hospitals), and turn to develop the low-end market, namely retailed pharmacy and rural areas; Second, in the following year they will carry out concentrated medicine bids in other areas, and will strive to win a tender at a relatively high price. Therefore, with words inside trade, most "low-price tender" end with nobody bidding for it.

Without a doubt, if "medicine as income" is not put under control, in terms of medical security for all people, or corporatizing public hospitals, patients will be unable to obtain attractive and reasonably priced medicines. How to eradicate the harm of "medicine as income?" The "New Medical Reform Plan" presents two ways of thinking. First is zero-rate policy of medicine; second is reform of the basic medicine system.

The zero-rate does not cancel the government's improper control, and only changes the highest markup of medicines from 15% to 0%. If income cannot be gained this way, medical institutions will certainly make it up from other places, leaving everything unchanged.

Reform of basic medicine system is the second measure. Its main target is similarly to rectify unrealistic high medicine price. But, regarding the basic system frame of the basic drug system, the "New Medical Reform Plan" does not give a clear description. On August 18, 2009, nine ministries and commissions, including the Ministry of Health, issued "Opinions on Establishing a National Basic Medicine System" and "Measures on the Administration of a National Basic Medicine Catalog (Provisional)," and officially started construction of a national basic medicine system. At the same time, the "National Basic Medicine Catalog (for Grass-roots Medical and Health Organizations)" (edition in 2009) (hereinafter referred to as "National Basic Medicine Catalog (Grass-roots Edition)") was officially promulgated, including 205 kinds of chemicals and biological preparations and 102 varieties of traditional Chinese medicine, in total 307 varieties of medicine, as well as decoction of some traditional Chinese medicine. The Ministry of Health announced "Ministry of Health Order" No. 69, and declared that this edition of basic medicine catalog be in force starting September 21, 2009.

At present, selection of basic medicines and the formulation of basic medicine catalogs are still carried on under nontransparent situations. The grass roots edition has already been issued, but people's understanding towards public hospitals remains in mystery. The use of medicine catalogs by medical security is renewing, and the relations between the two entities' catalog are unclear. The purchase and allocation (namely intermediate links) of basic medicine system take the concentrated bid. But, existing concentrated medicine bidding system is not limited in basic medicines, even not limited to medicine which may be reimbursed by medical security, rather it applies to the majority of medicine sold in public hospitals. Under this situation, is the system of concentrated bidding of basic medicine different than that of non-basic medicines? If the difference is not big, there is no substantial difference even in setting up the concentrated tender independently for the basic medicine system. Finally, the use of medicines is also very important. The "New Medical Reform Plan" has stipulated that "all urban and rural basic-unit medical and health organizations should equip and use basic medicines completely." Among them, what does "equip and use completely" mean? These expressions have two explanations. First, it means that they only use (sale) basic medicine; second, all basic medicine should be in stock, but may also use (sale) other medicine. Which explanation will become policy is still unclear at present. As for "other all kinds of medical institutions need to put the basic medicines as the first choice and to determine the use proportion", the key is how to determine what the proportion should be. If it is too high, it will limit the option of medical institutions and patients in medicine use enormously, which will cause negative repercussions; if it is too low, it will not have material significance because the public hospital are massively using the basic medicine.

In summary, because there is no clear diagnosis to the symptom of "unrealistic high medicine price," the curative effect of the two new medicines of the "New Medical Reform Plan" (namely zero rate of medicine and basic medicine system) is pessimistic. Even more crucial, although these two new medicines have not yet been implemented, it has already attracted widespread attention and confusion in medical institutions and medicine enterprises. Many people look forward to the "New Medical Reform Plan" but at the same time are uneasy because of the uncertainty revolving around the policy.

ANALYSIS ON PUBLIC ORDER IN 2009

Fan Zaiqin, Song Dongyan and Yan Congbing

I. *Overall Situation of Public Order Maintains Steady Progression*

Starting from 2009, public security organs closely revolved around the general requirements of "guaranteeing growth, guaranteeing livelihood of the people, and guaranteeing stability" to effectively deal with the impact of the international financial crisis to the public order; to unceasingly maintain crackdown on all kinds of prominent criminal offenses, and to unceasingly enlarge rectification strength to public order, which created good public order environment diligently for the celebration of China's 60th anniversary. From January to October, the overall situation of public order maintained stability, public security order was steady, and various celebration activities for the 60th anniversary were not disturbed and influenced by illegal and criminal acts. But it is to be noted that, because of influences from many factors, it was difficult to have ultimate containment to high frequency of illegal and criminal cases in a short time, where the pressure of maintaining sustained stability of public order was still big.

A. *Criminal Cases are Unceasingly Faced with Increased Pressures*

From January to October 2009, public security organs registered 4,443,000 criminal offense cases in all, a 14.8% increase from that of 2008. Criminal cases registered by the public security organs of 25 provinces, autonomous regions and municipalities increased from that of 2008. It should be noted that, in 2009, public security organs of various areas vigorously carried out work of case registration according to the requirements of the Ministry of Public Security, and a mass of "small cases" which involved people's vital interests were investigated by public security organs, which promoted growth of criminal cases registered objectively.

B. *Serious Criminal Cases of Murder, Raping, Arson and Robbery to a Certain Extent have Increased*

From January to October 2009, public security organs registered 12,000 cases of murder in all, which were as much as the ones in 2008, which resulted in the death of 12,000 persons, a 0.4% increase from the previous, in which 5779 cases occurred in resident houses; there were 28,000 rapping cases, a 11.4% increase; 6064 arson cases, a 26.4% increase; 1045 cases involving dangerous substances, a 37.5% increase; 237,000 robbery cases, a 6.7% increase, and 17,000 burglary cases, a 0.2% increase. Because the quantity of serious violent offenses was relatively small, it was easy to obtain a higher increased range in the statistics, but generally speaking, serious violent offenses were still relatively little.

C. *Gangster Activities and Harmful Events are Disappearing*

Since 2009, public security organs further enlarged the work strength of crackdown on organized crimes and such. From January to October, in total 45,000 criminal groups were ferreted out, a 3.1% decrease from 2008; a total of 181,000 group members were exposed, a 2.7% decrease from the previous year; and there were 244,000 criminal cases, a 23% decrease from the previous year. A total of 181 gangster criminal groups were destroyed, a 25.7% increase; 1737 group members were ferreted out, a 20% increase; and there were 1345 cases, a 6.8% increase. Under continuous strict crackdown and pressure, besides organized crime, other criminal activities from other groups also decreased from 2008. With the strengthening of crackdown on organized crime and criminal activities, the space for organized crimes to multiply and spread had been greatly compressed, and tendency of criminal activities has largely been contained.

D. *Order of Public Security Management Maintains Stability*

Public security organs pay even more attention to strengthen the source of rectification to public order, and pay special attention to small cases and symptoms to investigate general illegal case under the situation of frequent conflicts, which maintained the stability of public order. From January to October 2009, public security organs investigated 8,275,000 cases against public security management, which grew 19.9% over that of 2008; 6,271,000 cases of public security lawbreakers, which grew 17.5% over that of the previous year. Total 209,000 criminal cases of impairing the social management order, which grew 16.2% over the ones in 2008, in which 107,000 cases of "Pornography, gambling and drug abuse and trafficking", which grew 28.5% over previous year; 88,000 cases of harassing the public peace and order, including impairing the official business, gathering a mob to have brawls and stirring up fights and causing trouble etc., which grew 17.9%.

E. *Juvenile Delinquency Remains Stable and Dropped*

Juvenile delinquency is an important target in evaluating public order. From January to October 2009, in youth involved in criminal cases captured by public security organs, individuals under the age of 25 below dropped 2.1% from that of 2008, which since 2006 has continuously dropped. Among them, 18–25 year-olds dropped 1.8% from the previous year; minors under the age of 18 dropped 14.8%. In youth involved in criminal cases captured by public security organs, students in school dropped 26% from 2008, where elementary school students dropped 25%, junior high school students dropped 29.6%, senior high school students dropped 18.4%, and college students dropped 24.3%. In recent years, the number of juvenile delinquents, especially minor criminals, no longer increases but has rather steadily dropped, which reflects positive development in the public order situation.

F. *Many Disputes Among the People on Public Security have been Effectively Mediated*

In view of the situation which contradictions and disputes among the people in the economic and social transformation period and the criminal offense cases initiated thereby were increasing unceasingly, public security organs of various regions continuously increased its strength in mediating disputes among the people on public security, thus fulfilling its function of handling disputes, and public security organs have become a normal channel for handling disputes. From January to October 2009, the public security organs mediated 2,696,000 cases of public security in all, which accounted for 32.6% of total cases of public security investigated, a 29.1% increase from that of 2008. The effectiveness of this function causes intensifying contradictions to be avoided, and has eliminated possible malignant criminal cases.

G. *Traffic Accidents and Fire Accidents, etc. have Obviously Decreased*

From January to October 2009, there were 185,000 traffic accidents throughout the whole country, which caused 52,000 deaths, injured 221,000 persons, and 710 million yuan in property was loss, which respectively dropped 14.8%, 10.1%, 13.2% and 16.7% over that of 2008; in total there were 106,000 fire accidents, which caused 831 deaths, injured 509 persons, and 1.06 billion yuan in property was loss, which respectively dropped 3.8%, 26.2%, 15.3% and 21.3% from the previous year.

H. *People's Sense of Security Remains at a High Level*

National investigations of people's sense of security in 2008, regarding the present public order environment, presented the following results. Feelings of "very secure," "secure," and "basically secure" by interviewees accounted for 94.6%, which increased by 1.3 percentage point over that of 2007. Regarding what affected people's sense of security, 26.6% answered "criminal offense," a 1.8 percentage point increase from the previous year. Confusion of public order, criminal offenses and traffic and fire accidents are always the most prominent factors affecting people's sense of security. From the data from 2009, and the tendencies of these development trends, Chinese people's sense of security still remain at a high level.

II. *Current Contradictions and Problems that Affect Social Stability and Order*

Beginning in 2009, the financial crisis has initiated various complications all over the world, and has caused a series of unstable events one after another, which have badly impacted social stability and order in some countries. It is evident that from when the crisis first began up till now, it has gradually evolved from an economic problem into a social problem. It is observed that during the first stage of the crisis, key words are 'finance', 'economy' and 'enterprise'; key words at the second stage are 'economy', 'society' and 'government'. From experiences abroad, global financial crises occurred throughout history all have widespread and profound influence to the world political and economic patterns and the internal affairs of main countries; although

China is different than Western countries in its developmental stage, it is possible for the impact of financial crisis to greatly affect Chinese society. Looking at the domestic situation, since the Reform in China, although China undergoes a course of development that took other developed countries hundreds of years, many social problems and contradictions have also been created, especially some medium- and long-term contradictions and problems which affect China's social stability. Thus China is still in a critical period with complex struggles, contradictions among the people and frequent criminal offenses. The ability to withstand non-traditional security risk is also low relatively, and the foundation is also quite weak. Therefore, properly looking at the influences of the financial crisis to China's social stability and order is important in evaluating social stability in 2009.

A. *The Impact of Financial Crisis, to a Certain Extent, has Intensified the Uncoordinated Economic and Social Development in China, and has caused an Increase of Negative Factors, to Induce and Multiply Illegal Acts and Crimes, which has Brought about New Pressure to Public Order and Stability*

The crime problem is a combination and reflection of all kinds of social contradictions and negative factors. The fluctuation of crime and the quality of public order, depend on the control over the entire society, and the strength of the positive factors (will suppress and control crime) compared to negative factors (will cause crime to multiply). In 2009, with the increasing impact of the financial crisis to the Chinese economy and society, problems such as, regional economic development being unbalanced, ability transfer employment being insufficient in cities, coverage of social security being small, and so on, became even more prominent. In a short time, unemployment increased suddenly, unemployed persons were found everywhere in society, and the poverty problem initiated by unemployment multiplied and spread, which brought tremendous pressures for public order and stability to be maintained.

First, criminal activities such as burglary, robbery and looting, which impose on wealth occurred frequently, which caused criminal offenses to unceasingly grow. Because social security did not yet completely cover peasant workers working in the cities, their salary was their basic security to livelihood. Once out of work, they would quickly fall into poverty, and illegal and criminal activities, such as larceny, burglary or impulsiveness robbery and looting, to obtain money. Statistical data indicated that, from January to October 2009, public security organs registered 3,860,000 criminal cases of infringement to wealth, a 16.1% increase from that of 2008, where criminal cases of infringement to wealth registered at under 5000 yuan increased by 408,000 cases compared to 2008, a 16.9% increase. Although the value of objects stolen in these crimes were lower, and the amount stolen was not too big, the social harm was relatively weak, but these cases occurred frequently, and would become the main cause to the rise of criminal cases in 2009 according to its growth trend.

Second, illegal and criminal activities of stirring up fights, causing trouble, and gathering mobs to have brawls, etc. increased, which possibly negatively influences people's sense of security. Because of unemployment of individuals in alien land, stirring up fights and causing trouble, gathering a mob to have brawls, hindering official business and personal injury often become methods unemployed persons use to let out their emotions, settle disputes and express complaints. Hence illegal and criminal activities occur more frequently, which have badly influenced public order in urban society, urban and rural integrated areas, and medium and small towns. Statistical data indicated that, from January to October 2009, public security organs registered 209,000 cases of harm done to social management order, an increase of 29,000 cases from 2008, a 16.2% increase. Among them, there were 33,000 cases of stirring up fights and causing trouble, a 10.7% increase from the previous year; 4812 cases of mob gatherings to have brawls, a 23.3% increase. It is noteworthy that, in recent years, investigations on people's sense of security showed that, regarding public security affecting the sense of security, disorder of public order caused by general illegal crimes was of greatest impact. It was first in 2005, and second only after traffic accident from 2006 to 2008. The increase of these types of cases will intensify people's reactions to all kinds of unstable factors, will strengthen their worry and anxiety about all kinds of social problems, and will result in objectivity to the work of public security.

Third, because unemployed persons increase and are found throughout, population that may participate in crimes increased. Peasant workers go from being part of a "acquaintance society" ("熟人社会" Shu Ren She Hui) in villages to an "anonymous society" ("匿名社会" Ni Ming She Hui) in cities and go from being temporary "enterprise individuals," to "social individuals." They are confronted with unemployment and unfamiliarity with both people and place, therefore they generally faced huge psychological problems, and left deprived in the city. This marginalization situation easily causes them to organize into gangs, using the relations of fellow villagers and co-workers. In recent years, the offence of peasant worker gangs increased; illegal and criminal activities, such as stealing bicycles, organizing minors to steal from communal facilities and equipment or raw materials, were common occurrence, and had a professional disposition. It is noteworthy that, because of the shut down and bankruptcy of small- and medium-sized enterprises, not only did many idle personnel emerge, but huge debt disputes also emerged, creating a market of potential members for gangs, and a small number of those unemployed may be recruited by gangs.

B. *Under the Dual Influences of a Shrinking Market Demand and Macroeconomic Regulation and Control Policies, the Enterprises' Contradictions and Problems Accumulated in many Links such as, Fund Procurement, Production and Operation etc., Appear in Causing the Negative Factors to Multiply and Induce Economic Crimes*

Presently, the impact of the international financial crisis to the Chinese economy is unceasingly expanding; it not only threatens finance security and industrial security, but also aggravates trade risk and enterprise risk, also impacts traditional domains, such as commodity production and sale etc., and affects emerging markets, such as real estate, credit and the negotiable securities etc., and has an especially serious impact to China's manufacturing industry. The contradictions accumulated by small- and medium-sized enterprises, which undertake export-processing trade in sectors of policy guidance, industrial support, financing and credit, production and operation have been greatly exposed. Problems of difficulty obtaining loans, shrinking of the market, increase in cost and increase in price of raw material, all simultaneously appeared, which created an environment for economic crimes, such as the fraud in fundraising, illegal banks, false report of capital, fraud in export tax reimbursement, false invoices of value added tax, the false contracts, embezzlement by those in power, and so on.

First, in terms of fund raising, economic criminal activities, such as illegally absorb public deposits and cheat in money collection have high frequency. Under the impact of the financial crisis and the shrinking of the world market, the fund chain where small- and medium-sized enterprises maintain regular production and operation is very weak, and under the limitation of bank credit and the influence of a tight monetary policy, it is difficult for the majority of private enterprises to obtain financial support from regular channels, thus creating an environment for crimes of illegally absorbing public deposits and fraud in fundraising to occur. Statistics indicated that, from January to October 2009, criminal cases of illegally absorbing public deposits and of fraud in fundraising registered by public security organs increased by 60.3% and 48.1%, respectively from the previous year. It is noteworthy that, compared with other economic crimes of harming the market economic order, economic crimes involving many people harm a larger scope of people, reaching even those in weak situations. It does not simply harm order to the market economy, but also creates other factors that are unstable, thus impacting social stability.

Second, in terms of production and operation, the situation where a few CEOs take part in criminal activities of false contracts and establish an enterprise to illegally make profits, has increased. Since 2009, in "Zhujiang Delta" and "Changjiang Delta" areas, some small- and medium-sized enterprises that shut down, went bankrupt, or lost foreign capital, occurred as a result of massive acts of malicious tax evasion, bank loans and private loans, owing money to workers and suppliers, etc. It is noteworthy that, these types of cases often involve a mass of the legal income of the enterprise's staff and payment for materials of enterprises concerned. Thus it is easy to initiate group events, where the victims gather in great numbers to appeal for help from the party and government organizations.

Third, in terms of export tax revenue, crimes of swindling export tax reimbursement and false invoice of value-added tax, which harms collection and management of tax revenue, has increased. At present, it is difficult to radically alleviate the difficult position of small- and medium-sized enterprises in a short period of time. Because they are on the brink of closure and bankruptcy, a few enterprises resort to tax evasion and false reports of exports to swindle export tax reimbursement and reduce economic loss. Sometimes they even collaborate with tax administration to specially produce false special invoices for value-added tax to swindle tax reimbursement for export receipts. Statistical data indicated that, from January to October 2009, public security organs 7417 cases of abusing tax revenue were registered to be investigate, a 11.6% increase from the previous year.

C. *Facing the Dual Difficult Position of Large Growth in Unemployment and Decrease in Demand of Market Employment, Employment Situation Becomes More Severe, Posing a Greater Threat to Social Stability. Employment is the Foundation of People's Livelihood*

Speaking of social stability, stable and continuously growing employment means that more populations can share in the achievements of the Reform and the economic development through their own work. They can move up in economic and social position through employment, which can reduce the differences between urban and rural areas and between rich and poor. Presently, under the impact of the financial crisis, China's export-oriented growth pattern has serious crisis, and all kinds of contradictions accumulated over a long period of time in terms of employment have all simultaneously appeared, which has largely impacted social stability.

First, under the influence of economic growth and elasticity of employment, its rise and fall, in a short period of time, employment will be the most prominent social problem affecting social stability. On the one hand, with the rapid advancement of industrialization and the unceasing upgrading of industrial structure, the driving force of economic growth is obviously weakened with employment. Statistical data indicated that, in the 1980s, each time GDP grew a percentage point, employment would increase by 2.4 million persons; this statistic dropped to 900,000 persons in 2008. Since September, under the impact of the US financial crisis, the Chinese economic growth speed has obviously dropped, and the employment situation has gotten more severe. According to statistics from the Ministry of Labor and Social Security, in the third quarter of 2008, there was a decline in labor demand, which never occurred in recent years, appeared in China; the labor demand dropped 5.5% in the whole country; half of enterprises lost positions, and newly increased employment posts and lost posts balanced out to negative growth. On the other hand, the manufacturing industry, which was most severely impacted by the financial crisis, was the key industry in admitting transfer employment of rural surplus workers, and the areas of "Changjiang Delta" and "Zhujiang Delta," which suffer the most serious impact, is also the crucial areas for employment of rural surplus workers. As a result of these two factors, many small- and medium-sized enterprises went bankrupt, thus initiating even more unemployment. It is noteworthy that, social problems caused by unemployment are widespread, and the impact to social stability is most prominent. Under the combination of the above two factors, the impact of the financial crisis to China rapidly spreads from the economic domain to the social domain in a short period of time, and all kinds of contradictions and conflicts accumulated in the process of China's economic and social transformation have a level of "resonance," which will influence social stability in the current and coming periods.

Second, unemployment causes the amount of medium and low income groups to increase, and the scope to enlarge, which will intensify the popularization between the rich and poor and intensify the contrast in the social strata. Since the Reform, with the transformation of the interest structure and acceleration of social mobility, the Chinese social stratum structure has profound changes. But, under the influences of many factors, the social stratum actually presents a pyramid shape where the proportion on the bottom is excessive, and the middle level is too small. It is calculated according to a 1% sampling of the population in 2005. Industrial workers and agricultural workers, as well as the jobless, unemployed and semi-unemployed persons found at the bottom approximately accounted for 60% of the total. Looking at the present situation, this group has an inclination toward further development and expansion. Statistical data indicated that, by the end of 2007, problems regarding transfer employment and social security of 150 million rural surplus labors and large numbers of land-levied farmers needed to be solved. Because of the imbalanced of regional economic development and the lagging social security system, getting employment in other regions or sectors has become the main method for rural surplus workers to find work and for farmers to increase their income. During the first three quarters of 2008, average income per farmer was 3321 yuan, where wage income was 1139 yuan, and approximately accounted for 34.3% of gross income; wage income was an important source of rural family income. After losing their job, their living conditions become uncertain and unstable. It can be foreseen that, in the current and coming periods, under the impact of the financial crisis, for urban and rural jobless, unemployed and semi-unemployed groups, feelings of being deprived will increase, and an environment suitable for all kinds of negative thoughts and social conflicts will emerge.

Third, it is more difficult for graduates to get employment, and they may become the new social marginalized group, which will have an adverse effect to social stability. Education is an important mechanism for in social mobility. With the rapid development of higher education in China, the number of graduates of institutions for higher learning rise year by year, and by 2009, reached 6.11 million persons. Guaranteeing graduates' full employment is an important criterion of social employment policy, and is also an objective to maintain social stability. Looking at the present situation, the manufacturing industry, which is at the end of the world industrial chain and admits a high level of employment, does not require high technological skills, and thus there need not be a high educational level when choosing employees. This has an adverse effect to the graduate group's employment. Statistical data indicated that, the registered graduate employment rate is at about 70%, but because of the impact of the US financial crisis, large quantities of small and medium-sized enterprises closed down, many large-scale state-owned enterprises' profits reduced, and massive foreign-funded enterprises reduced their staff, causing the social employment environment to further worsen. At the same time, under the influence of the declining European and American economy and shrinking overseas employment market, massive high-end talents have returned to the homeland to seek jobs, thus causing the already tight positions for gradates to be further tightened, causing employment competition to get more intense. If calculated according to statistics of employment rate, the graduate group, which is found throughout society, waiting for a job, has become a large group. It is important to note that, although it is not an independent interest group, the graduate group has high social attention in terms of social problems of unfair allocation, embezzlement and corruption and the gap between rich and poor, has intense psychological sensation, and is easy to form unified group consciousness and value judgment; simultaneously this group is at the stage where world views, philosophy and values are being formed, and has relatively low social adaptive capacity and universal frail psychological bearing capacity; once they encounter a difficult position in employment, and the huge contrast between expectation and reality, some students easily fall into depression or psychology frustration, which not only possibly induces suicide or illegal and criminal activities, but also easily transfer and blaze malcontent mood to other social objects, and then poses a latent threat to the social stability.

D. *The Drop in Satisfaction with Standard of Living and the Rise of a Sense of Frustration Sense is Intertwined, which Seriously Influences People's Psychological Anticipation, and the Bad Morale of a Few Groups may Evolve into a Prominent Problem*

With economic globalization and the development of social informatization, fluctuations in the world economy is more and more so connected to people's vital interests, and people's sensitivity and attention to economic life is also further enhanced. The financial crisis has not only brought direct impact to China's economic and social development, but through various medias' spread of ideas, people's worry and dread of economic recession magnified. Especially for some social vulnerable groups, under the dual pressure of difficult position in unemployment and difficult life, their sense of frustration and sense of depravity easily increases, causing pessimism, disappointment, negativity, etc., and when they undergo a specific situation or event, they make that the opportunity and retaliate against the society.

First, life pressure increases, which possibly causes individual mental and physiological disorder, and induces criminal cases of harming public security for purposes of suicide or retaliating the society. Under the situation where the employment contradiction becomes increasingly prominent, and where social competition becomes increasingly intense, once they are balked of work and life, it is easy for a few illiberal extreme unemployed persons to initiate individual mental and physiological disorder, and to intensify the contradictions and conflicts between the people, to evolve into suicide or intense violent offense, even where the object of the crime is directly towards public security and innocent people. On May 19, 2009, an extraordinarily serious murder case occurred in Daye of Hubei, because he was out of funds to treat an illness, the criminal suspect was malcontent with society and wantonly used a knife and attacked people ont eh street; he killed 4 and injured 2; On June 5, a bus arson case occurred in Chengdu of Sichuan, a pessimistic man wanted to retaliate against society intentionally because he did not attend properly attend to his business and caused family dissension; he set fire to a bus, and caused death to 27 persons and injury to 74 persons.

Second, if the social malcontent mood accumulates and ferments in specific regions and special groups, group events "without immediate interest conflict" may be easily induced. Because of the slowdown of economic development and backflow of population, driving role of economic growth to social development has reduced, and the slow release function of population movement to social contradiction has obviously weakened. In some specific areas where the economy is underdeveloped, the coverage of social security, and proportion of low-income group is high, all kinds of malcontent feelings are easy to accumulate, enlarge and ferment, and to intensify the social opposition and to expedite social listlessness. Once people are stimulated through some event, although some people do not have immediate interest conflict with the inducing event, the common social circumstances and identification intensify the mood and enlarge the mental anger, and considerable amount of people may join in the conflict and relieve malcontent feelings, which forms a bigger scale gathering in a short time, and causes situation spread and conflict aggravation, which induces a group event "without immediate interest conflict." The sudden group event regarding public security occurred in Shishou of Hubei in June, 2009 had such characteristic.

Third, realistic benefit is damaged, mental anticipation suffers setbacks, and people's bearing capacity to unstable social events reduces, all which become important factors that affect the people's sense of security. With the unceasing improvement of material standard of living, public security becomes an increasingly urgent public demand of all social members. Generally speaking, resident's sense of security and overall evaluation to public order are positively correlated with economic development and income level on the whole; residents in a society, where the more developed the economy is, the higher the income level is, possibly have higher and higher overall evaluation to public order and sense of security; the less developed, the lower. In recent years, Chinese people's sense of security increased year by year, which was realized based on sustainable, healthy and steady economic development. Presently, under the influence of the financial crisis and economic growth slowdown, people's mental anticipation, which develops the economy and improves the standard of living, is affected to a certain extent; psychological sensation to many disharmonious and factors causing instability is further strengthened, which has an adverse effect to people's sense of security and to degree of satisfaction to public security work. It is noteworthy that, with the unceasing development of social informatization, social hazard caused by individual vicious crime cases and disaster accidents of public security, has not only been limited, especially through the bamboo telegraph of more and more advanced modern media, but the impact to mental anticipation of all people that live and work in peace and contentment will be further intensified. It is foreseen that, it will be more difficult to unceasingly keep the rising trend of people's sense of security 2010.

III. *Countermeasures on Maintaining Public Order*

Through review to public order in 2009, we see that, although the economic development fluctuation brought by the financial crisis impacted China's social stability, it was better than the situation esti-mated as a whole. Looking into 2010, with the stabilization and rise of the world economy, China's economic growth speed will speed up recovery, promotion and driving role of economic development to social stability will be further strengthened, social contradictions will overall relax, the situation of social stability will get better, and the foundation of social harmony will become more reliable. But, we must have level-headed awareness, in order to deal with the impact of the financial crisis to China's social stability, we must focus on solving medium- and long-term problems and contradictions that exist in the society and affect China's social stability. If we do not so, it is difficult for short-term actions to have a lasting effect; social stability mainte-nance work with a view of key objects, key fields and key links should be done well, social contradictions should be targeted, and grass-roots foundation work should be strengthened earnestly to consolidate the foundation of social stability. Regarding public order work in 2010, we must do target current main contradictions and prominent prob-lems from the overall situation and strategic level by firmly grasping the characteristics of economic and social development at this stage, to best control and reduce harmful factors of inducing crime growth, and to enlarge unceasingly the strength of crackdown and rectification to prominent crimes and highly frequent disaster accidents of public security, which guarantee sustainable stability of the overall situation of public order.

A. *Accurately Grasping Social Psychology and People's Psychology, and Strengthening People's Sense of Security and Degree of Satisfaction*

Currently, in the special historical period where criminal offense fre-quent occur, by insisting in strict law enforcement, we can protect the legal sanctity and promote social justice, can effectively maintain social harmony and stability, and strengthen people's sense of security and degree of satisfaction. Judicial agencies must further innovate the idea of law enforcement, further improve the way of law enforcement, put forth effort to solve prominent problems in law enforcement work, insist in strict, fair and civilized law enforcement, insist in rational, gentle and standard law enforcement to enhance unceasingly the credibility of law enforcement, maintain the social fairness and justice earnestly to promote the social harmony and stability; must insist in integrating strict crackdown with strict precaution, strict administration and strict control, strictly crack down on serious criminal offenses, rectify prominent problems of public security that people complain about, manage earnestly various administrative items, achieve initiative attack, effective rectification and rational management, solve the problems that fail to be effectively attacked and problems of lax management; must earnestly learn the profound lessons of serious malignant events initiated because of improper law enforcement in recent years, concretely study the practical situation of different law-enforcement objects to improve the law-enforcement way, pay attention to law-enforcement art, earnestly achieve taking the law as the basis, and convince people through reason and evoke people's emotions, and integrate the law, principle and emotion to solve the problem of simple and mechanical law enforcement; must closely revolve around the law-enforcement domains of public security management, fire management and road traffic management etc. which easily have problems, closely grasp law-enforcement links of interrogation and examination, search, pursuit and capture, interception and capture etc. which easily can help to further consummate each law-enforcement system and procedure, guarantee that police have laws to go by and have regulations to follow in each law-enforcement activity to solve the problem of arbitrary and unmannerly law enforcement.

B. *Deepening Rectification Action of Public Order Unceasingly, and Strengthening the Target-Oriented and Effectiveness of Crackdown on Illegal Acts and Crimes*

To deal with the impact of the international financial crisis effectively in regards to public order, in April 2009, the Ministry of Public Security made the overall deployment, which launched the national rectification action of public order, and organized and launched a series of special crackdown action, which made preliminary progress. Public security organs must, on the basis of local practical situation of public security, according to the requirements of the Ministry of Public Security, and in accordance with the principle that "emphatically rectifies prominent problems of public security; solves the problem that is prominent in public security; emphatically cracks down on the crimes what people most hate," together investigate the prominent problems which influence local public order and chaotic places of public security that people have reflected, organize and launch regional crackdown and rectification action as circumstances permit, and creatively deepen the national rectification action of public order unceasingly; Must further give prominence to the target of attack, severely crack down on organized crimes, sternly crack down on serious violent offenses of detonation, poisoning, kidnapping and murder etc., sternly crack down on crimes of burglary, stealing and robbing vehicles, robbing people's property by driving motorcycle or telecommunication cheating etc., which infringes upon wealth, severely crack down on serious economic crimes of illegal attracting savings, fraud by raising funds, financial swindling, taking money to flee to other place and so on, severely crack down on crimes of swindling and children and woman trafficking which infringes personal rights, together rectify the vile social evils of "Pornography, gambling and drug abuse and trafficking" etc., which the people abhor, and firmly beat the tendency of high frequency of current criminal offense activity, to guarantee that the overall situation of public order has sustainable stability, and guarantee people's sense of can be obviously enhanced.

C. Strengthening and Improving Social Management Work, and Maintaining Stability of Public Security Order

Organs concerned must insist in the guideline of fair treatment, good services, reasonable guidance and good management, positively innovate the new mentality of supervisory service work for the floating population, gradually realize the change of administration from "administering population by certificates" to "administering population by real estate," and using informatization means and shock action to clean up and rectify the regular ordered management, firmly maintain legitimate rights and interests of floating population, firmly attack illegal and criminal offenders hidden in it; Must establish record of highly frequent crime group for persons released upon completion of a sentence, persons that have fulfilled a sentence outside prison but under surveillance, drug addicts and waifs and children of persons serving sentences etc., consummate scroll investigation and dynamic control working mechanism, grasp their active track and practical situation promptly, and prevent and reduce illegal and criminal activity; Must explore positively and strengthen new action of public security management regarding places of special trade and public entertainment services, synthetically take the ways of quoted rectification, on-site urging to handle and track accountability etc., earnestly enlarge inspection strength regarding places of special trade and public entertainment services, duly grasp the conditions of public security, legally investigate illegal cases, and eliminate prominent hidden trouble of public security; Must jointly with departments concerned positively strengthen security check on units of production, storage, transportation, sale and use of guns and ammunition, explosives and dangerous virulent chemicals, supervise and urge implementation of safety control system and technical specifications, severely attack illegal and criminal activities that secretly conceal, deal and transport dangerous goods, and control and reduce occurrence of cases involving guns, explosion and narcotics; must prevent public security disaster accidents, such as fire and road traffic etc., positively carry out concentrated investigation and rectification of the hidden danger of fires and road traffic, aimed at rural areas, and firmly contain the tendency where the death toll rises in rural public security disaster accidents.

D. *Further Consummate the Prevention and Control System for Public Order, and put forth Effort to Enhance the Control Ability of a Dynamic Society*

Under the background of a period of social informatization, strengthening the construction of prevention and control system for public order has been endowed with new connotations, and the prevention and control domain has been expanded from stressing prevention and control of illegal acts and crimes in the past to various aspects, including investigation, attack, and social management. To meet the demands of the new situation, organs concerned must positively build the three-dimensional prevention and control system for public order which integrates prevention and control, and comprehensively cover the inside and outside Internet to effectively enhance control ability to dynamic society; Must positively advance information integration construction, put forth effort to enhance information compilation study and determination ability, and realize foreknowledge, early-warning and prevention; Must take information as the link to diligently discover the target of attack in guard management and to discover the weak points of prevention and control in attack and rectification, to realize the integration operation of attack, prevention and control; Must positively build the omni-directional, all-weather, three-dimensional social dynamic prevention and control net which is composed by the prevention and control network of the street front, the community, work unit content, video monitoring, regional police cooperation and the "virtual society," which integrates the site, line and coverage, people's air defense, material and technology, attack, prevention, management and control and the inside and outside Internet to furthest reduce blind areas of management and prevention, to furthest extrude the space of crimes, and to furthest reduce opportunities for illegal acts and crimes.

ENVIRONMENTAL PROTECTION UNDER INTERNATIONAL FINANCIAL CRISIS IN 2009

Qian Yong and Yan Shihui

I. *Deepening Environmental Management to Guarantee Growth*

In 2009, guaranteeing GDP's growth at 8% was the key to whether dealing with the international financial crisis was successful or not. Therefore, guaranteeing growth became the core task of the whole year. Facing the serious threat of comprehensive economic decline and the drop in profit for enterprises, how to handle correctly the relations between guaranteeing growth and strengthening environmental management was the new task for work of environmental protection. For one year, the work of environmental protection closely revolved around the core task of guaranteeing growth to promote structural readjustment in strengthening the environmental management and quickening energy conservation and discharge reduction. Controlling old and new pollution sources expanding domestic demand, guaranteeing growth, readjusting the structure, and benefiting the livelihood of the people became more closely related. To speed up focus on controlling regional pollution, blind startup of projects with "high energy consumption, high pollution and resource product" ("两高一资" Liang Gao Yi Zi), capacity surplus and low-level construction of redundant projects were strictly controlled to positively push industrial restructuring and transformation of economic development.

A. *Speed Up Structural Readjustment, Goal of Conserving Energy and Reducing Discharge*

On June 5, 2009, Premier Wen Jiabao stressed in the Conference of the National Leading Committee on Climate Change and the State Council Leading Committee on Energy Conservation and Pollutant Discharge Reduction that, it was a decisive year when the goal of energy conservation and pollutant discharge reduction was realized in the "11th Five-year Plan" in 2009. Various areas and departments must push for energy conservation and pollutant discharge reduction in order to maintain steady economic growth. Energy conservation and pollutant discharge reduction need to be regarded as key to economic structural readjustment and development. As the important content of dealing with the international financial crisis, expanding domestic demand, guaranteeing growth and readjusting structure, and as important methods of adapting to climate change and promoting human sustainable development, policy measure on energy conservation and pollutant discharge reduction must be comprehensively implemented. An in order to strive for greater results, guaranteeing fulfillment of a scheduled goal in terms of energy conservation and pollutant discharge reduction needs to be in line with implementation progress of the "11th Five-year Plan." Various regions and departments implemented and earnestly carried out requests of the Party Central Committee and the State Council, paid special attention to carry out projects of pollutant discharge reduction, structural pollutant discharge reduction and management pollutant discharge reduction. They sped up monitoring and assessment of pollutant discharge reduction, and unceasingly strengthened the guidance function of environmental protection target assessment in economic and social development, where the work of energy conservation and pollutant discharge reduction had positive progress.

In order to guarantee the goal of energy conservation and pollutant discharge reduction, the pace of industrial restructuring step was further quickened, and the capacity of pollution prevention and control has been obviously strengthened. First, the replacement of primitive capacity has quickened. In the three years before "11th Five-year Plan", through the policy of "setting up large units and shutting down small units," the thermal power generating units of 34.21 million kilowatts were shut down, and primitive iron-smelting capacity of 60.59 million tons, primitive steel-making capacity of 43.47 million tons and primitive cement capacity of 140 million tons were eliminated. In the first half of 2009, thermal power generating units of 19.89 million kilowatts were eliminated, and industrial structural readjustment of high energy consumption and high pollutant discharge, including steel and iron, cement, coking, papermaking, ethyl alcohol, monosodium glutamate etc., also made new progress. Second, the ability of pollution prevention and control has been enlarged. By the end of 2008, countrywide coal-burning power plants capacity amounted to 360 million kilowatts, where the proportion of electricity generation of coal-fired power plant was enhanced from 12% in 2005 to 60%. During the first half of 2009, coal-burning units of 42.35 million kilowatt were also completed. Total centralized urban sewage treatment plants reached more than 1,500; daily sewage treatment capacity was nearly 100 million tons, and the urban sewage treatment ratio was enhanced from 52% in 2005 to 66%, which increased the urban sewage treatment capacity by 5.68 million tons per day.

In the first half of 2009, work unit GDP energy consumption dropped 3.35% from that of 2008, the ratio compared to total discharge of two main pollutants, sulfur dioxide and chemical oxygen demand (COD) reduced respectively 5.40% and 2.46% from that of 2008. It is forecasted from the present situation of pollutant discharge reduction that the goal of sulfur dioxide discharge reduction in the "11th Five-year Plan" would achieve in advanced by the end of 2009, and the goal of COD discharge reduction is also possible to be achieved as scheduled.

Environmental monitoring indicated that, since 2008, the water quality of countrywide big basins slightly improved, and the annual average concentration of permanganate index in the sections of national controlled surface water was 5.7 milligrams/liter, which achieved Class-III water standard for the first time. In the first half of 2009, the water quality in sections of national controlled surface watera unceasingly improved, and the permanganate exponential average concentration was 5.3 milligrams/liter. In 2008, the average concentration of sulfur dioxide in the air of 113 key environmental protection cities was 0.048 milligrams/m3, which dropped 7.7 percentage points from the previous year, and dropped 15.8 percentage points from that of 2005. In the first half of 2009, the air environment quality of key environmental protection cities unceasingly improved, and the average concentration of sulfur dioxide was 0.045 milligrams/m3.

B. *Implementing the Demands of "Three High-Quality Guarantees" and Strengthening Supervision of Environmental Law-Enforcement*

"Guaranteeing growth, guaranteeing livelihood of the people, and guaranteeing stability" is the basic policy the central government strives for in order to combat the financial crisis. Environmental protection is not only a problem that effects the economy, but also the livelihood of the people. All levels of environmental protection departments closely followed the requirements of the "three guarantees" in environmental law-enforcement supervision to expand their work domain, to improve their methods, and to solve prominent environment problems, which hinders economic development.

Environmental protection law enforcement is continually developed. In 2009, the Ministry of Environmental Protection jointly with 8 Departments and Commissions including the National Development and Reform Commission continually launched special actions of environmental protection, which rectified illegal pollution discharge enterprises to guarantee the public's health. Three focuses of these actions are as follows. First, it strictly administered that industries of "high energy consumption, high pollution and resource product" carry out special inspections of steel and iron and arsenic contamination; Second, it strengthened sources of drinking water, and continuously supervised environmental protection; Third, it put forth effort to rectify illegal acts regarding urban sewage and harmless waste treatment, and guaranteed that the effect and benefits of pollutant discharge reduction fully be brought into play. By the end of September, various regions altogether sent environmental law-enforcement officials of 1,800,000 persons-times, inspected 750,000 enterprises-times, and investigated 7669 illegal cases regarding the environment. According to incomplete statistics, 119 liable persons were investigated because of illegal acts on environment and environmental pollution. In some areas where there was lax environmental protection supervision to order to promote growth, 313 enterprises and projects in 72 prefecture cities of 23 provinces (regions, municipalities), and 62 enterprises and projects were inspected and had committed illegal acts regarding the environment, which accounted for 19.8%. At the same time, centralized inspection to more than 44,000 heavy pollution industrial enterprises and key pollutant discharge enterprises in key regions was investigated, and 1690 enterprises were prosecuted, where the pollutant discharge exceeded the allowed figure; more than 100,000 construction projects were inspected, which started operation in 2007, 1,824 projects were prosecuted, where construction began without approval, and 3,167 projects prosecuted, which did not carry out the "three simultaneous" ("三同时" San Tong Shi, namely simultaneous design, simultaneous construction and simultaneous production and use) of environmental protection. They were supervised and urged to improve.

The complaint hot-line of the Ministry of Environmental Protection is opened. On "June 5," 2009 World Environment Day, the Ministry of Environmental Protection opened the report hot-line for environmental protection "010-12369" to take people's reports on sudden environment events, inter-provincial pollution as well as other complaints regarding the environment, which would be investigated and handled by the Ministry of Environmental Protection. Regarding reports and complaints which local departments of environmental protection are authorized to handle, according to the principle of jurisdictional management, they will be handed to the provincial and municipal departments of environmental protection concerned through the networking operating system of environmental protection report hot-line. For those reports which provincial (autonomous region, municipality) departments of environmental protection fail to solve, the people may bring to the Ministry of Environmental Protection through the phone number "010-12369." They can learn how the handle the complaint thorugh this number. Since the opening of the hot-line, within four months, over a thousand reports on environmental pollution have been accepted, and all were dispatched to verify and solved the first time, which has provided an effective way for people to report and solve problems relating to environment.

Regulations to the heavy metal pollution enterprises are carried out. From January to September 2009, the Ministry of Environmental Protection received reports and handled 136 sudden environment events, which increased 22.5% from the previous year; all these events were properly handled, especially events since August; for example, the lead pollution event that occurred in Fengxiang of Shanxi, and the cadmium pollution in Liuyang of Hunan. According to the Party Central Committee and instruction of State Council leaders, the environmental protection system was urgently mobilized and deployed to begin prevention and control work of heavy metal pollution. Special inspection was rapidly organized to be carried out throughout the whole country from October to December, and enterprises dealing with lead, cadmium, mercury, chromium and metalloid arsenic were comprehensively investigated; heavy metal pollution events frequently occurred in such enterprises. Departments concerned should formulate polices on prevention and control of heavy metal pollution, create special funds for the prevention and control of heavy metal pollution, and strengthen the Popular Science Propaganda on hazard of heavy metal and health protection. Up to present, 15 events of heavy metal pollution have been handled properly, greatly limiting the danger of these events.

C. *Treatment of Key Regions Improves, and Water Quality of 70% of Sections Reach the Standards*

To strengthen the work of pollution prevention and control in key regions, the State Council General Office retransmitted the provisional measures of the Ministry of Environmental Protection on the assessment to the implementation of policies on water pollution prevention and control in the key regions. In late June to early July of 2009, the Ministry of Environmental Protection jointly with the National Development and Reform Commission, the Ministry of Supervision, the Ministry of Finance, the Ministry of Housing and Urban-Rural Development and the Ministry of Water Resources, respectively assessed the 2008 annual implementation of the "11th Five-year Plan" regarding water pollution prevention and control in 21 provinces, autonomous regions and municipalities in some key regions including Haihe River, Liaohe River, the Three Gorges Reservoir Region and upper, middle reaches of the Yellow River, Chaohu Lake, Dianchi Lake and Tai Lake, and so on. The results indicated that, by the end of 2008, the anti-pollution engineering projects of the "11th Five-year Plan" and total investments were about 40% complete, and water quality of 70% reached standards in water-quality supervision assessment.

Since the "11th Five-year Plan", according to the requirements of the plan, the local people's governments concerned in key regions have strengthened organization to work on water pollution prevention and control. Reducing discharge of main pollutants and improving the quality of water environment were most important, as well as speeding up construction of anti-pollution engineering projects. Strength of structural readjustment was increased; the environmental protection access system was rigorously enforced, and construction of urban sewage and waste treatment facilities was quickened. By the end of 2008, in terms of water quality, in 115 assessment sections, the water quality of 80 sections reached standards, which accounted for 69.6% of the total. The Three-Gorges Reservoir Region and its upper reaches, Haihe River, middle and upper reaches of Yellow River, Liaohe River etc. were assessed using the permanganate index, and the standard reach rate was respectively 100%, 87.1%, 81.8% and 77.8%. Tai Lake, Chaohu Lake and Dianchi Lake etc. were assessed using the permanganate index, ammonia nitrogen (total nitrogen) and total phosphorus respectively. Taking the permanganate index as assessment, the standard reach rate of section water quality was respectively 93.8%,

85.7% and 66.7%; assessed by ammonia nitrogen (Total nitrogen), the standard reach rate was respectively 50%, 47.6% and 0%; assessed by total phosphorus, the standard reach rate was respectively 75%, 71.4% and 50%. In terms of anti-pollution project construction, 773 out of the 1834 anti-pollution projects specified in the "11th Five-year Plan" were completed (including commissioning), which accounted for 42.1%; 500 projects were in progress, which accounted for 27.3%; 418 projects were in preparatory stages, which accounted for 22.8%; 143 projects were yet to be started, which accounted for 7.8%. In terms of investments, total investment of the "11th Five-year Plan" was 116.03 billion yuan, and actually completed investments was 43.75 billion yuan, 37.7% of total investments. Generally speaking, projects in Haihe River region progressed quicker, and projects in Three Gorges Reservoir Region and its upper reaches had slower progress.

Although the work of water pollution prevention and control in key regions had positive progress, the planned project investment gap of pollution prevention and control in key regions was still big, the operating efficiency of urban sewage treatment facilities was not high, and the contamination problem of ammonia nitrogen (total nitrogen) and total phosphorus magnified; the task of water quality improvement was still very arduous.

D. *"Promoting Environment Protection by Reward" to Promote Comprehensive Reform in Rural Environment*

At the beginning of 2009, the State Council General Office transmitted the "Plan on Implementing "Promoting Environment Protection by reward" ("以奖促治" Yi Jiang Cu Zhi) to Speed up Solving Prominent Problems concerning the Rural Environment" to the Ministry of Environmental Protection, the Ministry of Finance, the National Development and Reform Commission to carry out comprehensive deployment of the "Promoting Environment Protection by Reward" and "Replacing Compensation by Reward" ("以奖代补" Yi Jiang Dai Bu) policies. One billion Yuan in funds were budgeted to boost the comprehensive treatment of rural environment. More than 1200 villages with prominent environment problems were treated, more than 170 villages and towns of ecology model got rewards, and 9 million persons benefited from it directly, causing rural areas to invest nearly 1.5 billion Yuan for environmental protection. Through the implementation of "Promoting Environment Protection by reward", comprehensive environment treatment of villages and towns was promoted, which has carried on the beneficial attempt and practices to explore new mentalities, means and new actions of rural environment protection; it supported to carry out comprehensive rural environment treatment in the pilot areas of the Wuhan city circle of Hubei Province and of Changsha-Zhuzhou-Xiangtan urban group resource-conservation and environment-friendly society of Hunan Province to push construction for the local "two types" of society; it supported to carry out concentrated rectification how difficult problem regarding scattered breeding and domestic pollution in villages around Erhai Lake, which would reduce the pollution loads in the Lake, should be treated; it supported the rectification project of a wide range of villages around Dahuofang Reservoir of Liaoning Province, which explored jointly building and sharing of waste and sewage treatment facilities; it supported comprehensive rectification project in immigrant new villages of Ningxia to cooperate with the socialist new rural reconstruction, which explored efficient ways for ecology immigration work of similar areas.

E. *Consummating the Environmental Economic Policy, and Preventing Environment Risk*

In recent years, China studied, formulated and implemented a series of policy measures on green credit, green insurance, green securities, green trade and green tax revenue etc., and has made good progress, where the basic structure to policy security system for environmental protection and economic growth has been formed.

Green credit. Green credit is a finance monitoring measure where commercial banks implement credit squeeze or collect loans in advance from enterprises concerned according to information provided by the department of environment protection regarding illegal actions of enterprises. Since it was implemented in 2007, the central bank credit management system has recorded more than 40,000 pieces of information regarding environmental protection, and more than 13,000 pieces of enterprise's illegal actions regarding environment have been given to various commercial banks through the Banking Regulatory Commission. In June 2009, the Ministry of Environmental Protection and the Central Bank further consummated the information sharing mechanism, and further increased three classes of information, such as environment impact assessment for enterprise projects, environmental protection acceptance for construction project, enforcement of clean production verification enterprise based on reservations on sharing enterprise's illegal actions regarding environment.

Green insurance. Green insurance, namely environmental pollution liability insurance, is where enterprises bear the responsibility of compensation to damages to a third if a pollution incident occurs. Since the green insurance became a pilot project in 2007, many areas have positively responded. Jiangsu Province released the shipping pollution liability insurance aimed at water-borne transport. Hubei Province, Hunan Province and Ningbo City of Zhejiang Province created environmental pollution liability insurance successively. Hebei Province and Shenyang City of Liaoning Province stipulated provisions on environmental pollution liability insurance in local laws and regulations concerned. Hunan Province had the first national case of compensation with the environmental pollution liability insurance. In September 2008, a chlorine hydride leakage accident occurred at Zhuzhou Haohua Agricultural Chemicals Company, and nearby the vegetable fields of nearby villagers suffered from the pollution. This enterprise's insurance company, Ping An Insurance (Group) Company Of China promptly compensated for the losses of more than 120 villager families, according to the insurance clauses of "pollution incident" through the professional loss assessment, which settled the contradiction and dispute.

Green trade. In 2007, the department of environmental protection started to formulate a directory of products of high pollution and high environment risk as an important foundation to limit the export of pollution products. In January 2008, the national department of environmental protection issued a directory of more than 140 kinds of products of high pollution and high environment risk of 5 industries including agricultural chemicals, inorganic salt, battery, coating and dye and so on, which are involved in over 2 billion US dollars of export trade. At present, three batches have been issued, and a directory of more than 280 kinds of products of high pollution and high environment risk exist. The departments of finance, commerce, tax affairs and customs have taken measures of canceling tax reimbursement for export and forbidding the processing trade to products of high pollution and high environment risk found in the directory, which has reduced China's environment price of export products. Through preliminary assessment, after the directory of products of high pollution and high environment risk was issued, enterprises in industries of agricultural chemicals, inorganic salt, coating, dye and battery were given more restrictions in the examination and approval of projects, bank loans, enterprise listing application and refinancing etc., which has powerfully impelled the enterprises to expand investments for pollution treatment and move toward technical innovation.

Green tax revenue. The environmental tax policy is the core of environmental economic policy. Until now, China does not levy an independent environmental tax, and only gradually makes "ecological transformation" to the existing tax system, and some categories of taxes have manifested the demand of environmental protection and resource conservation. In tax reimbursement for export, the products of high pollution and high environment risk are lowered or cancelled in export rebates. In terms of income tax, enterprises are allowed to offset and remit enterprise income tax by 10% of investment cost used in purchasing special equipment for environmental protection. In terms of excise tax, besides increasing the excise tax rate to wooden chopsticks and the large output volumes of automobiles, products made using heavy pollution technology will join the excise tax. In value-added tax, products of comprehensive utilization, which meet demands of environmental protection, are given preferential policy of value-added tax, and products rid of sulfur, and utilizing recycled products, etc given preferential treatment in value-added tax. At present, the departments concerned are studying and formulating independent environmental tax policy as quickly as possible.

In addition, many other types of environment economic policy are being also studied and formulated quickly. In terms of green price, the reform of resource price products advanced, resource tax standard of coal, crude oil and natural gas adjusted, reform of refined oil price and of expenses of taxation implemented, and enterprises limited and eliminated in 8 high energy consumption industries have been implemented the different electricity price. The green electricity price policy charges desulphurization power plants a price increase of 0.015 Yuan for kilowatt-hour, and price policy reform to pollution discharge charge and town sewage treatment cost etc. is also steadily advancing. By the end of 2008, the average water price (including tap water price, sewage treatment cost and charge for water resources etc.) of resident domestic water and industrial water in 36 big- or medium-sized cities was respectively 2.35 yuan and 3.19 yuan per ton, which respectively increased by 12.4% and 17.2% from that of 2005. Among them, resident domestic water, the actual collection standard of industrial water and sewage treatment cost was respectively 0.70 yuan and 1.00

yuan per ton, which respectively increased by 29.6% and 38.9% from that of 2005, and the adjustment range of sewage treatment cost standard surpassed the final value of water. In terms of green purchase, the "Government Procurement List on Environmental Products" has expanded, and presently it includes more than 10,000 classes of products. At the same time, compulsory government procurement has been implemented to 9 classes of energy-conservation products. In terms of green investment, to deal with the impact of the international financial crisis, and to maintain steady quick domestic economic development, the Chinese government promptly adjusted the macroeconomic policy, and released a package plan to stimulate business recovery, focused on energy conservation, pollutant discharge reduction and ecological environmental protection as important sectors for investment; in the newly increased 4 trillion yuan government investments, the Chinese government budgeted 210 billion yuan to be directly used in projects of energy conservation, pollutant discharge reduction and ecological construction, adding to the 370 billion yuan investments for independent innovation and structural readjustment; investments relating to environmental protection have reached as high as 580 billion yuan. In terms of green finance, reconstructive projects for energy conservation adopt the policy of "replacing compensation by reward," and reward enterprises according to energy conservation quantity, and financial subsidy is given to reconstruction for energy conservation.

F. *Plan Environmental Impact Evaluation Regulations and Program and Environmental Impact Assessment Integrated*

The State Council Order 559 promulgated "Regulations on Planning Environmental Impact Assessment," and it went into force on October 1, 2009. The promulgation and implementation of "Regulation" is a significant step for China's environmental legislation; the main content include 36 articles in 6 chapters, and through strengthening of planning environmental impact assessment work, and increasing the scientific nature of planning, guarantee of institutions' work on preventing environmental pollution and ecological destruction is given from the source, which symbolizes that environmental protection is beginning to have an impact on decision-making and macroeconomic regulation and control has entered a new stage. "Regulation" requests to regard the overall influence of ecosystem in regions, basins and coastal areas as the point of application of planning environmental impact assessment, which is beneficial to prevent problems relating to environment caused by unreasonable allocation of production force and resource allocation from the policy-making source. It is the important means to carry out the orientation of environmental protection policy that gives priority to prevention and integrates prevention and treatment. "Regulation" regards unified planning of economic benefit, social benefit and environment benefit as the key in advancing environmental impact assessment, which is advantageous to push innovation to establish and consummate a coordinated sustainable scientific progress system mechanism and corresponding managerial system, and is the guarantee of the legal system, which insists in ecology civilization construction as the instruction and explores new ways of environmental protection with Chinese characteristics. "Regulation" regards solving prominent environmental problems, which endanger people's health and affects sustainable development, as the starting point to advance environmental impact assessment, which is advantageous to maintain people's vital interests, and is an effective means to promote social harmony through being environmental friendly.

While formulating the supporting implementation measures for "Regulation," the Ministry of Environmental Protection established the linkage mechanism of planning environmental impact assessment and project impact assessment according to the provisions of "Regulation." It specifically requests that construction projects, which are not contained in the planning environmental impact assessment to not be included in documents of environmental impact assessment. Presently, the planning environmental impact assessment to industries of steel and iron, and cement etc. that have surplus capacity are emphatically strengthened. On the premise of planning environmental impact assessment to regional industries, acceptance, examination and approval of the documents on environmental impact assessment to high energy-consumption projects in the region may avoid new regional environmental problems caused by surplus capacity and construction of redundant projects. When making significant adjustment or revision to the implementation scope, available deadline, scale, structure and layout of the planning authorized, environmental impact assessment should be remade or created, and where there is no environmental impact assessment, documents on environmental impact assessment to construction projects should not be accepted. For planning which has had environmental impact assessment, contents of environmental impact assessment to its construction projects can be suitably simpli-

fied according to the analysis, and the actual contents which are sim-
plified, as well as those that need to be further assess should be defined
in the examination opinions.

G. *Mobilizing Social Strength, and Expanding Public Participation*

In 2009, government departments concerned further expanded the
channels for public participation in environmental protection, which
positively guided social strength to further develop environmental
protection.

Chinese public environmental protection index (2008). On January 16, 2009, the findings of investigation from the Chinese public
environmental protection index (2008), organized by the China Environmental Culture Promotion Association, were issued officially in
Beijing, this was the fourth time it was issued for society since 2005.
This investigation was done in 31 inland provincial capital cities and
in 4 municipalities, and those sampled was 9,593 people. The findings
revealed that the public's score on environmental consciousness was
44.5 points overall, the score on environmental protection behavior
was 37.0 points, and the score on environmental protection satisfaction was 45.1 points. Compared with the previous year, three index
signs increased. This score not only reflected that the government
strengthened environmental protection propaganda and made positive
progress in recent years, but also reflected that the public's consciousness toward environmental protection was also unceasingly enhancing,
as well as their satisfaction level to environmental protection work and
environmental condition. It should be mentioned, after the Beijing
Olympic Games, Beijing public's satisfaction to environmental protection has risen rapidly. But, overall, at present, Chinese public's
consciousness of environmental protection is remains at a low level.
This investigation reflected several issues; first, environmental pollution has become a public focus. In 2008, in investigations on "Chinese
public's social hotspot issues," environmental pollution ranked third
after "price" and "food safety;" the attention proportion was 37.7%.
Second, the public's consciousness of environment crisis has universally increased, but the public individual quality of environmental protection is remains low. The investigation showed that 72.2% of the
public did not know that June 5 is "World Environment Day;" 58%
of the public did not know "12369," the national unified environment
hot line; only 11.2% answered correctly that the organ "responsible

for environmental quality in its own area of jurisdiction" is the local people's government. Third, the public's satisfaction to government environmental protection actions is 56.74 points, which increased 1.18 points from the previous year, which reflected that the public approves of the government's efforts in environmental protection. The public especially marvels at enterprises' performance; their score of satisfaction reaches as high as 72.47 points, which increased 25.54 points from 46.93 points of the previous year, and show that enterprises have undergone a breakthrough in terms of environmental protection management, and have transformed from traditional passive management to initiative management. Fourth, environmental pollution threatens public's basic necessities in life. The investigation also indicated that waste treatment, noise pollution, pet management, as well as water and air pollution have become the environmental problem the public worries about most. Fifth, 62% of the public thought that there is great disparity between China's environmental protection level and that of developed countries, which showed that China's environmental protection domain in international cooperation and exchange is very broad.

Thousand youth environment friendly messenger action. June 5, 2009 is the 38th World Environment Day, the subject determined by the United Nations Environment Program (UNEP) is "Your planet needs YOU! Unite to combat climate change." According to China's national condition, the Ministry of Environmental Protection defined the Chinese subject of environment day of 2009, "Take actions to mitigate pollution." Two themes confirm that increasing consciousness and advocating participation are the goals. For this purpose, the Ministry of Environmental Protection jointly with the Commission of Environment Protection and Resources Conservation of NPC, the Human Resources and Environment Committee of CPPCC, the National Development and Reform Commission, the Ministry of Science and Technology, the Ministry of Education, the Central Committee of Communist Youth League and the All-China Women's Federation, initiate the project of thousands of youth environment friendly messenger action. The role of youth as pioneers, and where one individual transmits to a thousand, public's consciousness of environmental protection is increased; it urges the public to pay attention to prevention and control of pollution, and to positively participate in action of energy conservation and pollutant discharge reduction.

National energy conservation propaganda week. To further mobilize all circles to positively participate in construction of a resource-conservation and environment-friendly society, 14 ministries and commissions, including the National Development and Reform Commission jointly held a national energy conservation propaganda week from June 14 to 20 in 2009. The theme is "promote energy-conservation products, promote to expand consumer demand." During energy conservation propaganda week, some energy-conservation products were propagandized and promoted emphatically, including highly-effective illumination products, highly-effective energy-conservation air conditioning, highly-effective energy-conservation electrical machinery, energy-conservation environmental-protection automobile, etc., to guide the public's scientific consumption and green consumption. Various regions organized to carry out energy-shortage experience activities, propagandized and promoted energy-conservation, environmental-protection driving activities, such as lightly step on the gas, reduce stepping on the brakes, little use of air conditioning, often check tire pressure, drive with less weight, and so on. Drivers were encouraged to form good driving habits and to actively participate in energy conservation and pollutant discharge reduction.

II. *Arduous Tasks in Environmental Protection*

At present, China is at the stage of quick development in industrialization and urbanization. In the next 15 years, with growth in population, enhancement of urbanization level and gross economic expansion, according to present levels of resource consumption and contamination control, pollution capacity will increase 4 to 5 times, therefore the task of environmental protection is very arduous.

A. *Development of the Heavy Chemical Industry will Continue, and Industrial Pollution Control Remains under Stress*

According to the forecast of the State Information Center and the Chinese Academy for Environmental Planning, under the impact of the world financial crisis, the Chinese economy will still be in the stage of "double speed" development of industrialization and urbanization after phases of adjustment in 2008 and 2009. The steel and iron industry, and automobile industry are still the important forces to drive China's economic growth. Because the industrial chain is long, and inertia of acceleration or deceleration is large, the heavy chemical industry needs more time to adjust, therefore negative impact is also bigger; the proportion of energy source of raw material industry in all industries will reached its peak around 2020, thus the coal-based energy structure will remain for a long period of time, and treatment of sulfur dioxide, nitrogen oxide, smoke and dust, and industrial dust will be more arduous.

B. *Urbanization Quickens, and Gross Domestic Pollution Increases*

According to the forecast of the State Information Center, in the future, urbanization levels will remain at a 1 percentage point increase every year, will reach 58% by 2020, and the urban population will reach 820 million, where the urban population will be 1.4 times that of the rural population. In the urbanization process, waste water discharge and waste output increase. At present, construction of environment infrastructures in big cities is still in a period of historical "debt", the construction of infrastructural facilities in the overwhelming major-ity of small- and medium-sized towns and cities is seriously behind, garbage and sewage cannot be safely treated; after factory relocation, land pollution becomes more extreme, and high-tension development in coastal areas enlarge environment pressure. Similar problems are outstanding especially in medium and small towns of central and west-ern areas.

C. *Rural Economy Transforms, Consumption Increases and Pollution Becomes More Problematic*

In terms of domestic demand, rural areas have huge potential, and can help speed up rural economic and social development; therefore rural environmental protection must be strengthened. With rapid urbaniza-tion, the rural population will slowly decrease, domestic waste discharge will also drop, and under the transformed situation where the scope of seed area is not big, increase in usage of chemical fertilizer year after year will also enhance the pollutant output of crop production, live-stock discharge will reduce greatly if livestock breeding can use large-scale cultivation, but total pollutant output will still rise year by year along with increase of output value of livestock breeding. Increase in rural consumption level inevitably causes explosive growth to output of domestic garbage, and at present, the overwhelming majority of areas do not have methods of waste treatment; garbage is thrown in landfill, which not only breeds mosquitos and houseflies, affecting hygiene, but also has latent threats to bodies of water. "Garbage is blown away by the wind, and sewage is evaporated" is an accurate description of rural environments in many areas.

According to the forecast of the State Information Center, around 2020, Engel's coefficient of urban and rural resident families will be on average 35%, which gradually changes from having enough food and clothing as measures of life to enjoyment being the symbol of a well-off life. Change in consumption also will bring new environmental problems; consumer demand in basic necessities of life becomes varied, continuous demand of new products becomes the trend, causing resources and energy consumed for life to continuously increase every year. With the increase in resident income level, and number of automobile and other vehicles, the problem of atmospheric pollution brought by fast increase of urban vehicles becomes increasingly prominent, especially the ash haze weather of urban-group areas and some big cities that increases as a result. At the same time, traffic also faces pressure so that construction of infrastructural facilities, such as roads and bridges are unceasingly increased, which consumes large amounts of resources and energy consumptive products including cement and steel products etc. With the improvement of consumption living standard and speed up of urbanization, the growth speed of some home consumables, including electrical appliance, house and automobile etc. speeds up, and thus some home appliances being discarded as useless occurs. It is estimated that, in the next five years, 4 million refrigerators, 5 million washers and 5 million television sets need to be discarded. Recycling and safe disposal of worn-out home appliances, disused building materials and scrapped cars and tires etc. will become an important environmental problem in the next 10 years and longer.

III. *Green Transformation of Economic and Social Development in Structural Readjustment*

The impact of the financial crisis further exposes the contradictions within China's economic development way and economic structure. Domestic and foreign environment of "post-crisis time" development has obviously changed, therefore the development mode urgently needs transformation. This is a profound revolution. The world development trend tells us that the scientific development concept must be insisted upon to protect the environment and optimize economic development, and to realize green transformation of economic and social development.

A. *Expanding Investments for Environmental Protection, and Enhancing Material Support Capacity for Green Transformation of Economic and Social Development*

Money for pollution governance must be spent sooner or later, sooner administration the more initiative, and later governance the more passive. We must grasp the opportunity where the state implements the financial policy, and regard investment for environmental protection as the emphases of public fiscal expenditure, all levels of finance should readjust the expenditure structure, enlarge the support to environmental protection, and guarantee that the growth rate of environmental protection investment is higher than the growth speed of the newly increased financial resources. National capital investments should also unceasingly lean towards environmental protection; financial support strength to regional pollution prevention, control of key basins and projects of town environmental infrastructural facilities should be increased. The bank should give loan support to projects of environment infrastructural facilities and pollution rectification projects that have the ability to repay. Investment and financing channels for environmental protection should be expanded; enterprises should be encouraged to increase investments for environmental protection, foreign capital and social funds should be guided to enter the environment rectification market, and thus the multiplex investment pattern of environmental protection can be formed.

B. *Advancing Strategic Readjustment to the Economic Structure, and Alleviating the Structural Pressure on Green Transformation of Economic and Social Development*

Good environment quality and resource continuation ability is becoming a new competitive advantage of states and regions, protection to the environment is protection to productive forces, and environmental improvement can help develop the productive forces. In economic and social development, environmental capacity should be regarded as the important basis of economic development, access to environment as the important means of economic regulation, environmental management as the important measure of economic development way transformation, and environmental protection as the important gripping device of economic structural readjustment in order to promote optimized renewal of the industrial structure, and to quicken development of the advanced manufacturing industry, high and new technology industry and service industry, thereby to form an industrial system in favor of resource conservation and environmental protection. At the same time, the industrial policy and environmental protection standard should be strictly executed; high-consumption, high-emission, low-benefit primitive productivity should be eliminated, and construction projects that waste resources and pollute the environment must be strictly forbidden, thus the pressure of economic and social development on the ecological environment can be fundamentally reduced. We should develop vigorously the recycle economy to alleviate the contradiction of insufficient resource supply and to reduce pollutant discharge. Energy conservation, saving water, land, and materials and a comprehensive and recycle resource utilization must be advanced, and clean production should be carried out to realize increase in production and pollutant reduction.

C. *Consummating Measures on Environmental Economic Policy, and Consolidating the Power Foundation for Green Transformation of Economic and Social Development*

An economic policy in favor of environmental protection is the inevitable requirement to establish a long-acting mechanism of environmental protection. Resources, energy and environmental factors should be integrated into the system of cost and price as soon as possible to establish the finance and taxation system in favor of saving resources and energy and environmental protection, which realizes green transformation in the finance and taxation system, and further promotes high fusion of energy conservation and pollutant discharge reduction and economic development. The preferential electricity price policy to enterprises with high-energy consumption should be cancelled, and encouraging electricity price policy should be implemented in regards to biomass energy, solar energy, wind energy, water and electricity and nuclear electricity etc., and technical innovation projects of energy conservation should be given support and reward. Continuation of

policies on preferential on-grid electricity price, desulphurization subsidy, sewage treatment charge, promoting environment protection by
award and replacing compensation by reward should be guaranteed.
National departments concerned should opportunely start levying
independent environmental tax. They should bring into effect price
leverage, and establish a price and charge mechanism that can reflect
pollution rectification cost, which implements the charging policy of
town sewage treatment and domestic garbage treatment comprehensively. Pollution charge standards for industrial enterprises should be
gradually increased; an incentive mechanism for enterprises' environmental protection and restraint mechanism for pollutant discharge
reduction should be established. The systems of green credit, green
insurance, green tax revenue, green purchase and green trade should
be quickly consummated. Pollutant discharge trading system should be
opportunely released, and the pollutant discharge right trading market
should be established. According to the principle "one protects what
one develops, one restores what one destroys, one compensates what
one profits, one pays for pollutants one discharges," the ecology compensation policy should be consummated, and the ecology compensation mechanism should be established.

D. *Strengthening Ecology Transformation of Existing Industries, and
Strengthening Technical Support to Green Transformation of Economic and
Social Development*

According to the requirements where promoting economic development is changed from mainly depending on funds and material
investment into mainly depending on advancement of science and technology and human capital, new technologies and advanced applicable
technology must be widely applied to transform and push traditional
industries; former method that massively depended upon factors investment to advance industrialization must be changed, and the development direction of technological innovation and industrial optimization
should be paid great attention to. Technical renewal and equipment
transformation of traditional manufacturing industry should be paid
great attention to, and vanguard technologies, which do well in the
economy, have low resource consumption, less pollutant discharge and
are friendly towards the ecological environment should be developed
and utilized vigorously, where technological innovation may become
the formidable strength to push the optimization renewal of industrial
structure. Independent innovation should be integrate with introduc-

tion, digestion and absorption, and strength should be concentrated to tackle key problems, and to try and make a breakthrough in key technologies and common technologies of environmental protection. Studies on strategy and standard of environmental protection and environment and health etc. should be first carried out, prevention and control of pollution to water body, atmosphere, soil, noise, solid wastes and agriculture as well as studies and technical development on ecological protection, resource recycle, potable water safety and nuclear safety etc. should be encouraged, key and difficult technical problems on advanced sewage treatment, the desulphurization and denigration of coal-fired power plant, cleaning coal and the automobile exhaust purification etc. should be tackled, and new technologies should be applied to the environmental protection domain. Technical demonstration and promotion of achievement should be carried out positively to enhance technological contents of environmental protection. While transforming the existing industrial ecology, manufacturing of environmental protection equipment should be developed, the service industry of environmental protection should be strengthened, and all kinds of ownership enterprises should be supported to participate in pollution rectification and environmental protection industrial development. Policy support and market supervision must be strengthened, local and industrial protection must be broken to promote fair competition, and enterprises dealing with environmental protection and enterprise groups that have strength and competitive power should be cultivated. The construction of domestically produced standardized modern industrial system for the environmental protection industry should promote the environmental protection industry as an emerging pillar industry, which has good economic benefit and social efficiency. The new energy and energy-conservation industries of sustainable energy, green transportation, green construction etc. should be developed vigorously, and the green economy should be cultivated into a new point of growth for the current economy.

E. *Mobilizing Social Strength to Protect the Environment, and Forming Strong Combined Strength for Green Transformation of Economic and Social Development*

Environmental protection is the biggest project of livelihood of the people tied up with people's fundamental interests, the system security project tied up with long-term economic and social development, the important fundamental project tied up with great rejuvenation of the

Chinese nation, must closely depend on the masses, and the strength of the entire society should be mobilized to care, participate and support jointly. Only thus can we win. Propaganda strength to basic state policies for environmental protection and environment legal system must increase, the public opinion atmosphere for resource saving and environmental protection should be built diligently, the environmental culture should be carried forward, and the entire society should be impelled to create ideas of ecology civilization. Environmental protection talent training should be strengthened, young people should be strengthened in environmental education, and environmental protection popular science activities for all people should be carried out, which enhance the public's self-consciousness about environmental protection. All levels of institutions must take the lead in saving resources and protecting the environment, and become a model for the entire society. All kinds of enterprises must initiatively observe the environmental laws and regulations, and initiatively undertake social responsibilities. Each citizen, family, unit and community must start to do anything in their power, with the intention of treasuring nature, protecting the environment, and improving the environment, and make these actions common practices.

REPORT ON INVESTIGATIONS OF FAMILY FORMATION AND FAMILY RELATIONS IN FIVE CITIES

Li Yinhe

Abstract

To understand changes to urban family formation and family relation in recent years, the Institute of Sociology, Chinese Academy of Social Sciences carried out the "Five-city Family Investigation," a sampling questionnaire survey in five cities, Guangzhou, Hangzhou, Zhengzhou, Lanzhou and Harbin, from June to October 2008. The respondents are municipal district residents between ages 20 to 80 in five cities, the sample size is 800 families for each city, in total 4000 families for the five cities, and 4000 persons. At the end, total families sampled was 4013 families, and 4013 persons, where men accounted for 40.1% and women 59.9%. The average age is 47.27 years old, and the median is 46 years old. In terms of vocation, amongst all interviewees, employed persons accounted for 54.3%, unemployed persons 15.7%, and retirees 30%. In terms of marital status, single persons accounted for 5.9%, first marriage persons 81.3%, remarried persons 1.9%, divorcees 3.6%, ones who lost their spouse 6.5% and cohabitants 0.8%. In terms of educational level, illiterate persons accounted for 3.4%, elementary school 9.2%, junior middle school 26.9%, senior high school 34.3%, and junior college and above 26.2%. For this investigation, the response rate is low, especially in Guangzhou, where there was only 8.94% response. The highest response rate is in Hangzhou, but that was still only 36.77%. But because those sampled are sampled according to the random sampling principle, data from the investigation may deduce the overall situation.

I. Family Formation and Family Scale

Family formation refers to members of the family and how the family is composed. The first question in this investigation is, under China's specific circumstances, for urban residents, where is the boundary for a family? And which people are regarded as a family member? In former family investigations, family is defined with foundations of "marriage and blood relationship," which neglects some important family types especially types that have increased along with social transformation, such as the one-person family. The concept of "cohabitation" is also relatively fuzzy and is difficult to grasp. Therefore, we did not give a definition for family in the investigation, but first asked interviewee to confirm subjectively how his/her family composed, and which family members they recognized. Then focusing on those family members recognized by each interviewee, were asked "whether they lived cohabited" as well as "whether their financial conditions was a whole." From this, our findings have discovered three classes of families: "emotion family," family recognized subjectively by interviewee, "cohabiting family," composed of family members who live together, and "economic family," composed of family members with integral financial conditions.

The investigation discovered that, in five cities, average family size is 3.22 persons, with the three-person family as the principal mode, and its proportion is close to half (46.7%). Compared with total family population, the populations of "cohabiting family" obviously decreased, average is only 2.69 persons, and the three-person family is still the mainstream, and the proportion reaches 43.1%.

Parsons et al. argued that the transformation of family formation from large-scale joint family to small nuclear family is outstanding feature of family modernization. In this investigation, data of family formation indicated that, all classes of nuclear family (including its incomplete form) are the main type of current Chinese urban families, and account for 70.3%; next is all kinds of stem family (including its incomplete form), and account for 16.6%; one-person family accounts for 12.0%, joint family 0.2% and other types of family 0.9% (See Table 9.1).

Compared with investigations in 1982 and 1992, throughout the 26 years, we can see the miniaturization of urban families and the nuclear family tendency: the proportion of one-person family has increased approximately 10 percentage points; nuclear family has increased approximately 3 percentage points; stem family has reduced approximately 10 percentage points; joint family has reduced approximately 2 percentage points (See Table 9.1).

Table 9.1: Family Formation in Three Family Investigations Unit: %

Family formation	Investigations of five cities in 2008	Investigations of seven cities in 1992	Investigations of five cities in 1982
One-person family	12.0*	1.78	2.44
Nuclear family	70.3	66.96	66.41
Stem family	13.8	25.28	24.29
Joint family	0.2	2.19	2.30
Skipped generation family	2.8	2.17	–
Cohabitant family	0.8	–	–
Others	0.1	1.73	4.56
Total	100	100	100

* Note: in the investigations in 2008, the one-person family includes 1.57% of interviewees of collective households

II. *Husband / Wife Relations*

Conjugal relation is the most important relation in family relations. In family research, the most important theory regarding modernization of family relation and differences between Chinese and Western family relations revolves around emphasis on children and spouse. This theory believed that the ante-modern family relation gives priority to the parent-child axis; modern family relation has transformed into giving priority to the spouse axis; traditional Chinese family relation gives priority to the parent-child axis; but Western family relation gives priority to the spouse axis. Certainly, we did not simply equate Western family relation pattern with modern family pattern, and Chinese family pattern with ante-modern family pattern, but we discovered transformation between parent-child axis pattern and family axis pattern in Chinese family. Our issues of concern specially include spouse's selector mode, conjugal power relation pattern, family violence and conjugal emotion.

A. *Spouse Choice*

The marriage radius is an important survey index for spouse choice. Family vicissitude theory believes that, the marital radius of traditional family is quite small; but with modernity, the marital radius increases. In observations to marital radius of respondents in five-city samples, the proportion where spouses are from the same village, same urban residents' committee, same village and town and same street only accounts for 10%, same county and same district included, it is still less than 30%, but where the spouse is from same province and city, different provinces and cities, and different countries, the proportion is above 70%. For families in Guangzhou and Hangzhou, the proportion of marital radius within same province and city is more than 80% or close to 80%. This should be associated with higher modernization degree of these two cities. Generally speaking, it is observed that the marital radius of five cities is the typical urban marital radius pattern, and is very different from traditional family's source of finding a spouse.

Compared with five-city investigations in 1982, the data indicated that, in the past 26 years, the marital radius has enlarged; in previous investigations, where the spouse before marriage was from same village, same urban residents' committee, same town and same street, the proportion dropped from 12.27% in 1982 to 10.4%; where the spouse before marriage was from same county and same district, the proportion rapidly dropped from 29.26% to 17.3%, a 12 percentage points decrease; where the spouse before marriage was from the same province and city, the proportion increased from 45.66% to 63.3%, and increased nearly 20 percentage points; where the spouse before marriage was from different provinces and cities, the proportion slightly dropped from 12.81% to 8.9%. Among them, the most prominent change is the proportion where the spouse was from the same county and same district, which has largely dropped; but the proportion from the same province and city has greatly increased.

Methods of spouses becoming acquainted can be divided into three patterns, parents taking care of everything, through introduction (including introduction by relatives and friends) and getting to know each other themselves. In these three acquaintance ways, the first kind is obviously traditional, the third kind is most modern, and the second kind lies in between. In this investigation, the statistical result of spouse's acquaintance way indicated that, the proportion where they are introduced by relatives and friends accounts for 55%; knowing each other by themselves, 40%; parents take care of everything, only 3.3%. Comparing by cities, we discovered that, Guangzhou has the highest proportion of spouse's independent meeting, which is associated with a higher degree of modernization in Guangzhou.

Compared with the five-city investigations in 1982, recent findings indicated that, in methods for spouse acquaintance, the traditional way has gradually faded out, and the proportion of knowing each other themselves has greatly increased. The proportion where parents take care of marriage has suddenly dropped from 17.65% in 1982 to 3.3% at present; the proportion of introduction of relatives and friends has dropped from 65.97% to 55.8%; the proportion of knowing spouse themselves has risen from less than 1/3 (32.98%) to 40.1%.

The proximity of economic position and social status between the husband and wife's families is also an important target to examine and weigh conjugal relation. The investigation showed that, comparison of economic position of respective families before marriage presents a similar normal distribution pattern: where the two families have similar economic position, the proportion accounts for 70%; where the husband's family is wealthier, 17%, where the bride's family is slightly wealthier than the husband's side, 12%; where the husband's side family is much wealthier, 1.3%; where the bride's family is much wealthier, 0.6%.

Compared with the five-city investigation data in 1982, the pattern of well-matched families in terms of economic positions has increased, in the investigations in 1982, where the two families' economic position was similar, the proportions was 57.02%, and in this investigation, this proportion has risen to 69.0%, a 12 percentage point increase; where the bride's side of the family is wealthier, the proportion has dropped from 20.17% to 12.7%; where the bridegroom's side family is wealthier, the proportion also has dropped from 22.81% to 18.2%.

B. *Conjugal Power Relation Pattern*

The dwelling after marriage is an important index in conjugal power relation, and is very important in the issue of equality between men and women. After marriage, bride enters the groom's family for life, which is often the foundation for male power within the family, and then also becomes the foundation for male sexism. This investigation showed that, at present, in urban families, the proportion of independent conjugal new residence system after marriage has occupied a half, which manifests a new custom where male power within the family is no longer dominant. However, at the same time, we also see that, after marriage, the proportion that lives in the husband's home still occupies more than 45% in urban families, which is still a principal residence mode after marriage. But the proportion that lives in the wife's home after marriage is low. After marriage, the new residence system of independent family is level with the system of living in the husband's home, which shows that male power in the family still has a strong foundation.

The man sharing in housework is another important index in the equality of conjugal relation. With modernization in China and other countries, woman participating in the social productive work becomes a significant social change. But, at the same time, men do not share in the housework, thus the issue of woman's dual work burden in social production and housework has aroused the attention of feminists. The findings showed that, in present urban families, the housework division pattern where the wife primarily does all the housework has the biggest proportion, more than 30%; next is the situation where the wife does more of housework, close to 30%; it is noteworthy that, the proportion where husband and wife share the housework equally is 26.8%; situations where the husband does more housework and in where the husband primarily does all the housework account for 5% respectively. Adding together the situations where the wife primarily does all the housework and does more of the house work, male power two options which wife does more homework or does it primarily, the andocentric pattern in housework still accounts for 60%, equality pattern has approached 30%, and the feminist pattern only 10%.

Regarding the issue of conjugal equality, this investigation also designed a question that directly asked who has real power. The findings showed that 60% of persons replied husband and wife have equal power. Through the five-city comparison, equality pattern in Harbin has the lowest proportion, but the proportion of androcentrism and feminism is higher than the other four cities, which is not a pure androcentric pattern.

C. *About Conjugal Violence*

Conjugal violence is an issue that feminism pays great attention to. The findings showed that, in families of the five-city investigation, the proportion where there was violent behavior between husband and wife accounts for 12.2%, in which the violence is quite serious, 0.5%. Compared with the other cities, Lanzhou's family violence degree exceeds that of the other four cities, accounts for 21%, in which the violence is quite serious, 1.3%; the degree of family violence in Guangzhou is the lowest, 5%, and nobody is frequently beaten up by their spouse.

Through gender analysis on family violence, in situations where the spouse is beaten up frequently, sometimes or occasionally, the proportion of women being harmed is greater than that of men, which proved that violence between spouses is mainly imposed on women by men. Although the degree of family violence is overall quite low in this investigation, its gender difference still has distinctiveness in statistics. In the investigation, we also discovered that the nature of permanent registration is associated with conjugal violence; conjugal violence in registered agricultural households are higher than of the non-agricultural households. This indicated that conjugal violence is more so a rural phenomenon, and the degree of urban residents' violence is low.

D. *Conjugal Emotion*

This investigation used the method that directly asked interviewees' their subjective feeling to assess conjugal emotion. The findings showed that, in families of the five-city investigation, the proportion that responded saying conjugal emotion was "good" is close to 45%; "quite good", close to 55%; and "not bad" and "bad" add up to less than 3%. Harbin has the highest proportion with "good" conjugal emotion, and then in turn Zhengzhou, Lanzhou, Guangzhou and Hangzhou.

In the investigation on whom the respondents first seek out when grappling with difficulties or troubles, interviewees' first option is "pouring out to the spouse," the proportion occupies nearly 60%; next is "pouring out to schoolmate or friend," almost 10%; the proportion that pours out to parents and other family members or relatives is relatively low, less than 10%. It is noteworthy that, the proportion that pours out to parents is lower than that who pour out to other relatives, and is lower than the one to schoolmate and the friend; this result may be evidence that urban family relation has transformed from parent-child axis to husband-wife axis.

III. *Parent-Child Relation*

A. *Equality Model or Ruling Model*

The traditional Chinese society is a typical patriarchy society; the relation between elder and younger generation is the relation between higher authority and subordinate, namely ruling relations, and no equality. This situation radically transforms in the recent several dozen

years, especially in urban families. This investigation designed a group
of indexes to measure the parent-child power relation pattern. Among
them, the decision-making power of spouse choice is the index used
frequently in the sociology of family because the issue about happiness
in individual life being related with choosing one's own spouse has
conflict between the ruling model and equality model.

The findings indicated that, in the families of the five-cities, regarding the issue of decision-making power in choosing spouse, the proportion which decides by oneself and then solicits parents' opinions
accounts for 60%; decides by oneself but does not solicit parents' opinions, close to 20%; decides by oneself and parents together, more than
10%; decide by the parents and then solicit one's opinions, less than
10%; also 2.4% of marriages are altogether arranged by the parents.
Compared with wht five cities, Lanzhou has the lowest degree of modernization, the proportion of its arranged marriage is highest, and the
proportion where the parents decide the child's marriage and solicits
the child's opinions is also quite high.

B. *Intimate and Alienated Parent-Child Relation*

According to modern theory, with the transformation of family relation from giving priority to the parent-child axis to husband-wife axis,
the parent-child relation will become increasingly loose. But, in this
investigation, we discovered that, in family relation, the parent-child
relation did not have such a tendency, and instead appears to be very
intimate. Regarding the question of relation between respondents and
parents, nearly 75% interviewees replied to be very intimate; more
than 20% of people replied to be rather intimate; nearly 5% replied
to be average; and only few people replied to be estranged or very
estranged, which is statistically almost meaningless.

In looking at frequency of contact between respondent and parents, we may also deduct how intimate the parent-child relation is.
Generally speaking, frequency of parent-child contact is quite high
in the five cities; nearly 30% of people contact their parents nearly
every day; nearly 50% contact 1–2 times every week; 20% contact
1–2 times every month; less than 10% contact several times every
year; and only few people do not contact parents at all, which can be
statistically ignored. It is important to point out that not all 26% of
families who contact their parents nearly every day live together with
their parents; only 12.3% live together. In other words, although they

do not live together, 13.7% of children and parents contact each other nearly every day. In Western societies where parent-child relation are not highly regarded, the society has been nearly completely nuclear family, the child separates from parents' family after marriage, some do not live in same city, therefore having contact 1–2 times each week is unthinkable. But, in big cities of China, families that have contact with each other 1–2 times every week occupy half.

Regarding the distance between home of respondent and parents, slightly above 10% live in the same place; 20% live nearby; more than 35% live in the same city; 20% live in the same province; slightly above 10% live in different provinces; also a few live overseas. In comparison of five cities, the result indicated that, in the Lanzhou families, the proportion of parents and child that live nearby (28%) is far higher than the other four cities; the proportion of Guangzhou and Hangzhou parent-child families live in the same city surpasses the mean value of the five cities; the proportion of Zhengzhou parent-child families that live in the same province far surpasses the mean value.

C. *Parent-Child Economic Contact*

Economic contact is an important measure to the intimacy between parent-child relations. In the measurement of parent-child economic contact, this research uses two targets, one is desire and another is actual reality.

In the investigation of desire, we asked two questions, the first one, whether respondents will borrow from parents when they need a large sum of money. The findings indicated that, nearly 55% of the people said yes, and more than 45% said no. within the comparison of the five cities, the extent of desire to borrow money is ranked nearly completely according to the urban wealth degree: Guangzhou is highest, and then in turn, Hangzhou, Zhengzhou, Harbin and Lanzhou.

The second question, whether parent's help would be sought under condition of serious illness. The result is very similar to the first question. In the respondents, 55% said yes and 45% said no. The order of the five cities is still ranked according to the urban wealthy degree.

In actual parent-child economic contact, this investigation designed four groups of more in-depth questions. The first is respondents' help to parents; the second is parents' help to respondents; the third is respondents' help to grown-up children who have independent income; the fourth is grown-up children' help to respondents.

(1) *Respondents' Help to Parents*

For the question of whether parents' daily life needed to be bear by the respondent, nearly 25% people replied they subsidize and take care of their parents; 15% only give economic subsidy; Nearly 20% take care of parents by oneself; 40% replied there was no need to do this completely. 60% respondents subsidize and take care of parents' daily life; this is quite rare in Western individualism society, which fully reflects the important relationship between families in Chinese society.

For the question whether parents ought to be regularly subsidized, 30% of the respondents replied yes; nearly 70% replied no. In the comparison of the five cities, the result indicated that the proportion that regularly subsidizes parents is the highest in Guangzhou, and lowest in Harbin. The former accounts for 40%, and the latter 20%. The statistics showed that, those persons who regularly subsidize parents, the average subsidy is approximately 2988.49 Yuan per year, and the standard deviation is 3981.65 Yuan.

There are a variety of reasons for why parents are not subsidized, and they do not all necessarily reflect a bad relationship. Among the reasons why respondents do not subsidize parents, 70% of respondents said their parents did not need to be subsidized; nearly 30% of respondents had low income, and are incapable to subsidize parents. Within the five cities, the proportion where parents do not need to be subsidized is highest in Hangzhou (87.8%); lowest in Lanzhou (53.5%); and average in other cities.

(2) *Parents' Help to Respondents*

For the question whether parents' help need to be obtained in daily life or not, more than 60% people replied no; only about 10% people obtained subsidy, and 15% of respondents are taken care of by parents; and 15% of people are subsidized and taken care of. In the five cities, the result indicated that the proportion that never obtained parents' help in daily life is highest in Harbin (75.2%), and lowest in Guangzhou (43.1%).

For the question whether parents regularly subsidize respondents, only 10% persons replied yes, and 90% of the people did not regularly obtain parents' subsidy. The proportion where parents regularly subsidize respondents is approximately ranked by the urban wealth degree; the wealthier city the smaller the proportion; the poorer the city the bigger the proportion. The statistics showed that, for those people who accept parents' regular subsidy, the average subsidy amount per year is approximately 4390.93 Yuan, and the standard deviation is 4327.26 Yuan.

Reasons why parents did not subsidize respondents included 70% not needing parent's subsidy and 30% of parents having low income and being unable to subsidize their children.

(3) *Respondents' Help to Grown-up Children Who Have Independent Income*
For the question whether grown up children who have independent income need to be helped in daily life, more than 50% people do not subsidize and do not take care of the children; nearly 20% people subsidize and also take care of children's daily life; more than 10% people only give subsidy; and above 20% only take care of them. Generally speaking, 50% of parents subsidize or take care of the daily life of grown-up children who have independent income, this is a very high proportion compared with foreign cultures, especially Western culture, which reflects the intimacy between parent-child relations in Chinese families. In the five cities, the result indicated that the proportion that does not bear completely the daily life of grown-up children who have independent income is the highest in Guangzhou (58.8%), and the lowest (42.7%) in Lanzhou.

For the question whether respondents regularly subsidize grown-up children who have independent income, nearly 90% people do not subsidize; more than 10% people give subsidy. In the five cities, the result indicated that, the proportion that regularly subsidizes grown-up children who have independent income is the lowest in Guangzhou (3.7%); highest (16.3%) in Lanzhou, and average in the other cities. The statistics showed that, for those people who regularly subsidize grown-up children who have income, average subsidy is approximately 4691.02 Yuan per year, and the standard deviation 4393.74 Yuan.

Regarding why respondents do not subsidize grown-up children who have independent income, 70% of the people do not do so because the children do not need subsidy; 30% because of their own low income, causing them to be unable to subsidize.

(4) *The Help of Grown-up Children Who Have Independent Income for Respondents*
For the question whether to obtain grown-up children's help in daily life, 55% people did not obtain help; nearly 20% obtained subsidy and care; nearly 20% people only obtained care, and not subsidy; less than 10% people only obtained subsidy, and not care.

For the question whether grown-up children having income regularly subsidize respondents, more than 20% people obtained children's regular subsidy; nearly 80% people did not obtain children's subsidy. In the five cities, the result indicated that, the proportion of respondents that obtained children's regular subsidy is the biggest in Guangzhou, and close to 50%. The statistics showed that subsidy from grown-up children who have independent income for respondents is in average 4451.23 Yuan per year, and the standard deviation is 4707.03 Yuan.

Regarding why grown-up children did not subsidize respondents who have independent income, 75% of respondents did not need children's subsidy; 25% because the children's income is low, and incapable to subsidize. In the five cities, the result indicated that, the proportion of respondents that did not need subsidy is highest in Hangzhou, more than 90%; lowest in Lanzhou, only 60%.

In addition, this investigation also asked what parents have done for children after the children got married in order to understand the intimacy and actual content in the parent-child relation. The findings showed that, 41.8% people replied that parents helped during the months after a baby was born, 49.3% people replied that parents helped to take care of their child; 32.8% families replied that parents helped to do the housework; 22.6% people replied that parents provided economic subsidy; 22.1% people replied that parents provided spiritual comfort.

Regarding the parent-child economic relation, there is also an option about parents' one-time large monetary gift to children, namely parents' subsidy to newlyweds when the child got married. This investigation showed that, when respondents got married, the amount of money provided by parents is in average 7815.67 Yuan, and the standard deviation is 26980.49 Yuan; the highest was 1 million Yuan.

Compared with other society, especially with Western society, gift to a child at marriage may be a common phenomenon amongst both societies, but parents help after pregnancy of the child, help care for grandchildren, and help with housework, and so on, which are seen to be Chinese characteristics, and is significance to explain the intimacy between parent-child relation in China.

D. *Providing for the Aged Model*

China's pattern of caring for the aged is extremely different from that of Western individualism societies. In Western societies, people live in this world basically as individuals, one provides for ones' aged life by oneself when one reaches old age either at home or in a senior home, and people do not think this is pitiful. But, in China, people's basic living unit is the family, if an old person has no child to care for him during old age, and enters a senior home, other people will take pity on the old person. Even if the old person can provide for himself, if he does not have any child to care of him nearby, he will still be regarded as very pitiful person. Entering a senior home is logical in Western societies, but in China it is a nightmare.

In this investigation, we specially designed a question on people's idea of how the aged ought to be cared for in order to understand the situation and change of idea of caring for the aged. The findings showed that, for the question of how to arrange parents who are old and cannot take care of themselves, nearly 70% of respondents replied that children take care of parents; 20% replied that children spend money to hire other people to take care of parents. It is noteworthy that only 8.8% of people chose "we will send parents to a senior home if they are willing." On the one hand, this indicated that sending parents to a senior home is not popularized, but from another angle, reflects that the traditional supporting custom has begun to be challenged. In the five cities, the result indicated that the proportion of people that chose "we will send parents to a senior home if they are willing" in Hangzhou and Guangzhou is far higher than the other three cities, and the proportion of people that chose "parents hire other people to take care of themselves" is also higher than the other three cities. It is observed that, this reflects the urban development degree, the retirement facility consummation degree, as well as the people's idea variation degree.

This investigation also asked how one's own aged life should be arranged and cannot take care of own life, we discovered that this arrangement is very different than the arrangement for parents; less than 30% people chose to let their children take care of them; 15% chose to hire other people to take care for them; but as high as 50% chose to go to senior homes. The proportion that is willing to go to senior homes is high, which reflects that people believe the traditional family retirement way has been difficult to bear, where the elderly will be properly looked after. At present, under the influence of the family planning policy, middle-aged parents are entering old age, "Four-Two-One" families (one child has two parents and four grandparents) will become the mainstream pattern of Chinese cities, half of the elderly will find it impossible to live together with their child, and it will be impossible to obtain daily care; the traditional family retirement pattern where children look after the elders at home will be inevitably changed. Therefore, nearly 70% of urban residents are ready to depend on their own deposits, and not depend on their child to take care of them in their aged life. This is inevitably a new issue in the urbanization process, and is also a new complexity caused by the urban one-child policy. In the long Chinese history, it is a new question, and the result (urbanization result, and result of family planning policy) and reason (affects people's life style and idea) of social change, and we cannot estimate its practical significance, which changes the society, or its symbolic significance.

E. *Notion of Parent-Child Relation*

Because traditional Chinese society is a typical patriarchy society, the parent-child relation and change in ideas is a sensitive and significant domain. Therefore, this investigation designed a couple of questions regarding the idea of parent-child relation in order to observe the present situation and the change in parent-child relation idea.

In regards to the idea where "children should show filial piety and respect their parents," more than 80% chose very approval, 20% quite approved, only a few people did not approved and did not make public their stand. In the five cities, the findings indicated that the proportion that greatly approved of the notion that "children should show filial piety and respect their parents" is highest in Harbin (95.2%); lowest in Hangzhou (61.4%); and average in the other three cities.

The attitude regarding "must listen to parents' words whether they are right or not" is to measure the view about parents' absolute authority. Only 10% of respondents very approved; 25% quite approved; 45% did not approved partly; nearly 20% did not approved absolutely. In the five cities, the result indicated that the proportion that approved of parents' absolute authority in Harbin (23.7%) is far higher than the other cities; quite high (12.9%) in Lanzhou. The proportion that most denied parents' absolute authority is in Guangzhou, and about 30% chose "not approve absolutely," which is far higher than the other four cities.

For the issue, "parents are authorized to read child's letters and diaries," 55% of people did not approve; 40% did not approved partly; it is noteworthy that 7.5% people quite approved or approved very much the idea which parents are authorized to infringe upon children's personal privacy.

In the issue, "we may let parents enter senior homes as long as they are willing," more than 10% approved very much; more than 40% quite approved; 30% approved partly; about 15% did not approve absolutely. From the comparison of the answers to idea questions with concrete action to one's own parents, people are more receptive to the idea than they actually practice; they cannot actually do so in concrete practice because of pressure of public opinions or internal feelings. This is that more than half of respondents did not oppose to sending their parents to senior homes, but, as mentioned above, only 8.8% people actually planned to send parents to senior homes when they are faced with their own parents who are aged and cannot take care of themselves.

IV. *Conclusions*

In this investigation, the biggest theoretical harvest is the verification and challenge to the theory of family modernization. According to this theory, modernization (as well as urbanization) of society will cause the miniaturization of the family scale, formation of the nuclear family, equalization of conjugal relation, the center of gravity of family relation changing from giving priority to the parent-child axis into the husband-wife axis, reduction of difference between relatives of the same clan and relations by marriage, and relaxation and shrinkage of kinship relationship, and so on.

This investigation has verified the modernization theory in certain aspects, for example, miniaturization of family scale, formation of the nuclear family and equalization of conjugal relation, and so on. But, in the investigation, a more important discovery is the challenge to the modernization theory of classical family, and also the deviation between the specificity of Chinese family relation and the modernization theory. For example, the nuclear family does not cause estranged parent-child relations. Although families in big cities have become nuclear families to a large extent, married children often live in the same city as their parents, and the parent-child relation is far closer than that of Western families. Whereas in Western families basically give priority to the husband-wife axis, nuclear family from Chinese cities do not caused the family to transform completely from giving priority to the parent-child axis into the husband-wife axis, but a new pattern develops, which pays equal attention to the husband-wife axis and the parent-child axis, and this point can be validated from the contact frequency between children and parents, the distance between two homes, as well extent of economic contact.

The main significance of this discovery is, although Chinese urban families are experiencing unprecedented modernization process, they do not have the tendency that evolves into Western individualism society. In Western societies, a 'family' is the combination of two individuals, children; parents and relatives are unimportant, do not have lifelong companion relation—children basically separate from parents after they grow up and get married, and so do their children after growing up. Therefore, individualism is people's ultimate value and the individual is the basic measuring unit in Western society. But, the families in our investigation are different from West families, although Chinese families have experienced modernization, and become similar to Western families in many aspects, for example, equality of conjugal relation, family miniaturization and nuclear family etc., Chinese families still retain many differences, and do not completely conform to that of Western families. Among them, the most main difference is that, the family (not individual) is still the ultimate value and basic measuring unit of society, and the spirit and economic relation between parents and children and between relatives are different than that of Western families, not only in quantity but also in nature. In China, such a society without a religion, the family is the people's most main life value, and it nearly embraces the people's true-life goal (let family members have happy life), the goal of human life (carry on the ancestral line, and bring honor to ancestors) and the spiritual support of religious belief (ancestor worship). Speaking from a western's point of view, it is not that families do not have any value, but are simply one of many values, and in Chinese people's minds, families are not the only value, but an unequalled value. Even if our society has thoroughly modernized, China's family relation will also retain its unequalled importance. This is an important conclusion from this research, and also a challenge to research in family modernization theory.

INVESTIGATION REPORT ON RECONSTRUCTION AND REHABILITATION OF THE WENCHUAN EARTHQUAKE DISASTER AREAS

Zhao Yandong, Ma Ying, He Guangxi, Deng Dasheng
and Xue Shu

Abstract

The Wenchuan earthquake that occurred on May 12, 2008 caused more than 80,000 deaths or missing people, hundreds of thousands of injuries, damages to several million farmer houses, more than ten million people suffered from the disaster, and direct economic losses reached more than 800 billion Yuan, which was the strongest destructive earthquake disaster since the new China was established. The emergency rescue response after the Wenchuan earthquake enormously stimulated all Chinese people's patriotism and compatriot emotion. All levels of governments underwent severe tests in ability for disaster rescue, emergency response and social management, and their emergency rescue policies formulated had good effect, receiving praise from people around the world.

After the emergency rescue period passed, a more arduous task is to reconstruct the hometown. In September 2008, the State Council issued "General Plan on Post-Wenchuan Earthquake Rehabilitation and Reconstruction" (hereinafter referred to as "Plan"). As the document of rehabilitation and reconstruction of the disaster areas, "Plan" defined the goal, principle and specific requirements of reconstruction to disaster areas, and proposed a three year, 1 trillion yuan plan to complete the reconstruction of Sichuan, Gansu and Shanxi, to bring about "employment within every household, social security for everyone, enhancement of facilities, development of the economy, and improvement to ecology," and to raise the living conditions and social and economic development level in the disaster areas to achieve or surpass the level before the disaster. With the progress of reconstruction work in disaster areas, in March 2009, the 2nd Session of 11th National People's Congress also proposed that every effort be made to complete the reconstruction task within two years instead of three, and that by September 2010, the tasks as formulated in the "Plan" be completed.

Under the instruction of "Plan," reconstruction work has been carried out orderly in disaster areas. According to information issued by the State Council Information Office on May 8 2009, by the end of April 2009, post-disaster rehabilitation and reconstruction in three provinces Sichuan, Gansu and Shanxi had started more than 21,000 projects, and has invested approximately 360 billion yuan, about 36% of planned investment task. Specifically speaking, in housing reconstruction, in the rural areas of three provinces, 99.5% of housing maintenance and reinforcement finished, and 76.6% of housing reconstruction finished; the speed of urban housing reconstruction was slightly slower than rural areas, 48.9% of maintenance and reinforcement is completed, and 8.9% of reconstruction is completed. In infrastructural facilities, projects of transportation, correspondence, 60% of water conservation and energy started, the expressway is restored to the level before disaster, the trunk highway constructed above 93%, and the rural road completed 15% of reconstruction task. The majority of education and medical construction has begun, 75% of rehabilitation and reconstruction of all kinds of school began, and 7.8% have finished; 60.6% of medical and health care facilities started, 13% of them are completed. Because Sichuan suffered the most serious earthquake, most attention is placed on this region. By September 2009, in Sichuan disaster areas, permanent farmer houses of 1,238,900 households were completed, which accounted for 97.1% of demands. 2904 schools began reconstruction, which accounted for 86.9% of demands. 1226 medical and health care projects began reconstruction, which accounted for 91.5% of demands. 97.6% of large-scale industrial enterprises damaged have recovered production.[1] Because urban housing reconstruction has more difficulties, the progress was relatively slow; through efforts of departments concerned, by October 20, urban housing reconstruction of Sichuan planned to begin in 228,900 units, and the operating rate was 88.32%, where 107,300 units were completed, which occupied 41.4% of housing demands.[2]

In July 2008, Chinese Academy of Science and Technology for Development Task Group carried out a fast demand investigation of residents in Sichuan earthquake disaster areas to fully understand disaster-area residents' living conditions and policy demand at that

[1] CATV NET: http://www.dahe.cn/xwzx/gn/t20090927_1662940.htm.
[2] Sichuan Daily (四川日报): http://www.gov.cn/gzdt/2009-10/24/content_1447903.htm.

time.[3] In July 2009, to assist the national assessment work of the General Plan on Post-Wenchuan Earthquake Rehabilitation and Reconstruction at its middle stage, Task Group continued the research mentality and method of investigations of 2008 to launch an "investigation on Wenchuan earthquake disaster-area residents on rehabilitation and reconstruction" in the Sichuan disaster areas. The investigation followed the method of proportioning probability sampling (PPS) according to population scale, and resident families sampled were given visiting questionnaire interviews. The investigation covered 26 disaster-stricken counties (cities and areas) in the disaster areas,[4] altogether investigated 142 general communities (villages, residents' committees, urban communities) and 29 placement sites of board room zones, visited 5,549 households, and successfully visited 4,037 households, a success ratio of 72.8%.

This investigation's main target was to comprehensively understand disaster-area people' situation of production and life recovery a year after the earthquake, and contents of the investigation covered housing and infrastructure, basic demography information, education, medical and health care, labor employment, agricultural production, family-run operation, social support and social participation, social manner and assessment, and so on. The following data is from this investigation, and is the description and analysis on the disaster-area residents' living conditions and policy demands a year after the earthquake. It is to be explained that the data of this article reflects the situation investigated at that time (August 2009). With the continuous advancement of reconstruction, the practical situation possibly has had huge changes. We will unceasingly pay attention to and trace those changes in future researches.

---

[3] For the details and main findings of this investigation, See Wang Fenyu et al.: "Investigation Report on Resident's Living Conditions and Policy Demands in Wenchuan Earthquake Disaster Areas" in Pages 33–48 of "Yearbook of Social Development: Analysis and Forecast on China's Social Development in 2009" published by the Social Sciences Academic Press in 2009. The thereinafter all findings of investigation mentioned in this paper 2008 refer to this investigation.

[4] Investigation sampling took the method of proportioning probability sampling (PPS) according to the population scale, covered 26 counties and cities, including Dujiangyang, Pengzhou, Chongzhou and Dayi of Chengdu; Jingyang District, Mianzhu, Shifang, Zhongjiang, Luojiang and Guanghan of Deyang City; Fucheng District, Youxian District, Beichuan, Pingwu, An County, Jiangyou, zitong, Yanting and Santai of Mianyang City; Lizhou District, Chaotian District, Yuanba District, Qingchuan, Jiange, Cangxi and Wangcang of Guangyuan City.

I. *About Disaster-Area Residents' Housing Conditions and Housing Reconstruction*

Housing reconstruction is the most important task of post-disaster rehabilitation and reconstruction; the findings indicated that the progress in disaster-area housing reconstruction was basically smooth, 90% of families moved into permanent housing, and housing conditions improved, but a few families still faced difficulty with housing reconstruction.

A. *The Disaster-Area Residents' Housing Infrastructure and Living Environment have Improved Since the Initial Period after the Earthquake, and Life Support Facilities are Self-Contained in Board Room Zones*

At present, 99.1% of disaster-area households have electricity, which raised nearly 20 percentage points from the initial period (81.5%) after the earthquake. 79.3% of families use safe sources of drinking water (tap water or other water sources which are covered, in which the proportion of tap water is 25.4%). 37.3% of families have water filters within the house, nearly a 10 percentage point increase from the initial period (29.6%) after the earthquake. 25.7% of families have facilities for hot-water bath. But treatment of household trash remains a prominent challenge, and household trash of more than a half of disaster-area families (53.5%) is still dumped in the open-air landfill or simply discarded anywhere.

At present, the public life support facilities are self-contained in board room zones, the proportion of households that use tap water and water filters reached 86.7% and 83.0% respectively. In addition, households in board room zones with convenient shopping locations reached 86.7%, and the proportion with convenient doctors reached 82.7%.

B. *Post-Disaster Housing Reconstruction Achievement is Remarkable, and 90% Disaster-Area Families Presently Live in Permanent Houses*

The earthquake destroyed large quantities of houses, and many residents were homeless. The investigation showed that the houses of about 1/3 of families in disaster-areas collapsed or were seriously damaged, and needed reconstruction; the houses of more than 50% of families were damaged moderately or lightly, these needed reinforcements or repair. Therefore, the government listed housing reconstruction as the most important task of post-disaster rehabilitation and reconstruction.

At present, the progress in disaster-area housing reconstruction is smooth. By this investigation, in families with damaged houses, 70.6% have returned to own original house, 17.2% have moved into new house constructed after the earthquake, and 2.3% have moved into non-own permanent houses; total families that lived in permanent houses account for 90.2%. Families that still live in temporary house, including active board room and tent etc. only account for 9.8% of total, which is nearly 30 percentage points lower (40.7%) that in July 2008.

C. Reinforcement/Repair is the Fundamental Mode of Post-Earthquake Housing Reconstruction, and Self-Reconstruction is the Fundamental Mode of Post-Earthquake Construction of Houses

At present, in the families that have moved back to own original house, 62.3% reinforced/repaired their original house. Obviously, reinforcement/repair is the broadest reconstruction way of housing reconstruction in disaster areas. At present, in families that have moved into newly built houses post-earthquake, 96.1% of these homes were self-constructed, less than 4% of families obtained new home through replacement and purchase as well as other ways. Thus, self-reconstruction is the most universal way of new home reconstruction presently. Families that moved into new houses have a degree of satisfaction with their new house, and 86.2% expressed satisfaction with their new house.

D. The Subsidy Credit Policy for Housing Reconstruction is Carried Out Well, but it is Anticipated that Many Families will have Difficult with on Time Credit Repayment

In families that moved into house that have been reinforced or repaired, above 80% (83.9%) obtained reinforcement subsidy provided by the government; in families which moved into newly built permanent houses, 96.8% obtained housing construction subsidy provided by the government. 61% of families that have reconstructed their house obtained bank loans; in families that obtained loans, 50.7% expressed they can make credit repayment on time, 41.9% expressed they can repay with slight postponement, and 7.4% expressed they are incapable to repay.

E. *Families in Temporary Housing, Especially Urban Families, are not Optimistic Regarding Permanent House*

By this investigation, nearly 10% of disaster-area families still live in temporary housing such as the board room and tent etc. In these families, most are optimistic that they will into permanent housing, and believe that they may move into new permanent housing within a year; But 32.8% believe that they still need to wait more than a year. In addition, 16.1% even thought that they "have no way of solving" permanent housing issue, and this proportion of urban families (17.5%) is far higher than rural areas (4.3%), because the urban housing problem is more complex, and unlike rural areas where priority is given to self-reconstruction, some areas have situations where the solution is still undetermined. These families will become the key points and difficulty of post-disaster housing reconstruction work.

II. *Disaster-Area Residents' Employment Status and Training Demands*

A year after the earthquake, those in the disaster areas not only faced the destruction brought by the earthquake, but also withstood employment pressure brought by the global financial crisis. Helping the residents to rapidly recover production and employment has become an important part of the reconstruction plan. The findings showed that, in disaster areas, overall unemployment rate was controlled at a low level, but the problem of unemployment for board room zone and youth was still quite prominent. Looking at the long run perspective, disaster-area employment opportunities gives priority to unstable temporary work, thus future unemployment risk cannot be ignored. The pre-job training system construction should be further strengthened to meet disaster-area residents' demands, and strengthen achievements already made in terms of employment.

A. *Disaster-Area Unemployment Rate is Controlled at a Lower Level, but Specific Group's Unemployment Problem is Quite Prominent*

According to the standard definition of International Labor Organization (ILO) widely used internationally,[5] this investigation calculated

---

[5] According to the definition of the International Labor Organization, an unemployed person refers to these crowd which do not work at present, are willing to

that the unemployment rate of disaster-area economically active population[6] was about 1.9%. Among them, local urban residents' unemployment rate was slightly high, 3.6%, and the one of local rural resident was only 1.6%. This unemployment rate was not only far lower than the national urban unemployment rate estimated by some scholars, but also lower than the national urban registered unemployment rate announced by the Ministry of Human Resources and Social Security in 2008 (4.2%). Compared with the European and American developed countries (US unemployment rate reached as high as 9.8% in August 2009, and 9.6% in Eurozone),[7] the disaster-area unemployment rate is obviously lower.

But, the unemployment rate for some groups still remain relatively high. The unemployment rate of board room zone reached as high as 7.6% because severely afflicted residents possibly lived in board room zones together, many people lost the original means of production and livelihood, and it was difficult for them to resume production or seek appropriate work in a short time. The unemployment rate of 16 to 24-year-old youths reached as high as 6.0%. This was associated with an increase in supply of laborerss in this age category; many of them dropped out of school, and were at the stage of seeking employment, which was possibly "temporary" unemployment only.

B. *Disaster-Area Residents' Employment Quality is not High, and Hidden Unemployment Risk cannot be Neglected*

According to the fore-mentioned definition of International Labor Organization, the employment rate of disaster-area economically active population reached as high as 98.1%, but the disaster-area employed persons' work quality was not high. Regarding employed persons, 39.2% were engaged in agricultural production, 25.6% were self-employed, 19.2% were engaged in temporary work, and only 16.0% were engaged in the long-term work. Even amongst residents of urban

work, are actively seeking a job, and can start work immediately if get a job. Only if the above four requirements are met simultaneously, can one be defined as an unemployed person.

[6] Refers to the population who is 16 years old and above, has the ability to work or requests participation in social and economic activities including employed population and unemployed population.

[7] The investigation of European and American unemployment rate was done based on the related definition of International Labor Organization, which has certain comparability with the findings of this investigation.

registered permanent address, only 40.4% were engaged in long-term work. But for those people who got employment after the earthquake, the proportion engaged in long-term work was only 9.8%, which indicated employment opportunities after the earthquake in disaster areas gave priority to relatively unstable self-employment and temporary work. In addition, the income of employed persons were also generally lower than before earthquake; 38.4% employed persons reflected the income were lower than before the earthquake, only 11.6% had an increase in income; after earthquake, and as high as 57.9% of the people who changed jobs had a reduction in income.

Looking into the future, 12.2% of employed persons worry that they would lose their job in the next two years because of "depression in the market," "end of the reconstruction projects," "scarce capacity" and so on. Among them, 3.1% of all employed persons worried about unemployment due to "end of reconstruction projects;" this proportion was 4.2% in extremely afflicted areas, 4.7% in board room zones, and the proportion which obtained work was as high as 9.5% after the earthquake. On one hand, this explained that post-earthquake reconstruction projects indeed have provided massive employment opportunities for the above group; on the other hand, this also indicated that employment opportunities provided by reconstruction projects are very unstable, and the employment situation of disaster areas, especially to these groups is quite weak. With the gradual completion of large-scale reconstruction work in disaster areas, it is likely that the unemployment rate will increase. Departments concerned should take necessary precautions, and prepare for this situation.

C. *Disaster-Area Residents have Exuberant Demands to Pre-Job Training, but the Existing Training System cannot Meet Demands*

Disaster-area people have intense demands of pre-job training, 27.9% of residents expressed "urgently need" or "need" training of employability skills, and 7.3% regarded providing pre-job training as the government's responsibility. Unemployed persons' demand was especially intense, and the above two proportions reached as high as 76.0% and 20.8% respectively. But the investigation showed that, a year after the disaster, only 3.2% disaster-area residents in total obtained pre-job training; unemployed persons had a slightly high proportion, but was still only 4.8%. The huge gap between demand and supply showed that the existing training system could not meet the demands of the residents.

III. *Disaster-Area Residents' Agricultural Production and Family-Run Operation*

Agricultural production and non-agricultural family-run operations are important components to the economy of disaster areas, and also important channels to solve the disaster-area employment problem. Recovering agricultural production and family-run operation are important means of disaster-area economic reconstitution. The findings showed that, at present, the disaster-area agricultural production is overall stable, and family-run operations are active, but both face difficulties in production and operation after the earthquake, which need sustaining policy support.

A. *Disaster-Area Agricultural Production Situation is Pessimistic, and Agricultural Land Loss is Worth Paying Attention To*

Disaster-area agricultural production situation overall was stable, 93.3% of agricultural families are still engaged in agricultural production after the earthquake. But the agricultural production situation after disaster is actually pessimistic; 41.5% of agricultural families thought the agricultural production situation after the earthquake was worse than before, 23.4% of agricultural families lost land after the earthquake, where 4.7% of the people lost all agricultural lands. Post-earthquake reconstruction using the land is the main reason for loss of agricultural land; in agricultural families that lost land, 44.4% lost land because post-earthquake reconstruction occupied the land, this proportion reached as high as 56.5% in extremely afflicted areas. In these families that lost land because of reconstruction projects, only 26% obtained cash compensation; other compensation forms are unknown because the investigation did not involve them.

B. *Policy Concerning Agriculture is Carried Out Well in Disaster Areas, and Peasant Households Still have Very Strong Demands of Agricultural Subsidy and Agricultural Technology Policy*

The findings indicated that, disaster area preferential policy concerning agriculture has been carried out well, 85.1% of agricultural families had obtained some form of support regarding agriculture after the disaster. Among them, all kinds of direct agricultural subsidy policies benefit agriculture in the broadest scope, 76.3% of peasant households obtained direct subsidy for grain after the disaster, and 21.3% obtained direct subsidy for agricultural materials. In addition, 10% of peasant households also obtained free agricultural materials. Comparatively, support coverage of free agricultural technology was low, only 1.6% of peasant households obtained this kind of policy support after the earthquake.

82.5% of peasant households explicitly proposed they unceasingly needed government's preferential policy support. Among them, the demand for agricultural subsidy and agricultural technological support was most intense, respectively 43.1% and 18.3% of peasant households hoped to obtain policy support in these two aspects. Compared with the fore-mentioned coverage of free agricultural technology, we discovered that existing preferential policies for agricultural technology are difficult to meet demands of peasant households.

C. *Non-Agricultural Family-Run Operations are an Important Component of the Economy in Disaster Areas, but it Faces Difficulties in Development after the Disaster*

At present, disaster area non-agricultural family-run operations are quite active, 9.4% of families are engaged in this kind of activity, and they mainly concentrate in service trades including wholesale and retail sales, catering and the hotel industry, beauty culture and hairdressing industry etc. They not only meet the life style demands of people in disaster areas, but have also provided nearly 1 million employment posts in disaster areas, which have made significant contributions to solve the employment problem in disaster areas.

But the investigation showed that, at present, family run operations in disaster areas are faced big development difficulties; 49.2% of families expressed operating conditions are worse than before the disaster; lower income from these operations become a general phenomenon; in the past a year, the annual income of 25% of these families were still less than 2,000 yuan, in which 10.2% of families made no profit or even loss profit; the annual income of only 25% was more than 12,000 yuan.

D. *Disaster-Area Non-Agricultural Family-Run Operations Need More Policy Support and Good Conditions for Business*

More than 30% of disaster area family run businesses obtained preferential policy in taxes or loans after the earthquake. Among them,

24.9% obtained preferential policy in taxation, 10.8% obtained preferential policy in loans. 66.5% of families explicitly expressed they also needed more policy support, where deduction and exemption from taxes was the most universal policy demand, and 23.9% of families hoped to enjoy this policy; next was demands on loans, rate reduction on loans, up front costs of stores, help with market development; the proportion of families with such demands was 9.3%, 8.6%, 8.2% and 5.1% respectively. It is noteworthy that, as high as 33.5% of families explicitly expressed they did not need government's policy support. For them, it is possibly more important that the government reduces unnecessary management and intervention to create a more open market for family run operations.

IV. *Rehabilitation of Medical Services to Disaster Areas and the Conditions of Middle and Elementary School Education*

The earthquake largely destroyed medical facilities and educational facilities. The findings showed that, although medical quality still needs further improvement, at present the accessibility to medical services of disaster areas have reached high levels. By the time of the investigation, many elementary and middle school students still attended class in temporary school buildings, but a batch of new school buildings have been completed and are available, and school hardware facilities and quality of teaching have improved. But future development of these schools, which do not involve reconstruction of the school, is a crucial issue, and excessively high school expenses for many elementary and middle school students are still prominent.

A. *State of Health of Residents in Disaster Areas is Overall Stable, Professional Psychological Consultation Needs to Increase Coverage and Effect*

From disaster area residents' self-assessment of their own health status, the proportion of people who thought their own health status was "very good" or "quite good" is 5 percentage points more than the findings in June 2008, and reached 69%, only 1 percentage point less than the findings of investigation to Sichuan population in 2004,[8]

---

[8] In 2004, the National Research Center for Science & Technology for Development (predecessor of Chinese Academy of Science and Technology for Development)

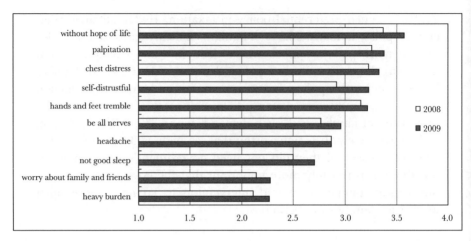

Figure 10.1: Scores of Disaster-Area Population's Mental Health (CHQ-12)
(2008–2009)[9]

which indicated at present the disaster-area residents' overall health
status is stable, and recovered to levels as before the earthquake.

Through measurement to disaster-area residents' mental health status using CHQ-12 measuring indicators, we discovered that, at present, every index has had slight improvement since the initial period
after the earthquake, but there is not a big difference in overall mental health condition (Figure 10.1). After the earthquake, only 2.3%
of residents received professional psychological consultation, where
29.7% thought it was of big help, 60% thought it was of some help,
10.2% thought it basically did not help, which expressed that coverage
and effectiveness of professional psychological consultation also needs
improvement.

B. *Coverage of Disaster-Area Medical Security is High, and Health Condition
has Distinct Improvement, but Service Quality Still Needs Enhancement*

At present, 94% of residents in disaster areas enjoy some medical security or insurance, which has greatly increased over the investigation

carried out a visiting questionnaire survey of 44,000 households in 11 western provinces. The Sichuan sampling scale reached 4,000 pieces, which the sampling design
can guarantee to deduce total Sichuan population. Hereafter the investigation in 2004
mentioned in this paper refers to this investigation.

[9] This measuring indicator uses self-assessment of 1–4 points, the higher the score
is, the less serious the problem is, namely healthier.

of Sichuan in 2004 where only 18.8% of people had medical security or insurance. Rural residents has a more obvious increasing trend, has rose from 13.0% in 2004 to 96.3% at present, and this mainly results from the promotion of new rural cooperatives medical insurance ("new rural cooperative medical system") in recent years—the insured rate of disaster area farmers has reached 92.9%.

At present, availability and attainability of disaster-area medical service have also improved. The proportion of disaster-area residents that are unable to see a doctor when unhealthy because there is no appropriate hospital nearby is less than 1% (0.6%); the proportion of residents who do not see a doctor because of economic hardship is 28.8%, which has reduced largely from 43.1% in 2004. But, the quality of hospital service still needs further improvement; about 23.2% of residents were unsatisfied with the service quality provided by the community hospital.

C. *Reconstruction of School Building of Disaster-Area Elementary and Middle Schools is Smooth, and Hardware Facilities and Teaching Quality Distinctly Improved*

The infrastructure of disaster area elementary and middle schools was obviously influenced by the earthquake. Up to June 2009, 38.6% of students still attended classes in the temporary school buildings (transitional houses), and as high as 66.0% in extremely afflicted areas. The construction progress of permanent school buildings was smooth, 5.3% of students moved into completely new school buildings, 8.5% moved into partially new school buildings, and 28.2% moved into school buildings that were repaired and reinforced.[10]

The new school buildings were reconstructed according to high quality and high standard requirements. 77.1% of students who utilized newly built schools thought that the school hardware facilities improved from that before the earthquake, and 48.7% thought that the quality of teaching also improved.

---

[10] It is to be explained that this was during the summer vacation when investigation occurred. Therefore, this paper describes the situation during the second term of the 2008–2009 school year. With many newly rebuilt school buildings being put into use at the beginning of the new term, the situation might possibly have sweeping change.

Table 10.1: Average Miscellaneous Expenses and School Fees Paid by Students of Disaster-Area Elementary and Middle Schools in the Past School Year (Yuan per person)

	Non-boarders	Boarders
Elementary schools	1012	2210
Junior middle schools	1882	3136
Senior high school	3397	6634

D. *Development of Non-Reconstructed Schools and High School Expenses of Many Elementary and Middle School Students are Worth Paying Attention To*

Unlike the hardware facilities of schools reconstructed, which have universally improved, the hardware facilities of schools that have been only repaired and reinforced are universally worse than the ones before the earthquake. Regarding these schools, only 28.9% of the students thought that the hardware facilities improved from that before the earthquake, and 29.3% thought they were actually worse. Therefore, in the reconstruction process, development of these middle and elementary schools, which were not reconstructed, should be specially paid attention to, to avoid new problems regarding educational resource inequality.

In total 51.0% of the students in disaster-area elementary and middle schools have enjoyed the preferential policy provided by all levels of governments after the earthquake, "living cost subsidy" (27.6%) and "deduction and exemption of miscellaneous expenses of school/school fee/lodging expenses" (26.2%) are most universal. But many students' problem regarding high school expenses still remains quite serious; 23.7% of students in elementary and middle schools paid above 5,000 yuan, for all kinds of expenses (including living expenses), to the school every year. The problem of boarders and high-school students was especially grave, and the proportion where the payment was above 5,000 Yuan is 29.3% and 58.8% respectively. The average expenses per high-school boarder amounted to 6,634 Yuan (Table 10.1).

V. *Disaster-Area Residents' Social Support and Social Participation*

Disaster area people obtained widespread support from the government and society after suffering serious losses. Meanwhile, the disaster area people also manifested an intense spirit, which helped and aided each other to overcome difficulties together, and spontaneously organized and actively participated in social commonweal events of disaster relief and reconstruction. The degree of unity amongst disaster areas has greatly enhanced, and social trust also has obviously increased, which is not only the source to overcome the disaster, but also constituted "the social capital," which is the most reliable when they reconstructed their hometown.

A. *Residents of Disaster Areas Obtain Widespread Social Support, the Government Remains the Most Important Supporter*

80.7% of disaster-area families obtained some form of outside social support. Daily necessities (60.5%), money (33.0%) and spiritual support (32.9%) were most universal, and help in housing construction (19.0%) and provision of temporary residence (17.7%) was also widespread.

55.7% of families thought that the government is the most important source of social support, and 32.8% thought that the help of relatives and friends and neighbors is most important. Although volunteers and NGOs played a major role in providing daily necessities and psychological comfort, only 1.3% thought that they were the most important source of support. Compared with the situation a year ago, the government's importance dropped, and the importance of relatives and friends and neighbors increased (the proportion of the two was respectively 60.4% and 22.0% at that time), which explained that as the progress of reconstruction was heading in the right track, people increasingly started to depend on traditional social support.

B. *Residents of Disaster Areas Actively Participate in Public Reconstruction Activities, and Commonweal Actions Organized Spontaneously is Vigorously Developing*

Within a year of the disaster, 42.4% of disaster-area residents have freely helped their relatives (35.0%), friends (29.6%) or strangers (20.7%). 43.1% participated in patrol, commodity distribution and construction of bridges and roads etc., and party members who did such reached as high as 58.2%. The proportion of people that participated in commonweal activity had a remarkable increase from 13.8% in 2008.

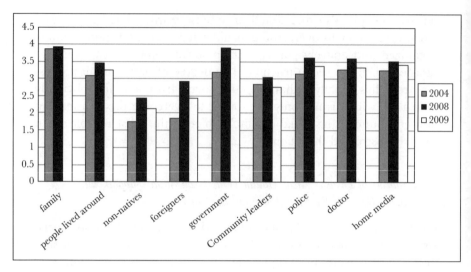

Figure 10.2: Average Score of Disaster-Area Residents' Trust Degree Toward Different Groups: 2004–2008–2009[11]

Basic-level organizations of village/residents' committees etc. were the organizers of the majority of commonweal actions, and 68.5% of commonweal actions that residents participated in were organized by them, but 17.1% of residents also spontaneously organized commonweal actions. This proportion has surpassed work units (9.9%) and government departments (6.7%) to become the second most important form of organization.

C. *The Degree of Social Unity Amongst Residents in Disaster Areas has Increased, the Degree of Trust Slightly Drops from the Initial Period after the Earthquake, but is Still Higher than that of before the Earthquake*

The earthquake has obviously strengthened the level of social unity amongst residents of disaster areas, 88.1% of disaster-area residents thought the residents from their village or community have become more united after the earthquake.

The degree of social trust of disaster-area residents toward other people and all kinds of organizations also maintained at a high level. From Figure 10.2, it is evident that disaster-area overall trust level

---

[11] The trust degree uses 4-point system. 4-point is the highest score, and represents "trusts;" 1-point is the lowest score, and represents "absolutely distrust."

reached its high point in the initial period after the earthquake; with society returning to normal, the trust level dropped slightly, but is still obviously higher than that of 2004. This indicated that, although the earthquake brought serious losses to disaster areas, it promoted the enhancement of people's trust level. This was the important spiritual strength for the people of disaster areas to defeat the natural disaster, and to rebuild their hometown.

VI. *Disaster-Area Residents' Policy Demand and Social Psychology*

The findings showed that the disaster-area residents' demand of reconstruction policy has changed from emphasis on survival to emphasis on development. Overall, the disaster-area social psychology was steady, residents' mood was positive and optimistic, and sense of social security was high. But some residents started to pay attention to inequality regarding the reconstruction process, and their confidence level and satisfaction degree to basic levels of government dropped.

A. *Disaster-Area Residents do not Fully Understand Post-Disaster Reconstruction Policy; their Emphasis of Policy Demand has Shifted*

Regarding the post-disaster reconstruction policy, 6.4% of disaster-area residents replied "fully understand," 43.0% "partially understand," 35.3% "not fully understand" and 15.3% "hardly understand." The overall level of understanding was as much as that right after the earthquake, still not high.

After more than a year of post-disaster reconstruction, disaster-area residents' emphasis of policy demand was obviously different than the initial period after the earthquake. First, residents became increasingly self-dependent, and the proportion that expressed "need not any help from government" reached 14.2%, which doubled from that of 7.0% in 2008. Next, the policy demand changed from paying attention to survival to paying attention to development. The demand of housing reconstruction and of reconstruction of medical and educational facilities largely decreased, and issues revolving around infrastructural construction concerning long-term development, such as maintaining local roads and strengthening facilities for irrigation and water conservancy etc., became disaster-area residents' primary policy concern. (Table 10.2). This reflected that disaster-area residents' survival

Table 10.2: Disaster-Area Residents' Policy Demand Changes from 2008–2009 (%)

Policy demand	In 2008	In 2009	More growth in 2009 than in 2008
Need not any help	7	14.2	7.2
Maintaining local roads	32.5	32.2	−0.3
Providing housing subsidy	46.7	22.1	−24.6
Facilities of irrigation and water conservancy	15.5	17.1	1.6
Improving medical services	27.8	14.7	−13.1
Deduction and exemption of child's school fees	22.6	11.7	−10.9
Providing job opportunities	23.3	11.3	−12
Improving inhabited environment	36.7	9.3	−27.4
Water, electricity and fuel gas	11.7	8.3	−3.4
Providing skill training	4.9	7.3	2.4
School reconstruction	16.2	2.8	−13.4

problem (mainly manifested in housing demand) has been solved well, and development naturally becomes the next primary mission.

B. *Satisfaction with Living is High amongst Residents of Disaster Areas, and Most Residents are Fully Confident of the Future*

79.8% of disaster-area residents were satisfied with life. 64.5% thought that living standards recovered to the level before the earthquake, 12.4% estimated that living standards would recover to the level before the disaster within three years, and 9.6% estimated it would need more than three years. It is important to point out, 13.5% of families had a pessimistic view on the recovery of living standard, where 8.8% did not know how long it would take before living standard would be recovered, 4.7% thought that it would be very difficult to recover to the original level. Families already in bad economic position before the earthquake would face more challenged in recovering previous living standards, therefore the "Matthew's effect" in post-disaster reconstruction should be paid great attention to.

Looking into the future, as high as 60.8% of disaster-area residents thought that life would get better in the next year, 31.7% thought there would be no change, and only 7.5% predicted that life would get worse.

C. *Disaster-Area Social Psychology is Steady Overall, and Public Order is Basically Stable*

Within the year of the disaster, only about 2.5% of total disaster-area residents participated in appeal and petition for help, and this proportion was as much as the one in the initial period after the earthquake. Moreover, when asked about the cause of the collapose of many elementary and middle school buildings, 84.6% of interviews thought that "natural disaster" was to blame, and 15.4% took an adverse opinion; compared with the situation the previous year, those people who regarded the collapse of school buildings as man-made calamities dropped 9 percentage points. Thus it can be seen the disaster-area people's psychology has become rational and calm.

D. *Some Disaster-Area Residents Start to Pay Attention to the Gap Between Rich and Poor and Inequality in Reconstruction, and the Appraisal to Basic Levels of Government Slightly Dropped*

The disaster-area residents' sense to social inequality strengthens. 39.5% of residents believed that the local gap between rich and poor increased slightly after the disaster. Moreover, quite a few people questioned the fairness of policy execution, and about 30% of residents thought there was unjust policy implementation after the disaster.

It is noteworthy that, although disaster-area residents' appraisal to the central government and the provincial-level governments still maintained high levels, their satisfaction degree toward basic levels of governments at the area- and county-level and below obvious decreased from the initial period after the earthquake. For example, the satisfaction rate in performance of county-level governments, villages and towns/sub-district committee as well as village/residents' committee in post-disaster reconstruction was 82.5%, 65.3% and 64.6% respectively, which respectively dropped 1.7, 7.2 and 8.0 percentage

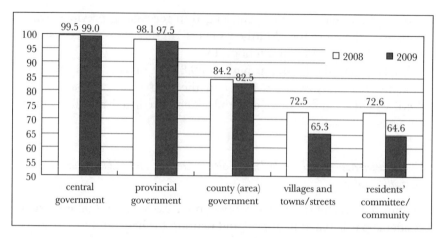

Figure 10.3: Disaster-Area Residents' Satisfaction Degree to All Levels of Governments from 2008–2009 (%)

points from that 2008 (Figure 10.3). This is possibly because there were unfair phenomena in implementation of reconstruction policy, and as concrete implementer and direct principal of the reconstruction policy, basic levels of governments have more opportunities to be in conflict with the people during this process.

E. *Sense of Social Security of Residents in Disaster Areas is High, but the Aftershock Still Casts a Shadow on Residents' Psychological Security*

92.8% of disaster-area residents thought they retained security levels if going out after 10:00 pm, and only 7.2% thought it was unsafe, which explained that disaster-area public order improved. Alternatively, residents of disaster areas worried more about the threat of an aftershock. Up to now, 62.7% of residents expressed they still felt the threat of an earthquake. It seems that recovery to people's psychology after the disaster is a longer and slower process than economic recovery.

CORE TASK OF SOCIAL CONSTRUCTION AT NEW STAGE: SOCIAL STRUCTURAL READJUSTMENT

Lu Xueyi, Song Guokai, Hu Jianguo and Li Xiaozhuang

I. *China Enters a New Stage That Emphasizes Social Construction*

Modernization practice indicates for different development stages of a country, there exists different development task and development models. At the early stage of development, the productivity level is low, products of labor are scare, and supplying enough food and clothing and meeting basic demands of life are the primary mission of social development. Therefore, at this stage, economic development is emphasized and economic development has precedence over social development. Therefore, as a characteristic of this development stage, the imbalance of economic and social development is rational to a certain extent. At the medium stage of development, lagging productivity has remarkable improvement, the problem about enough food and clothing and the demand of basic material life has been initially solved and met; people's demands of cultural life beyond material life and for integrated development become increasingly urgent. If the strategic targets for each stage are not readjusted to meet people's demands at that stage, the contradiction of imbalance between economic and social development will become more prominent.

A. *Coexistence of Prominent Economic Development Achievements and Incisive Social Contradictions*

On one hand, achievements of economic development are prominent. In the 30 years since the reform and opening, China GDP swiftly grows at an average rate of 9.8% per year, a rare rate in the world economic development history. The overall national power enters into a new stage, becoming the world's third-largest economy. If calculated using comparable price in 1978, the average disposable income per urban and rural resident and average net income per rural resident increased 7.16 and 6.93 times respectively from 1978 to 2008, and the living standard of the people has reached the well-off level overall.[1]

Since 2006, China has vaulted into the nation with the world largest foreign exchange reserve, the foreign exchange reserve grows on average by double-digit speed per month, and the remaining sum of foreign exchange reserves amounted to more than 2,131.6 billion US dollars by the end of June 2009, which accounted for more than 1/4 of the total amount of the world's foreign exchange reserves. This was unfathomed for China, who 30 years ago lagged behind economically, and also surpassed designers' blueprint at the beginning of the Reform. The transformation within China may be described as "earth-shattering."

On the other hand, social contradictions and problems are incisive and prominent. While economic development achievements are largely more than predicted, many social problems and contradictions are also unexpected. In 1978, at the beginning of the reform, it was socially accepted that China was faced with many contradictions and difficulties because of its poor and underdeveloped economic state, and if economic development was properly pursued, these problems could easily be solved. But, now, while economic development has made great achievements, social contradictions and problems have not decreased but rather increased. For example, issues about people's livelihood, such as housing, education, medical service and retirement security, become increasingly prominent; the gap between rich and poor, the disparity between urban and rural areas and the disparity among different regions are continually expanding; contradictions between social interest groups, such as the labor-capital relationship become increasingly obvious, and land requisition, housing relocation, the restructuring of enterprise and problems concerning law and litigation, which easily cause unstable events have been highlighted; in some areas, serious violent offense, such as murder and kidnapping have increased, and crimes of robbery, looting and burglary which infringe upon wealth have increased, creating new situations for public order. Particularly group incidents, from 1993 to 2005, group inci-

---

[1] Data from related years of "China Statistical Yearbook"; If thereinafter data quoted in this paper are not indicated specially, all are quoted from "China Statistical Yearbook".

dents increased by nearly 10 times.[2] Since 2008, group incidents, such as the Guizhou weng'an incident and Jilin Tonghua incident show the spread of such events, and issues regarding social stability become increasingly prominent.

Achievements in economic development are more than predicted, and likewise are social problems and contradictions, these "two unimaginable" occur at a key stage of China's development, namely after the medium stage of industrialization, which is new stage characteristic of the current Chinese economic and social development.

B. *China Enters a New Stage That Emphasizes Social Construction*

Overseas experiences of social construction have provided beneficial enlightenment. The current stage characteristic of China's development once also appeared in the development process of many modern countries. The end of the 19th century and beginning of the 20th century were the turning time of the United State's development, which had critical significance. Along with rapid economic development, social crises including a huge gap between the rich and poor and social disorder etc. appeared, but the government carried on social system reform promptly at this stage, and strengthened social construction to properly dissolve the social crises, which caused the social development to adapt to industrial advancement. After WWII, the Japanese economy grew swiftly, especially after 1960, economic growth was rapid, and occurred quicker than predicted, but simultaneously prominent social problems appeared, and the imbalance of economic structure and social structure caused people's life to be abnormal. At the end of 1970, some scholars commented that, "as for Japan's unbalanced situation of economic development and social development at that time, production was first-class, national income and consumption were second-class, and living environment such as housing etc. was third-class."[3] In order to solve the problem, Japan carried out large-scale social construction, but because of various reasons, social construction was not carried out effectively; Japan paid great prices

---

[2] Yu Jianrong (于建嵘): "China's Social Conflicts during the Transformation Period" published in Issue 176 of "Phoenix Weekly" (《凤凰周刊》) in 2006.

[3] Fukutake Tadashi: Page 107 of "Structure of Japanese Society" translated by Wang Shixiong (王世雄), and printed and published by East University Book Company in 1994.

at the expense of being an economic giant; for example, problems in living environment etc. are still not completely solved at present. "The Latin American development path" had indicated similarly the importance of social construction. In the late-1990s, the economic position in Latin American seriously worsened, the unemployment rate continuously rose, polarization of rich and poor became increasingly intense, and all kinds of social contradictions protruded and sharpened to form "the Latin American trap," which people thought was difficult to recover from. But the root of the issue was lack of understanding in social construction in Latin American nations, and the strength of social system reform was insufficient, which could not form the social structure to adapt to the economic structure.

Whether looking at the United State's successful experience, Japan' "price of success" or lessons from Latin America's mistakes, all present non-negligible and non-replaceable functions of social construction in the development process.

Let us understand now China's social development stage from the perspective of social construction. Since the 16th People's Congress, the importance of social construction has increased, and the government wrote the social construction task in the ruling party's party constitution. In 2004, The 4th Plenary Session of the 16th Party Central Committee proposed the strategic mission of "building a socialist harmonious society" and "social construction" for the first time. In 2005, the overall pattern of constructing socialism with Chinese characteristics was developed from a group of three: economic construction, political construction and cultural reconstruction into a group of four: economic development, political construction, cultural reconstruction and social construction. Social construction becomes an important part of overall development. Since entering the new century, while economic development remains key, the government repeatedly stressed that social construction must be placed in a more prominent position, and throughout paid great attention to social construction, which symbolizes that China is experiencing a second transformation, and has entered a new stage that emphasizes social construction.

C. *The Core Task of Social Construction Is Social Structural Readjustment*

The Report of the Seventeenth National Congress of the Communist Party of China pointed out that, "Social development is closely related to people's well-being. More importance must therefore be attached to social development on the basis of economic growth to ensure and improve people's livelihood, carry out social restructuring, expand public services, improve social management and promote social equity and justice. We must do our best to ensure that all our people enjoy their rights to education, employment, medical and old-age care, and housing, so as to build a harmonious society." Analysis from the sociological perspective, these contents of social construction may be summed up to social structural readjustment. If we can grasp social structural readjustment, we can grasp the core of social construction. Currently, through each work, building a modern social structure, which adapts to the economic structure, and advancing economic and social coordinated development are the crucial task that China is faced with and must put forth effort to effectively solve.

Social structure, in general, refers to a country's fixed resources and the opportunities society's members have to obtain them.[4] Social structure has important characteristics of complexity, integrity, hierarchy, relative stability etc., and an ideal modern social structure should have important characteristics of fairness, rationality and openness. Specifically speaking, social structure contains all kinds of important substructures, besides population structure as a basic factor, there is also family formation and social organizational structure, which manifest the means of social integration, urban and rural structure and domain structure, which manifest the means of spatial distribution, employment structure, income distribution structure and consumption patterns, which manifest the means of the survival movement, and the social stratum structure, which manifests the social position pattern, and so on. In these substructures, the social stratum structure is a core, and it directly or indirectly manifests the condition of social substructures in various aspects; changes within various substructures have an effect on other substructures. Readjusting the social structure also means readjustment of many of its substructures, especially the social stratum structure, and cause them to keep with advancement in economic and social development.

---

[4] About social structure, many sociological textbook define it as the composition way and situation of various places within a country or region. We thought that this summary does not fully reflect the factors and mechanism that composes the social structure, and this is just why it is indispensable analysis dimension to understand the social structure. Therefore, we thought that the social structure is the allocation of social resources to members of different social classes, as well as the result of the opportunity (i.e. fairness) where members of different social classes obtain the social resources, and this has the important theoretic and practical significance to the social structure condition as well as readjustment.

II. *Profound Changes in Contemporary China's Social Structure*

Since the reform and opening, China's social structure has had profound changes, and it is observed that these changes have never
occurred in the past several thousand years. The economic system
and social system reform have rapidly assisted the transformation from
agricultural society to industrial society, from rural society to urban
society and from traditional society to modern society; China's social
structure has had profound changes, and they are mainly manifested
in the following aspects.

A. *Basic Structure: The Demographic Structure Has Immense Changes*

The demographic structure is the basic structure of social structure.
From 1978 to 2007, China's fertility rate dropped from 18.25‰ to
12.10‰; human mortality was maintained at 6.5‰, and the natural growth rate of population correspondingly dropped from 12.00‰
in 1978 to 5.17‰ in 2007. Based on this, the Chinese demographic
age structure, quality structure and spatial distribution structure have
had momentous changes, and they are prominently manifested in,
the lengthen of average life expectancy, age structure enters the aging
stage, enhancement of culture quality, and movement of the population, spatial distribution of population massively moved and gath-
ered from rural areas to cities and from undeveloped areas to coastal
developed areas. The basic change of demographic structure affects
profound changes to the social structures such as family formation,
employment structure and social stratum structure.

B. *Social Integration Structure: Family Formation and Organizational Structure Continuously Change*

The family is the cell of society. Along with the change of population structure, family formation, structural pattern and its social integration function all have been affected. First is miniaturization of the
family. The average population per household obviously decreased,
which dropped from 4.41 persons in 1982 to 3.16 in 2008. Second is
diversification of family type. Along with the increase in love and marriage values and the movement of urban and rural population, family
type presents new diversified tendencies: DINK families, empty-nest
families and one-person families appear in the cities, the proportion

of skipped generation families rises in rural areas, and drifting families and separate nuclear families increase. Third is the change of family formation pattern. In the cities, it is manifested prominently in "Four-Two-One" pattern; and "Four-Two-Two" pattern (Four grandparents, two parents and two children) in rural areas. Fourth is the equalization of family relation. It is mainly manifested in the trend of equalization of husband-wife relation and family member relation.

The organizational structure and the integration function have changed. Since reform and opening, along with the disintegration of the planned economy and the establishment of a market system, the most sweeping change of organizational structure is to the allocation of resources and opportunities, along with the separation and growth of organizational structure, and the organization function is also unceasingly rebuilt. First, the method of control and function of government organization to the economy and society are transforming, from "omnipotent model" to "for the public" function. Next, with the increase and importance of enterprise organizations, the production function of state-owned enterprise is strengthened, non-production function is stripped, and private enterprise organizations and the individual units of industry and commerce have large-scale growth. Third, social organization starts to develop, and displays social integration function outside the state and market. For example, registered social organizations reached approximately 414,000 in 2008, in which social groups were about 228,000, the non-governmental non-enterprise units were about 182,000, and there were 1597 foundations, which admitted more than 4,758,000 persons for employment; they have become the important integration strength to build a socialist harmonious society.

C. *Survival Movement Structure: The Marketability Change of Employment, Income Distribution and Consumption*

People's survival movement structure mainly includes the employment structure, the income distribution structure and consumption patterns, and manifests the disposition of resources and opportunities and the disposition process.

The employment structure is manifested in labor disposition in the industry, vocation and post etc. Contemporary China's labor disposition has transformed from the natural economy before the founding of new China, the planned economy before the Reform, and into the current market economy, from agriculture employed population occupying the overwhelming majority into non-agricultural industrial employed population surpassing the agricultural employed population, and simultaneously employed population in the third industry surpassed the ones in the second industry. Until 1978, the distribution of the 400 million employed populations in the three industrial structures was still 70.5:17.3:12.2. After 1978, the employment structure had remarkable changes, up to 2008, the pattern of the three industrial distributions of total employed populations evolved into 39.6:27.2:33.2, and the non-agricultural employed population accounted for 60.4%. From 1978 to 2008, jobholders in the second and third industries averagely increased 11,664,000 persons every year.

Income distribution is not only related to the livelihood of the people, but also with social justice and fairness, and even with lasting peace and stability. Since reform and opening, the income distribution system reform has unceasingly deepened, the income distribution system and redistribution frame has had radical change, the huge change in the income distribution structure has broken the situation of equalitarianism and "Big Pot Rice" ("大锅饭" Da Guo Fan— extreme equalitarianism), and has formed a distribution system that gives priority to distribution according to work, which has stimulated the vigor of members of different social classes, as well as of numerous industrial departments, has aroused enthusiasm, and has powerfully promoted economic and social development. Presently, the problem with China's income distribution is mainly that the income differential between urban and rural areas, among various regions and between social strata is oversized, there is polarization between the rich and poor, which is disadvantageous to social harmony and stability.

Consumption not only pushes social differentiation, but simultaneously is also an important social integration mechanism. Since the Reform, resident consumption pattern has changed from a model of survival into a model of well off and wealthy. The Engel's coefficient of urban family dropped from 57.5% in 1978 to 37.9% in 2008, and has reached the wealthy level; in the corresponding period, the Engel's coefficient of rural family dropped from 67.7% to 43.7%, and has entered well-off society. Although this is still 30% below levels of developed countries, it is significant; in the consumption pattern, the consumption expenditure proportion of science, education, culture and health etc. is unceasingly enhancing, which presents the important characteristic where modern social consumption pattern becomes increasingly high-grade. Moreover, the dominant force, which impels the change of resident consumption pattern, has radical change, and the consumption function becomes more diverse, what is especially important is that the social market function is gradually strengthening.

D. *Spatial Structure: Continual Readjustment of Resource and Opportunity Disposition between Urban and Rural Areas and among Various Regions*

The urban and rural structure and the regional structure are the structural condition where social resource and opportunity form in spatial disposition.

The urban and rural structure change is first manifested in urbanization, namely with industrialization, large numbers of rural population shift into urban population, and the traditional rural society gradually transforms into urban society. The urbanization rate was only 12.8% in 1952, and only 17.9% in 1978, only 5.1 percentage point increase in 26 years. After 1978, urbanization sped up; if calculated according to the urban resident population, the urbanization rate reached 45.7% in 2008, which generally approached accepted urbanization level were the urban population accounts for 50% of total populations. Next, it is manifested in the transformation of urban and rural dual system, namely the development of the market economy has broken the administrative monopoly in urban and rural resource and opportunity disposition, which has loosened the urban and rural dual social structure formed under the planned economy. The rural reform, started in 1978, first broke through the restraint of urban and rural dual property system, and rural areas obtained relatively independent rights in resource allocation, which has induced a series of changes in the urban and rural system. Since entering the new century, the state proposed the strategy of unified planning in urban and rural development, and released a series of agricultural preferential actions, where rural areas and farmers have obtained many actual benefits. However, the disparity between urban and rural areas is still prominent.

Since reform and opening, the regional development had obvious differentiation; the interaction mechanism between various regions changed from unitary to multiple, the regional economic and social development pattern in eastern, central and western areas gradually formed, the difference of economic and social development model and speed are obvious in the different regions, the decrease in living standard and development opportunity among members of different social classes gradually enlarged. Generally speaking, in terms of developmental level, the highest is found in eastern regions, next in central regions and lowest in western regions, and the development disparity among the three regions is obvious. In 2008, eastern regions,[5] which occupies 9.5% of total land areas and 40% of total populations, produced 58.4% of gross national product; central and western regions, which occupies 90.5% of total land areas and 60% of total populations, only created local total output value which accounted for 41.6% of gross national product. Imbalance of regional structure is currently the situation in China, and coordinating regional development is an important aspect to readjust the social structure.

E. *Status Structure: The Modern Social Stratum Structure Has Begun To Form*

With the evolution of historical progress and changes of system and structure, changes to resource allocation and opportunity acquisition deeply changes the social stratum structure, which has become Contemporary China's characteristic of social structural change.

From 1949 to 1978, the vicissitude of China's social class and stratum was a process of structural simplification, through the establishment of socialist public ownership and the planned economic system, the social class and stratum structure of "two social classes and a social stratum," composed of workers, farmers and intellectuals was formed. Since 1978, with the profound transformation of economic system, means of resource and opportunity allocation tremendously changed, the original unitary centralized means of allocation has transformed into such where the state, market and society jointly distribute, which has promoted profound changes to social structure, has expedited some new social strata and groups, such as private businessmen and the off-farm workers etc., and has divided the society into a social stratum structure of "ten big social strata."[6] In terms of opportunity acquisition, overall, since 1978, especially at the initial stage of reform and opening, the arrangement of national system policy played a vital and even decisive role to people's social position, where the function of "ascribed factors" was obvious. But afterwards, the entire society

---

[5] Including 11 provinces and cities Beijing, Tianjin, Liaoning, Shanghai, Jiangsu, Zhejiang, Shandong, Fujian, Guangdong, Hainan and Hebei etc.

[6] Lu Xueyi (陆学艺): Pages 9–23 of "Contemporary China's Social Flow" published by Social Sciences Academic Press of Beijing in 2004.

became more open, and "acquired efforts" gradually become the primary method for upward mobility.

In the 60 years since the establishment of the New China, and especially since the Reform, profound changes of social structure have promoted the preliminary formation of a modern social stratum structure. The distribution of resources and opportunities in social strata has composed the objective basis of stratum position, and the ability of social stratum members in obtaining resources and opportunities has become the important factor in change to social stratum position. The structure before the Reform, of "two classes, one stratum" has gradually disintegrated, new social strata have formed, and the social stratum structure has changed from unitary to many and from closed to open, where the modern social stratum structure has basically formed. In addition, in this new social stratum structure, the scope of the middle stratum is unceasingly expanding, which manifests the current situation in China's social stratum structure. According to our survey, China's middle stratum accounted for 22% of total employed populations in 2007, which increased 7 percentage points from 15% in 1999; now the proportion of middle stratum approximately increases one percentage point every year, and about 8 million persons enter the middle stratum. Certainly, we must see that China's modernization transformation of social stratum structure is not completed, the proportion in the middle and lower stratum is still large, and the proportion of middle stratum is somewhat small, thus creating a pyramid shape for the entire structure.

III. *Contribution Social Structure Change has to Economic Development*

The change of social structure has significant contribution to economic development. In modern society, besides state interference and market regulation, the transformation of social structure is another "invisible hand" that affects resource allocation and economic development, and is not only the result of economic growth, but also the driving force of social change.[7]

---

[7] Li Peilin (李培林): "Another Invisible Hand: Social Structural Transformation" published in Issue 5 of "*Social Sciences in China*" in 1992.

A. *The Restoration of Family Economy Function Pushes Economic Development*

After 1949, with the completion of socialist transformation, rural land
was returned to collectives, and the production function of rural families were seriously damaged. After 1978, with the implementation of
the household contract responsibility system with remuneration linked
to output, taking the family as a unit, farmers obtained usage rights of
land production and operation, and the production function of farmer
families were restored, which enormously released farmers' enthusiasm
in production, and China's agricultural development entered a new
stage of swift growth.

In cities, family's economic function was transformed after 1956.
On one hand, with the transformation of the individual economy, the
individual economy was replaced by the work unit; on the other hand,
along with the establishment of a national rationing system, as well as
the arrangement of "high accumulation and low consumption" policy
in economic construction, urban families' consumption was controlled
by the national institutional arrangement, and lost independent consumption space. After the emphasis of the reform shifted from rural
areas to urban areas, the development of individual economy was first
permitted by the policy, urban families obtained possession and control over productive materials, individual businesses rapidly emerged,
which opened the doors for urban reform; At the same time, along
with the development of a commodity economy and the market prosperity, the family's consumption function returned, which enormously
promoted the development of a commodity economy.

B. *Employment Structural Readjustment Causes Rationalization of*
Labor Disposition

Before the Reform, the employment system was organized by the state,
the employment structure was rigid, and labor flow was blocked. After
reform and opening, with economic restructuring, massive agricultural
workers have quickly transferred from the first industry to second and
third industries, farmers have obtained the right and opportunity to
non-agricultural employment, which not only solved the problem
where the second and third industries urgently needed massive cheap
laborers, and agricultural workers needed other forms of income, but
also caused China to become the "World Factory," which with globalization has given the products a competitive advantage. From another

perspective, with large numbers of rural labors entering the cities, this not only sped up urbanization, and changed the urban and rural structure, but also brought about urban and rural optimization allocation of human resource, which has important meaning for promoting the integral development of the economy.

C. *Return of Autonomous Social Organization Function Promotes Economic Restructuring*

Before the Reform, the state had overall control over the entire society to form a kind of overall organizational structure.[8] After 1978, with the change in organizational structure, the functions of three big organizations, the state, economy and society started to regain their independence. First, national overall control continuously diminished, and evolved towards standardization and legalization, thus gradually changed the former situation where the state had total power. Second, the production function of enterprise organization strengthened, if enterprise's social function can be progressively separated out, this would have significant meaning for the development of the market economy. Third, independence in the social life domain strengthened unceasingly, and relatively independent social organizations increased. Social organizations are developed in the process where the state unceasingly withdrew from the social domain, and where economic organizations as key to the market failed to undertake the due social responsibility. Social organizations thus have the function of filling the gap left in the social life domain after the state and enterprise organizations withdrew. From these changes, the return of all kinds of different organization functions strengthened the diversification of resource allocation mechanism under specialized differentiation; in other words, resource and opportunity allocation transformed from complete control by the state into joint allocation by the state, market and society, thus allocation efficiency greatly increased, which largely contributed to economic growth and social development.

---

[8] Sun Liping (孙立平): "Transformation and Break—China's Social Structural Changes since Reform" published by Tsinghua University Press in 2004.

D. *Urban and Rural Structural Readjustment Has Spatial Aggregation Effect on Resource and Opportunity*

The city is the regional structural arrangement to reduce the resource allocation cost, the larger the urban scope, the lower resource allocation cost is. Structural change of urban and rural areas since the Reform is actually the rearrangement of resources and opportunity in urban and rural areas. Although today urbanization lags behind industrialization, and the urban and rural structure is still irrational, but since the Reform, urbanization enhanced the efficiency of resource and opportunity allocation between urban and rural areas, which powerfully promoted economic development. First, it promoted the growth of occupation production; second, it promoted industrial structural readjustment; third, it promoted the growth of consumption, and growth of consumption advances economic growth.

E. *The Rise and Development of New Social Strata Redoubles the Vigor of Socialist Market Economy*

While new social stratum structure unceasingly developed since the Reform, the social stratum, which grasps and operates economic resources, emerged and strengthened; they include the private businessmen stratum, the manager stratum and the stratum of individual units of industry and commerce. Since reform and opening, sustainable and swift economic growth is associated with the strengthening of these strata that operate the economic resources. It is observed that, without growth and strengthening of these new social strata in the market economy, it is impossible for China's economic growth to attain large achievements. In 2007, countrywide private enterprises accounted for 62.25% of total domestic enterprises, registered capital was 9,387.3 billion yuan, and tax payment was 477.15 billion yuan, which is an important force to push China's market economic development. In addition, appearance of off-farm worker stratum in the new social stratum structure created huge profits for the state, and the achievements of off-farm worker stratum have very important status in China's history of industrialization, modernization and urbanization.

IV. *Currently the Crux of Many Social Contradictions Rests with Lagged Social Structure Change*

In the process of economic growth, placing efficiency first in resource and opportunity allocation does not always create fairness. That is, the change of economic structure does not always impel rational change of social structure. Once social structure lags behind change of economic structure, and all kinds of social structures also uncoordinated, social contradictions and problems emerge endlessly.

Since the Reform, although social structure has profound transformation, and has positively impacted the economy, in the long run, in seeking quick economic growth, social construction was to a degree neglected, and resource allocation was obviously insufficient, therefore social structural readjustment lagged behind. Meanwhile, some system, such as the household register system, formed under the planned economy was not changed, moreover some policies, such as distribution adjustment policy, formulated since the reform and opening was not promptly readjusted along with changing situations; these issues caused or intensified inequality of social resource and opportunity acquisition to varying degree. Thus, within social systems, on one hand, the irrationality of resource allocation mechanism causes the social structure change to lose contact with the evolution of economic structure, and development disparity of members of different social classes is expanded; on the other hand, the difficulty that many members of different social classes have in obtaining resources and opportunities of development increases, where social structural readjustment is delayed. This delay has surpassed the reasonable limit.

A. *China's Social Structural Change Lags about 15 Years behind Economic Structural Development*

Certain important indexes in practical development indicated that currently China's economic structure has entered the medium stage of industrialization, and some indexes indicated that it has entered the late stage of industrialization. Looking at industrial structural change, the industrial structure has transformed from the "one-two-three" pattern (first industry-second industry-third industry) at the early stage of industrialization into the "two-three-one" pattern at the medium stage of industrialization; through the per capita income level, average

GDP or GNP per person US dollar, indicated the industrialization level is at the medium stage of industrialization as a whole. But, social structure indexes do not have similar transformation along with the transformation to economic structure; most social structure indexes are still at the early stage of industrialization. For instance, urbanization rate of urban and rural structural change should reached above 60% at the medium stage of industrialization, by 2007, China's urbanization rate was still at 44.9%; moreover, at the medium and late stage of industrialization, the middle stratum scope in a state or region is generally between 22.5%–65%, but according to the studies of this Task Group, China's scale of middle stratum was about 22% in 2007, which indicated that the middle stratum scale was still at the early stage of industrialization.

Economic structure and social structure not only present structural deviation, but this deviation is rather large. For instance, in China's employment structure, following that jobholders in the first industry are calculated by the average drop rate of 1% per year since the Reform, the present employment structural transformation does not reach the corresponding target at the medium stage of industrialization, and probably needs another 25 years; moreover, as for the urbanization rate, if calculated according to the speed that the urbanization rate on average grows 1% per year since the Reform, the urbanization rate should reach above 60% at the medium stage of industrialization, but it probably needs another 15 years. In addition, as for Engel's coefficient in consumption pattern, if calculated according to urban and rural residents' Engel's coefficient decrease of 0.82% and 0.71% respectively every year for 30 years, and drops to the target below 30% at the medium stage of industrialization, this coefficient needs respectively another 9 years and 16 years; Finally, as for the middle stratum scale, compared with the middle class scale of developed countries, if calculated according to a 1 percentage point increase of the middle class per year, for the middle class to account for 40%, another 18 years is needed.

Integrating these indexes and considering other factors, such as the economic development situation in recent years, the social structure lags about 15 years behind the economic structure. If corresponding social system reform is not carried out in the near future, and the strength of social construction is not increased, according to the present development pattern, social structure will not enter the medium stage of industrialization until about 2025.

B. *Other Deviation among All Kinds of Social Structures within the Social Structure*

According to general international experiences of modernization process, modernization transformation of urban and rural structure must experience three breaking points in turn: First is the breaking point of output value structure, namely the proportion of non-agricultural output value in GDP rises to above 85%; Next is the breaking point of urban and rural structure, namely the proportion of urban population in total population rises to above 50%; Third is the breaking point of employment structure, namely non-agricultural jobholders rise to above 70% of total jobholders.[9] Up to 2008, total agricultural output value only accounted for 11.3% of GDP; the proportion of town resident population in total population was only 45.7%, 5 percentage points lower than the target of above 50%; workers who were engaged in non-agricultural industry only accounted for 60.4% of total employed population, nearly 10 percentage points lower than the target of above 70%. There is structural deviation among the three, and explains why issues regarding agriculture, farmers and rural areas cannot be solved in a long time and why farmers have difficulty getting rich, even after obtaining enough food and clothing. Another example, according to development experiences of industrialized countries, for every 100 people, there exists on average one social organization. Modern social organizations are important integration strengths in industrial and urban society, and play crucial roles in social management. According to statistics from departments concerned, by the end of 2008, for every 3,115 people, there can exist a social organization in China, which is 30 times less than industrialized countries.

Generally speaking, social structural change lags behind economic structural development, and within the social structure, there exists all sorts of deviations, which is precisely why society has structural tension, and why many social contradictions and problems emerge.

---

[9] Ru Xin (汝信), Lu Xueyi (陆学艺) and Shan Tianlun (单天伦) as chief editors: Page 6 of "Analysis and Forecast on Chinese Society in 2001" published by Social Sciences Academic Press of Beijing in 2001.

V. *Policy Orientation of Social Structural Readjustment*

The essence of social structure is the allocation of resources and opportunities among members of different social classes. When the resource and opportunity allocation is appropriate, the social structure is also reasonable; otherwise the social structure will be uncoordinated. Therefore, the basic principle of social structural readjustment is how to bring about the most reasonable allocation of resources and opportunities. Speeding up social structural readjustment, changing the aspect that social structure lags behind economic structure, and coordinating economic and social development, all are goals of current social structural readjustment.

A. *Main Points of Social Structural Readjustment*

First, speeding up urbanization, and readjusting the urban and rural structure. Presently, China's urbanization rate is not only lower than the average world level, but is even lower than that of many developing countries, moreover included in this urbanization count are more than 100 million off-farm workers who are counted as part of the urban resident population, and strictly speaking, this part of the population is not absolute urban dwellers. Therefore, advancing urbanization vigorously and changing the current unreasonable urbanization pattern are urgent tasks. Certainly, this involves a series of policy readjustment in the urbanization policy, such as, the readjustment of household register, employment, education and social security etc. But, giving peasant workers who worked in cities the status of urban dwellers causes modern industrial workers' economic status to be consistent with their social status, which is the historical trend.

Second, consummating the income distribution system, and adjusting the income distribution structure. Regarding the income distribution structure, the income distribution system should be progressively consummated to solve well the unfair problem on primary distribution and redistribution. First, the income distribution pattern macroscopically should be readjusted to increase the proportion of labor income in primary distribution. Next, reform and consummation of the social security system should be quickened. The current social security system has many unreasonable parts, for example, welfare and social security of developed areas, preponderant departments and preponderant social strata and groups are greatly higher than for general social groups, especially over vulnerable departments and social strata. The secondary allocation system, such as the social security, should not become "the welfare network" of the preponderant social strata, but "the safety network" of the vulnerable groups.

Third, normalizing the labor market, governing the labor-capital relationship, and adjusting the employment structure. Generally, at different development stages of a state or region, the primary mission and pattern of development are different; the employment structure and labor-capital relationship will be also different. At the initial stage of development, to attract investors, many developing countries or regions usually utilize their own national or regional inexpensive labor, and reduce labor protection correspondingly to the requirements of investors, where "strong capital and weak labor" becomes the universal characteristic of labor-capital relationship at this stage. But, along with industrialization, labor laws and regulations inevitably need corresponding readjustment. On one hand, the profit unbalance and conflict caused by the labor-capital relationship pattern of "strong capital and weak labor" is not only unfair, but also affect efficiency. On the other hand, along with industrialization, the labor-intensive enterprise substituted gradually by technology-intensive enterprise become the tendency, further readjustment and upgrading of the industrial structure inevitably occur, where workers are given higher requirements to meet new demands of industrialization. Therefore, the basic standpoint of labor relation legislation at this stage has been changed from controlling labor cost into encouraging development of highly skilled workers, who grasp high skill and productivity, and promptly realizing this kind of change is the determining factor to whether a country can successfully transform their development model.

Fourth, promoting the growth of middle stratum, and advancing the formation of the modern social stratum structure. As for the present social stratum structure condition, social policy regulations should be launched around strengthening the middle stratum, reducing the lower stratum, and coordinating and integrating the social stratum interest relations. First, the middle stratum must be strengthened. In many aspects, some positive policies, which expand the proportion of mid-income earners, enhance resident property income, increase higher education, etc., have been released, and have made good progress in practice. Certainly, at present, policies concerning support to small- and medium-sized enterprise, as well as concerning housing, medical service and social security for the middle stratum, also need to be further consummated and implemented. Next, the proportion of the lower stratum should be reduced. The scope of the agricultural worker stratum and of the jobless, unemployed, semi-unemployed strata should be reduced, and simultaneously the economic and social status and treatment of these social strata should be improved. Therefore, employment must be actively increased, transfer of rural labors should be promoted to create employment opportunities for the jobless, unemployed and semi-unemployed persons; the rights and interest security of off-farm workers' also needs more attention, thus allowing them to better integrate into the city; at the same time, the overall coordination of interest relations between the upper stratum and bottom stratum should be paid attention to in order to reduce the conflicts of interest between the two.

B. *Concrete Policy Suggestions on Social Structural Readjustment*

First, speed up advancement of social construction, readjust the public resource allocation pattern, and enhance generalized preferences level of public product supply. At the new stage of social construction, departments concerned should make a resolution to readjust the public resource allocation pattern, turn from being inclined towards economic development into being inclined towards social construction, and increase investment to education, medical service, science & technology and culture etc. to quicken the development of public utilities, which will bring about reasonable resource allocation. This can change the unbalanced and uncoordinated position of economic development and social development.

Second, advance social management system reform. Formerly the emphasis on economic management system reform and economic structural readjustment was inevitably due to the time period. But now social management system reform should be emphasized to promote social self-development and growth. The current key point is to quicken the reform on household register, employment, social security, and community construction systems, and this is an important link to solve many economic and social contradictions and to build a socialist harmonious society.

Third, continuously expand construction of the benefit integration mechanism to guarantee social stability and order. Because China's social structural transformation is launched under the background where policy systems are changing, the economic system is transforming, and interest pattern is readjusting, differentiation between various interest groups appear with it. Generally speaking, the current benefit integration mechanism readjustment lags behind the demand of economic and social development, and all sorts of interest relation situations are prominently manifested in benefit contradictions and conflicts between urban and rural areas, among regions and between the social strata. Meanwhile, the tendency of structurization, systematization and even immobilization appear. Thus expanding construction of the social benefit integration mechanism and guaranteeing social stability and order appear more important and urgent.

Fourth, actively promote transformation of government functions. For a long time, the Chinese government was "the government of economic development." Under the planned economy, the government was the direct force of economic development. Since the Reform, even though a socialist market economy was established, as a result of influences from the planned economy, the problem that the government excessively intervenes in the microscopic economy is not yet settled, and it is unavoidable that public services are neglected and marginalized. Furthermore, these problems are not simply solved based on economic development and government intervention. As a result, the Report to the Seventeenth National Congress of the Communist Party of China proposed to construct a "service government," to further straighten out the relations between the government and market. The government should also make social construction key, and should focus on developing the economy and enhancing the efficiency of the market.

Fifth, develop and strengthen social organizations. First, the social organization registration managerial system, the dual managerial system and the level-to-level administration system should be reformed as soon as possible, the non-competitive principle should be gradually abandoned, and the "difficult position in registration" of social organization development should be resolved. All social organizations that do not violate the constitution and the related laws and aim at promoting social benefit and common interest of legitimate members should be directly permitted to register. The difficult position, where the present system causes organizations to be unwilling to undertake the management responsibility should be solved. Social organizations should become independent juridical associations that can independently undertake necessary legal and political liabilities. Next, social management system reform should be deepened, the separation of government and social organization should be earnestly implemented, and simultaneously the distribution system of public resources and social resources, which are closely linked with the development of social organization, should be reformed to resolve "the financial difficult position" of social organization development. Through the reform of separation of government and social organization, the administrative "umbilical cord" relationship between the state and social organization should be solved to bring about social transformation in administrative social organizations as soon as possible. The quantity of government-oriented social organization should be massively reduced, and the quantity of society-oriented social organization should be increased.

ISSUES ON POPULATION IN CHINA IN 2011–2015

Zhang Yi

Abstract

2010 is the last year of the "11th Five-year Plan," this indicates that China, a country of government-oriented development, soon must summarize former experiences and lessons in the past, and according to new situations, formulate a recent development plan, determine new development targets, find out major issues that need to be solved, formulate the "12th Five-year Plan," and maintain stable growth of the Chinese economy and harmonious development of Chinese society. So, what new problems exist regarding the Chinese population? Or what new problems need to be considered in the next five-year plan?

I. *Chinese Population Shrinkage*

A. *Shrinkage of Chinese Population Pyramid Base*

Population shrinkage mainly refers to the shrinkage of the population pyramid base, and the gradual steady drop of annual birthrate of the newborn population because of the birthrate reduction under restraint of the family planning policy or social and economic development. Two main reasons cause population shrinkage; First, the restraint of the family planning policy causes the drop in birthrate; Second, ideological mindset of giving birth changed due to cost of living, education cost, employment cost and social security, decreases the birth level.

Since family planning was brought into the "five-year plan" starting in the 1970s, China's birthrate gradually dropped. First non-agricultural household population dropped under the restraint of "one child policy," and then birthrate of agricultural household population started to drop in the 1980s. By 2008, China's population birthrate dropped to 12.14 %, the mortality rate rose to 7.06 % gradually in the process of population aging, and the natural growth rate dropped to 5.08%. In fact, from 2003, the natural growth rate of Chinese population was lower than the mortality rate. Although some demographers fore-casted that China would present "the fourth population birth peak" or "the population birth small peak" at around 2005, by the end of 2009, this "population birth peak" forecasted did not clearly appear.

From Figure 12.1, we may see the shrinkage situation of the Chinese population pyramid base. When a census was completed in 1953 and 1964, the results show that the population sex and age structure chart is genuine "pyramid" shape. The 10 year old and under children population shrunk in the third census in 1982. Under the influence of the "baby boom" in the 1980s, the 0–4 year old population increased, and therefore the fourth census indicated the pyramid base expanded in 1990. After the population policy stabilized in the 1990s, the pyramid base started to shrink—from the pyramid chart shape showed of the census in 2000, we obviously see that the children population shrunk.

After entering the 21st century, the shrinkage situation of the population pyramid base becomes more obvious. Total birth population was 16.47 million in 2002, 16.17 million in 2005 and 16.08 million in 2008. The death toll was 9.35 million persons in 2008, and after subtracting the death toll from the birth population, net increased population was only 6.73 million. The growth speed of Chinese population further slows down. If the net increased population is also less than 7 million in 2009, then by the end of 2010, China's total population will be controlled at about 1.35 billion, which is less than the goal of 1.36 billion determined in the population and family planning development program of "11th Five-year Plan."[1]

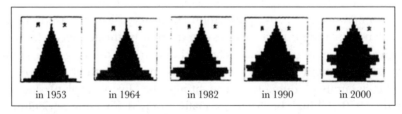

in 1953   in 1964   in 1982   in 1990   in 2000

Figure 12.1: China's Age Pyramid and Pyramid Base Shrinkage in All Previous Censuses[1]

---

[1] Data from Wu Cangping (邬沧萍), Wang Lin (王琳) and Miao Ruifeng (苗瑞凤): "Population aging process with Chinese characteristics, prospect and countermeasure" published in Issue 1 of "Population Studies" (《人口研究》) in 2004.

Although total Chinese population still grows under population inertia, the newly increased population actually drops during fluctuation.
Table 1 is the demographic data of various age sections counted by
"1/1000 population change sampling investigation in 2008;" we discovered that the population of 0–4-year-old age section account for
5.13% of total population, 5–9-year-old population account for 5.46%,
10–14-year-old population 6.73%, and 15–19-year-old population
7.87%. From this, we may see that, in the population pyramid base,
the younger the age section is, the lower the population proportion is.
Therefore, it has been very difficult to define the Chinese population
chart by age section and sex as a "population pyramid." In fact, this
is an "irregular component" composed of irregular inverse trapezoid
underneath a pyramid.

B. *Problems Initiated by Chinese Population Pyramid Shrinkage*

(1) *Aging of Population is Quickening, and Regional Distribution is Unbalanced*
Chinese population pyramid base shrinkage, on one hand, reduces the
dependency ratio of children population while reducing the population
birthrate; on the other hand, increases the proportion of 15–64-year-old
labor populations, and has brought unprecedented "population bonus"
to China. But because the population shrinks quickly, and aging is
accelerating, the "population bonus" period will end about 2020, the
retirement pressure will increase, and the phenomenon of "population

Table 12.1: Proportion of Population of Various Age Sections in 2008

Age	Proportion in total population (%)	Man	Woman	Sex ratio (woman = 100)	Age	Proportion in total population (%)	Man	Woman	Sex ratio (woman = 100)
0–4	5.13	2.83	2.3	123.26	50–54	7.8	3.93	3.87	101.36
5–9	5.46	3	2.47	121.4	55–59	6.58	3.33	3.25	102.7
10–14	6.73	3.61	3.12	115.91	60–64	4.47	2.27	2.2	103.27
15–19	7.87	4.19	3.68	114.1	65–69	3.32	1.68	1.64	102.39
20–24	6.86	3.39	3.47	97.85	70–74	2.83	1.4	1.42	98.87
25–29	6.48	3.18	3.3	96.34	75–79	1.87	0.89	0.97	92.14
30–34	6.96	3.45	3.51	98.13	80–84	0.99	0.44	0.55	80.08
35–39	9.27	4.58	4.69	97.75	85–89	0.41	0.16	0.25	65.34
40–44	9.65	4.81	4.84	99.23	90–94	0.1	0.03	0.07	45.17
45–49	7.19	3.57	3.62	98.64	95+	0.02	0.01	0.02	41.17

Data from Tables 4–7 of "China Statistical Yearbook" in 2009.

debt" will also gradually appear along with it. China entered the aging society around 2000—the proportion of people above 65 years old in the total population was close to 7% in 2000, more than 7% after 2001, and 8.3% at the end of 2008.

Moreover, non-agricultural household population mainly lives in the city, and the agricultural household population mainly lives in rural areas. The "one child act" is mainly implemented in urban areas, and the urban population birth level suddenly dropped in the 1970s. Up to the present, the population birth level of an overwhelming majority of the big cities is lower than the policy fertility rate. This phenomenon where actual fertility rate is lower than the policy fertility rate has caused negative growth in urban household population, like Shanghai. At present, although urban household population has the influence of mechanical increase, the aging level is actually getting higher and higher. For example, Shanghai's aging level has surpassed 21%. Under the situation of more and more only-child families, the urban family's retirement system will become extremely frail; is something were to happen to the only-child, the family retirement support system of his/her parents will be broken.

(2) *The Gender Ratio of Birth Population Increases with Population Shrinkage*
China's birth gender ratio has rapidly increased along with the strict execution of the family planning policy since the mid-1980s. The birth population gender ratio in 1981 from the third census in 1982 was 108.47; the one in 1989 calculated in the fourth census in 1990 was 111.92; the one announced in the fifth census in 2000 was 116. Observing the unbalanced condition in recent years by gender ratio in 0–4-year-old age population, the gender ratio was 118.38 in 1995, 119.98 in 1996 and 120.14 in 1997, the gender ratio from the fifth census in 2000 was 120.17, and the one from population change sampling investigation in 2003 was 121.22. The gender ratio of 0–4-year-old population from 1% population sampling investigation in 2005 was 122.66. That is to say, not only is there an increase in gender ration of Chinese baby and infant population, but it is far higher than the normal value where 107 is set as the highest warning limit.

Moreover, as shown in Table 12.1, in 2008, the sex ratio of 0 0 4-year-old population rose to 123.26 (this indicated that for every 100 girls between 0–4 years old, there correspondingly is 123.26 boys), the one of 5–9-year-old population rose to 121.4, the one of 10–14-year-old population rose to 115.91, and the one of 15–19-year-old population rose to 114.1. The younger the age of the birth group, the more serious the gender ratio disproportion. That is, the younger the age section, the more serious the shortage of female population in this age section over the male population. The disproportion of gender ratio in 0–19-year-old population will result in chances of men for marriage to decrease once this population enters marriageable age. And the period of the "12th Five-year Plan" is precisely when the population of 15–19-year-old age enters marriageable age, one after another.

II. *Structural Transformation of Population Movement and Floating Population*

The current population movement is initiated mainly by the labor population employment demand, but flow caused by child education, retirement care, immigration and relocation has increased. Moreover, the current population movement in China is different than that of developed countries, and is actually similar to developing countries migrating to developed countries. This similarity not only manifests a "pulling force" of non-agriculture and urbanization, but also manifests "attraction" brought by the shrinkage of urban population pyramid base. In the new century, the internal structure of the floating population actually has many tremendous changes.

A. *New Changes of the Floating Population Internal Structure*

(1) The growth speed of floating population with a junior middle school education and below starts to slow down, the floating population growth speed of graduates of secondary vocational school and of university speeds up. Since the Reform up to the end of the 20th century, the quantity of floating population from rural areas to urban areas has rapidly grown. But from the census in 2000 to the 1% population sampling investigation in 2005, the Chinese floating population grew from 144.39 million to 147.35 million, which only grew about 2.96 million persons in 5 years. Off-farm workers in the floating population, especially physical labor off-farm workers are lacking[2] mainly

---

[2] Even if during the financial crisis in the second half of 2009, the demand to off-farm workers brought by standing firmly and rise also appeared shortage. Various

because the supply of workers with a junior middle school education and below dropped. The consummation of nine-year compulsory education and the rise of student recruitment at the stage of senior high school, especially at secondary vocational school education, have greatly increased the proportion of students entering from junior middle school to schools of a higher grade. Because graduates of secondary vocational school increase—in the future, there will be above 8.1 million every year, because college graduates increase year after year—above 6.1 million persons graduated in 2008, where the population who had obtained high school education and above in the floating population started to rise rapidly. Although some provinces promulgated the policy where university students obtain household register after they get employment, the "job-hopping rate" of the employment market remains at a high level because the jobs of university students do not match their specialized subject. Although they are registered, they become part of the floating population. In the future, along with the rise in number of graduates and the high pressure of the employment competition situation, in this part of the population, more people will join the floating population—especially into the big cities.

(2) In the floating population, the proportion of men and women will stabilize, and the women floating population quantity may exceed that of men in big cities. At the initial stage of industrialization, with the construction of urban real estate and municipal transportation etc., the city create massive blue-collar jobs, and attracts the rural men floating population to enter the city for work. At the later stage of industrialization, with the shrinkage of urban capital construction recruitment quantity and the expansion of recruitment quantity in manufacturing and service industry, the woman floating population increases rapidly. Now, in Beijing, Shanghai, Guangzhou and Shenzhen etc., the amount of women in the floating population is close to or exceeds that of men. In some middle and small-scale cities, the amount of women in the floating population has also increased rapidly. During the period of the "12th Five-year Plan," along with the enhancement

---

regions were different in worker recruitment. "4 trillion" investments incline towards railway, highway and other infrastructures etc., which has accelerated the difficulty of off-farm worker recruitment in construction sites. This has caused directly the rapid rise of off-farm worker's wages in building industry—is higher than off-farm workers in manufacturing industry at present.

of post-industrialization characteristics in the megalopolis or provincial capital cities, more women will be attracted to work in the cities.

(3) Industrial upgrading in the coastal area, industrial transfer from coastal area inland, implementation of the rising strategy in central China and of the strategy of western development etc., all cause the flow region of floating population to go from unit concentration to multiple concentration. Under the impact of the financial crisis, this tendency will become more obvious. It can be said that, during the latter 20 years of the 20th century, the floating population mainly moved from rural areas to the cities and from the central and western areas to the coastal areas of eastern China. In the coastal areas of eastern China, the economic zone around Bohai Sea Gulf, the Changjiang Delta area and the Zhujiang Delta area became the main inflow areas of the floating population, and about 50%–60% of inter-provincial floating population flowed into these areas. Under the influence of industrial transfer, especially the transfer of low-tech labor intensive industry from coastal areas to central and western areas, the labor employment situation in 2009, especially the employment situation of the floating population, which gave priority to off-farm worker, looks different. In some big provinces that admitted the transferred industries in eastern areas, off-farm workers' employment had the tendency of transfer to other industries on the spot or nearby. Although at the beginning of the year, some reports said that more than nearly 20 million off-farm workers were out of work, in the end of first quarter, some reports said above 95% of returning off-farm workers had "successfully" gone out for business.

Although the economic zone around Bohai Sea Gulf, Changjiang Delta, and Zhujiang Delta areas are still the main inflow regions of the floating population, the ability of central and western areas to take in population actually strengthened greatly. In the new round of "labor shortage," some provinces that encouraged floating laborers to go out to work and to do business for developing economies even made the decision to "first meet the demands of their own province" in the third quarter of 2009, and advocated strongly that floating laborers get employment nearby to meet demand of local development of labor-intensive enterprise.

Moreover, emphasis on developing the service industry, advancing the manufacturing and high-tech industry in the Changjiang Delta and Zhujiang Delta areas, as well as treasuring the innovation and the science and technology in Beijing, all strengthened the requirements to the labor capital. It is observed that, with the increase in industrial upgrading in the coastal area, the low-end industries originally situated in these areas have transferred to central and western areas where the labor resource is quite rich.

(4) In the floating population, the proportion of population at 35 years old and above starts to increase. With the deepening of population shrinkage and the drop of laborers from elementary and junior middle school education background, the demand of urban floating population—of heavy physical labors has a shortage. In the third quarter of 2009, the wage level of laborers in the construction industry surpassed that of the manufacturing industry. The average age of floating population in the architectural construction industry increased. But for many years before the financial crisis, the proportion of the floating population at 35 years old or 40 years old and above was quite low. It is observed that, the increase in numbers of the floating population at the 35 years old and above age section is a new phenomenon.

(5) The family movement phenomenon of floating population becomes increasingly prominent. At the initial stage of industrialization, mainly, physical laborers moved to the city to find a job. For these people, there existed family relationship, mainly father and son went out to work jointly, and the grown married woman left behind in the rural areas worked the fields. After the middle stage of industrialization, the increase of employment demand to the floating population, especially to woman, in the cities caused a family-type migration of the floating population to manifest in the migration of couples and their children. In recent years, along with the gradual opening of urban public resource to the floating population, the number of family migrations becoming increasingly more, and this is manifested obviously from the increase in floating population children.

In brief, at present, not only has the flow of people from rural areas to the cities changed the immigration characteristic, but also immigration from city to city has increased. The movement of newly graduated college students has also increased the complexity of floating population group. Moreover, the degree of openness of cities and the accumulation of floating population work funds have also strengthened their ability to live in the city, thus to be able to stay for a longer period of time. Their children, so-called "second generation" off-farm workers, have lost interest in returning to their native place but identify with the city.

With the strengthening of post-industrial social characteristics, enhancement of work specialization degree, as well as substitution of graduates of secondary vocational schools for students of junior high schools, the population who has accepted vocational training within the floating population has largely increased, which will strengthen the immigrant characteristic of the floating population. The floating population will no longer be manifested in short-term migration, and will increase townsmen and immigration characteristics.

B. *Problems Brought About with the Floating Population*

(1) With the rise of the proportion of floating population in the total urban population, problems with social integration have appeared. In China, for the overwhelming majority of the floating population at the initial stage of industrialization, the main objective to working in the city was to make money. But after the middle stage of industrialization, along with the increase in capital of the floating population, the increase of proportion of graduates of secondary vocational schools, higher vocational-technical schools and colleges and universities, as well as the extended duration of stay for the floating population in the city, they not only seek to make money in the city, but also want to pursue "the significance of life," and request a sense of belonging and identification. The living area of floating population is relatively centralized, and they live in so-called "inside of a city village." There exist more than 100 of these "villages," in which above 10,000 floating persons live in the urban-rural intersections of Beijing. Once there is conflict, it is difficult to control.

(2) With the increase in floating woman population, problems regarding reproductive health of the floating population become more and more prominent. The mobile nature of the floating population causes problem relating to the spread of birth and venereal disease to be difficult to control. The urban-rural intersections that the floating population migrate to and are densely packed are also exactly the places in which there is a lack of public health and service resources. On one hand, this highlights problems about unmarried women giving birth to floating population and about the babies born exceeding the stipulated limit of the birth-control policy; on the one hand, this also causes many crisis in marriage and health of the floating population. In recent years, the divorce rate of floating population went up, and the morbidity rate due to AIDS is also increasing.

(3) The flow direction of floating population has changed from unitary to multiple, which has increased the difficulties in the management and service for the central and western areas. The government

departments in the big cities, Changjiang Delta and Zhujiang Delta areas have accumulated many experiences in the management and service of floating population, and also have built related facilities. But the small and medium-sized town and cities in the central and western areas, which in the past hardly took in floating population, do not have established the necessary facilities of management and service. Therefore, in these cities, under the situation where the back flow of off-farm workers gradually increase, there is big gap in public resource demand.

(4) The extension of living time of floating population in the city has increased their residential characteristic. Off-farm workers' re-lease of their own contracted land causes them to not have an income if they return to their native place. Thus the city needs to provide necessary social security. But, at present, it is difficult to transfer urban social security, especially the retirement security. Off-farm workers pay the endowment insurance premium, and actually they totally "make the contribution" to the city. Even if they are allowed to "withdraw from endowment insurance" at the end of the year, they can only be repaid the part of the individual account. In some cities, once the farmer becomes an urban resident, their land is hurriedly taken back, which is radically different from other developed countries where the state forbids the free trading of land but formally retains the legal tenure.

(5) Although urban education resources have been opened up to the floating population, the degree of openness is not big. Some elementary and middle schools that have good educational resources do not accept off-farm workers' children. In some areas where there are many off-farm worker children, so long as the off-farm workers' children surpass a certain number, the local town dwellers may transfer their own children to other schools with better educational resources. Moreover, the flowing characteristic of floating population causes transfer of floating population children to become the norm. For this reason, when many off-farm workers arrive in a city, their biggest difficulty is not obtaining a job, but rather finding a suitable school for their child's education level.

III. *The Chinese Population Starts to Gather Rapidly*

Because the birthrate of urban household population is lower than the rural household population for a long time, this causes the shrinkage situation of urban population to be quicker than that of the rural areas. Therefore, under the influence of population movement, the rural population pyramid also has a shrinkage situation. On one hand, the population pyramid shrinks; on the one hand, the population movement increases the population in the economical prosperous regions, where the Chinese population starts rapidly gathering, driven by industrialization. The gathering is manifested that the big agglomeration brought by urbanization and the small agglomeration brought by small town construction start parallel development.

A. *Gathering Situation of the Chinese population*

(1) *Urbanization Drives Population Gathering*

Urbanization refers to process of increase to the urban population. If the urbanization level of a state or region is more than 30%, this state or region enters the stage of fast urbanization. From Figure 12.2, we may see that, between 1949 and 1958, China had fast urbanization. But after the big crop failure from 1959–1961, China fell into a long-term low tide of urbanization—the proportion of urban population in total population not only did not increase, but instead decreased or suffered from fluctuations. Since 1978, China's urbanization level rose once again, and rose rapidly after 1995, when checked in 1990. By 2008, China's urbanization level reached 45.7%.

The result of urbanization first causes the population to gather in big cities, and then expands the population scale into small and medium-sized towns and cities. In recent years, Shanghai's resident population was only 14.74 million in 1999, but increased to 17.78 million by 2005, grew to 18.88 million by 2008, and it was estimated that Shanghai's population would surpass 19 million at the end of 2009. Beijing's resident population was 15.38 million in 2005, increased to 16.95 million by the end of 2008, and it was estimated that the population would surpass 17.4 million at the end of 2009. Shenzhen is another example of a city with prominent population gathering. The resident population was only 300,000 in 1979, and it was estimated that the resident population would surpass 16 million by 2008. Moreover, Guangzhou and Tianjin etc. also had more than 10 million people. Harbin, Wuhan, Xi'an, Chongqing, Shantou, Nanjing, Shenyang and Chengdu all might gather large numbers of population during the "12th Five-year Plan," to form the regional internal population gathering places. Now, the proportion of floating population in most big cities in resident population has surpassed 20%. Moreover, besides the explosive growth of population in big cities, the loose domicile system in medium-sized cities and the growth of real estate in medium-sized cities have also added to the population to those regions.

(2) *Urbanization of Small Town and County Has Promoted Population Gathering*

Besides population concentration driven by urbanization, small town construction has also driven the rapid gathering of rural population. At first, money made by off-farm workers was used in constructing houses. Now, after returning to their native village, some off-farm workers discovered that it is more cost-efficient to buy a commercial house in a nearby county than to reconstruct or expand their own house at the original house site. The progress of agricultural science and technology and the enhancement of mechanization level have reduced crop farming time; and improvement to traffic resources has caused people who buy houses in the county town to go to the countryside to farm in the daytime and return at night to the city.

Moreover, under the influence of industrial transfer, some labor intensive industries or industries which cannot survive in small and medium-sized towns and cities have been gradually transferred to the county, which has also driven local population gathering to those regions. The development impulsion of county town, the old-city transformation implemented in the county town and the construction of developing zone etc., all have stimulated population gathering to different extents. Under the government-oriented development mode, the county town has become the most flourishing area inside this administrative regionalism. Moreover, the county town expansion is due to its increasingly convenient transportation resources and investment attraction. Since the Reform, the population of an overwhelming majority of county towns has doubled, and the county-level city population in southern or coastal developed provinces has doubled several times.

Therefore, we may think that, during the period of the "12th Five-year Plan," the population of county-level city or county town will still have accelerated growth. This will greatly promote county territory population gathering, and accelerate the consumption progress of county territory, including housing.

In brief, the improvement of agricultural technology has released farmers from staying on their land, and has reduced their manual labor time. In the flatlands, people's manual labor time in farming has reduced to 20–30 days every year. Other time may be spent engaging in trade. In semi-mountain and semi-plain areas, the farming time is possibly longer, but does not surpass half a year. And non-agricultural development has driven population urbanization. People start to gather, from the villages to the towns, from the mountainous areas to the plain areas, to the flourishing county towns and to the central city nearby. This sort of gathering, on the microscopic level has constructed the short-distance and long-distance immigration process of Chinese population. The expansion of county town, and the cheapness of county land, can accelerate the reduction in village population, especially the population of remote mountainous villages, during the "12th Five-year Plan." Additionally the young people have already dispelled the nostalgic notion of provincialism, which possibly causes the emptiness of remote villages.

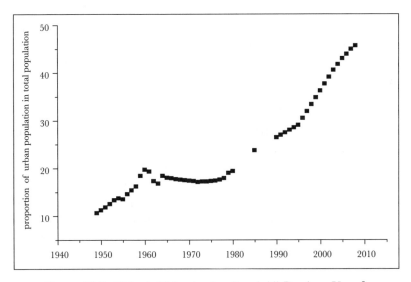

Figure 12.2: China's Urbanization Level All Previous Years[3]

---

[3] Table 3-1 of "China Statistical Yearbook" in 2009.

IV. *Policy Suggestions During the "12th Five-Year Plan"*

The shrinkage and flow of the Chinese population have not only brought about accelerated gathering of population, but will also radically transform China's social structure, where China will transform from a big power where farmers are the main force into one where workers are the main force.

During the "12th Five-year Plan," China's urbanization level will surpass 50%. Durative shrinkage of urban household population pyramid and durative demand of urban society to labors will still stimulate rural population to flow to or gather in the cities. The rural population gathering in cities and small towns will also bring a series of problems to cities or town society besides the possibility of a large-scale land circulation phenomenon. Therefore, the following are suggestions to policy-makers.

A. Steadily *Advance Urbanization*

China has entered the fast urbanization stage. China's urbanization will move forward, one by one, in turn, under the influence of stratified economic development from eastern area to central area and then to western area; eastern urban population growth will continue during the "12th Five-year Plan." China's insufficiency in urbanization development will seriously influence China's social construction in the future. From the employment structures three times, in 2008, the job-holders in the first industry dropped to 39.6%, but compared with the 11.3% proportion in the first industry in GDP, it was still very high. The proportion of second industry in GDP reached 48.6%, but the proportion of jobholders was actually 27.2%. Besides the statistical omission, urbanization insufficiency was also a primary cause. Therefore, only by advancing urbanization development continuously, can Chinese workers transfer from the first industry to the second and third industries and from rural areas to cities.

Moreover, with the extension of the floating population work time in the city, the second generation of floating population is either born in the city, brought into the city by their parents, or enter the city after studying in and graduating from the rural areas. The second generation of floating population is familiar with the city, but unfamiliar with the rural areas. Their life has been urbanized, but they do not have urban household register, and actually cannot become integrated into the city. Therefore, the second generation of off-farm workers becomes off-farm workers who cannot return to the rural areas.

B. *Accelerate Urban Clustered Development*

Decentralized population distribution may waste more cultivated lands and water resources, thus if development circles can be formed around one or several megalopolis or central cities, and support the industrial chain, this will strengthen the global competitive power of Chinese cities. Whether Europe, the United States or Japan, in their fast urbanization process, they presented the clustered urban group strategy. But as for urbanization of the world's largest population, China may have different urbanization methods than European countries where there was a small density of population, but may have a similar urbanization strategy with Japan, the East Asian country with a population of 100 million. It is counted according to the fact that the population of big Tokyo circle has surpassed 35 million, by constructing dozens of urban groups like those at the Changjiang Delta, Zhujiang Delta and the economic zone around Bohai Sea Gulf, China's future development will accelerate even faster. The urban group of clustered development will continue to change the distribution tendency of the Chinese population, and will continuously increase.

C. *Consummate the Protection of Off-Farm Worker's Rights and Interests*

The flow of floating population, especially of off-farm workers, is not only from rural areas to cities, but also frequently within the city, which has an adverse effect to enhancing the vocational and post technical level. Although the low technical skills needed for labor-intensive enterprise allows off-farm worker to easily transfer from job to job, job flexibility and unskilled abilities actually have affected accumulation and innovation of technical capital. Therefore, during the "12th Five-year Plan," under the environment where the negative impacts of the financial crisis gradually abates and where the competitive power of "made in China" continues to rise, the labor shortage will unceasingly enhance the common workers' ability of bargaining to form the situation of wage increase. The instability of work and high mobility rate may actually affect off-farm workers' resident process.

In consummating the protection of floating population's rights and interests, besides emphasizing improvement of work environment and the guarantee of on time wage payment, an important aspect is to release the resident policy that can cover all floating populations, and based on population residential areas, to design urban welfare and urban public service facilities. But the current emphasis is to strengthen the construction of public service facilities at the urban-rural intersections that off-farm workers reside in.

D. *Establish Management and Service System for Floating Population Based on Residential Areas*

Establishing a management and service system for floating population based on residential areas, on one hand, prevents the floating population and the native household population to become social isolated, on the other hand, prevents large-scale collective resistance occurrences of the floating population, which maintains a stable social situation. The existence of large-scale "inside the city villages" is a deficiency of urbanization. Although some megalopolis, especially megalopolis of above 10 million people, have dispersed "villages" based on the floating population in urban center through urban relocation and transformation, some new outstretched cities are not yet actually aware that "villages" have dangers of forming collective resistance. Mixed habitation is beneficial for social integration, and divided habitation will possibly lead to social isolation. After the first generation of immigrant reach old age, the second generation of immigrant may manifest more collective social resistance.

E. *Gradually Reform the Household Register System*

The emphasis on household register system reform is to weaken the influence of social welfare system concerning the household register system. Currently, the household register is still the main system and policy barrier that prevents the floating population from becoming urban resident. Therefore, if household register system reform of big cities has difficulties, small and medium-sized towns and cities should unceasingly advance household register system reform based on local conditions during the "12th Five-year Plan," learn from the experiences of Zhejiang, and should also carry out institutional innovations from the generalized experiences of urban and rural integration development of Chongqing. In brief, household register reform is important, and is impossible not to do. Only through floating population's localization and becoming residents can consumer demand be driven; their domestic demand ability will be enhanced. Although the new rural areas still have positive significance to them, under the background of an empty-shell village, the phenomenon of off-farm workers is actually a big waste of social resources.

F. *Strengthen Vocational Training to the Floating Population*

Under the background where secondary vocational school is gradually popularized, to enhance the work skill of the floating population, professional training in the inflow areas should be considered. The emphasis on training is not through learning in the classroom, but should be on hand training, and fixed enterprise training center should be established. Urban governments must be integrate with the urban development strategy in the training of floating population work skill, and pay equal attention and jointly manage them. Problems from various regional trainings to off-farm workers in 2009 must be learned to prevent waste of funds and of fraud in training. Short-term and one-week training should be lengthened into medium and long-term training of about three months to enhance the work skill of the floating population, which enhances the international competitive power. Training in the construction of advanced manufacturing industry and advanced service industry in "Zhujiang Delta" and "Changjiang Delta" areas especially needs strict planning. Because, along with the regional transfer of industry, potential ability from this kind of training will also create opportunity for the development of central and western areas in the regional transfer of labors.

G. *Strengthen the Reasonable Operation of Land*

Population gathering caused by population shrinkage and population movement inevitably brings about a phenomenon of an empty shell in remote rural areas or the vanishing of remote villages. Therefore, local governments must pay attention to the phenomenon of abandonment of arable land in the mountainous areas, strengthen environmental protection and forest plantation, and carry out policies of returning land for farming and forestry; at the same time, must pay attention to disputes or contradictions from land circulation in the flatlands or mountainous areas. In the process of farmers becoming town dwellers in some areas around the cities, or after off-farm workers join the household register of small and medium-sized towns and cities, authorities should not take back their contracted land due to desire for instant benefit. It should be known that, the result of farmers with land becoming town dwellers is distinctly different from that of the West where farmers became town dwellers becaue they were deprived of land. Land is the essential security for farmers during the initial process of becoming a town dweller, and is the effective support for farmers during periods of economic fluctuation.

H. *Reform the Family Planning Policy*

Under the trend of population shrinkage, reforming the family planning policy into a policy where "one is not too little, two is just enough, and three is forbidden." Authorities must pay attention to the vulnerable nature brought by family population reduction to the family, must realize the negative influences of population shrinkage to domestic demand, must learn from the lessons of developed countries where population shrinkage and aging population pressure affected economic growth; at the same time, must earnestly pay attention to disproportion in distribution of public retirement resources and nursing organizations.

DEVELOPMENT AND CHANGES OF PUBLIC EXPENDITURE STRUCTURE IN CHINA

Huang Yanfen and Lin Fan

Abstract

China's social development is closely related with the transformation of national finance and construction of public finance. Since 1998, after the national finance conference established the reform goal of building the public finance frame, the public finance system has been unceasingly consummated, the fiscal expenditure has tended towards the livelihood of the people, and public services has become an important component and focus of the government fiscal expenditure.

I. *Evolution and Development of the Public Expenditure Structure in Recent Years*

During the period of the planned economy, the financial administration was "big and comprehensive," and the scope of expenditure was extremely widespread. The reform and opening in 1978 started the public transformation of the financial administration, which became especially intense after 1998, after the public financial administration became the strategic target of finance reform. This sped up the gradual reform of constructing the financial administration into the public financial administration, where China's public expenditure structure presents the following tremendous changes:

A. *The Proportion of Expenditure on Economic Construction in the Fiscal Expenditure has Reduced*

The "expenditure on economic construction" in the fiscal expenditure basically contained all productive expenditures, and they are basically divided into capital construction expenditure, funds to tap the potential of existing enterprises and three types of expenditure in science and technology, and allocation of circulating funds for enterprises, and so on. In terms of the proportion of expenditure on economic construction in fiscal expenditure, the proportion in gross fiscal expenditure reached as high as 64.08% in 1978, along with gradual deepening of reform and opening, this proportion dropped unceasingly, and reduced to 26.56% by 2006 (See Figure 13.1).[1] The declining trend indicated that the fiscal expenditure structure has made positive adjustment along with the advancement of market reform and readjustment of government functions; the proportion of investments used directly in the productive domain of financial resources has dropped, the government has gradually withdrawn from competitive projects, and the degree of intervening private product domain has reduced unceasingly. This is not only advantageous to control fiscal expenditure in its function of preventing extraneous government functions, but also make up for the lack of presence in public services and social enterprises due to limitations in money, which may strengthen the government's public service function effectively.

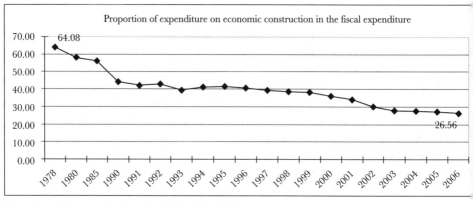

Data from "Finance Yearbook of China" in 2007.

Figure 13.1: Proportion of Expenditure on Economic Construction in the Fiscal Expenditure from 1978–2006 (%)

---

[1] Because the classification items of financial revenue and expenditure has been carried on the large reform according to "Notice of the Ministry of Finance on Printing and Distributing the Plan on Government Revenue and Expenditure Classification Reform" (Cai Yu [2006] No. 13) after 2007, the expenditure specification has changed, therefore, in this paper, data before and after 2006 are not compared.

B. *Swift Growth of Social Security and Welfare Expenditure After a Poor Start*

Since the 1990s, China has quickened the social security system reform. In terms of endowment insurance, "Decision on Establishing a Unified System of Basic Endowment Insurance for Enterprise Employees" issued by the State Council in 1997 has unified the measure of "integration of unified planning of individual accounts" of various regions, stipulated the unified payment proportion, individual accounts, measures on calculation and payment of basic pension and control measures, and has established the basic frame of basic endowment insurance for enterprise employees. In terms of medical insurance, the State Council issued "Decision on Establishing the System of Basic Medical Insurance for Urban Employees" in 1998, started full-scale reform to public expenses and the system of labor protection medical care, established the system of basic medical insurance for urban employees which covered all urban employers and their staff, integrated social unified planning payment of individual accounts, work-units and workers and staff. Since 2003, the medical security system has expanded to rural areas and urban non-employed residents, and pilot programs of the new rural cooperative medical system and of basic medical insurance for town dwellers has been carried out successively, which has gradually brought about comprehensive coverage of the medical security system.[2] In terms of minimum social security for urban dwellers, the State Council issued "Notice on Establishing the System of Minimum Social Security for Urban Dwellers in Whole Country" in 1997, and by the end of 2006, 22.4 million people were receiving minimum social security for urban dwellers, which had brought about coverage of basically all insurable people. In total, 2,133 counties (city) in 25 provinces (autonomous regions and municipalities) have implemented the rural minimum social security system, and insured persons have reached 15.09 million.[3]

The construction of the above social security systems reflected in the expenditure structure is that, social security expenditure and welfare expenditure were increased from 18.268 billion yuan 1996 to 436.178 billion yuan in 2006, a growth of 22.88 times! Its proportion in fiscal

---

[2] See Dong Keyong (董克用) and Guo Kaijun (郭开军): "China Social Security System Reform for 30 Years" published in "China Information" (《中国信息报》) on December 25, 2008.
[3] Data from "Finance Yearbook of China" in 2007.

expenditure grew from 2.3% in 1996 to 10.79% in 2006, and proportion in GDP grew from 0.26% in 1996 to 2.26% in 2006. Although
the data in 2007 and in 2008 cannot compare with ones before 2006,
we still see that expenditures on social security and welfare in 2007
and 2008 unceasingly maintained stable growth, its proportion in fiscal
expenditure rose respectively to 2.18% and 2.26%, and proportion in
GDP respectively reached 10.94% and 10.87% (See Table 13.1).

C. *The Proportion of Government Expenditure on Health in Fiscal Expenditure
has Reversed the Unceasing Downtrend before 2002, and the Proportion of
Government Expenditure on Healthcare Rises Quickly*

From 1985 to 2002, medical and health development was influenced
by the state-owned enterprise reform; the medical institution gradually
adopted the market principle, and some areas publically auctioned and
sold public health centers of villages and towns and local state-owned
hospitals. Although the absolute amount of government investment on
health increased year by year, the proportion of government expenditure on health in terms of total cost of health and in fiscal expendi-

Table 13.1: Expenditures on Social Security and Welfare and Its Proportion
in GDP and Fiscal Expenditure from 1996 to 2008

Year	Expenditures on social security and on welfare (hundred million Yuan)	Proportion in GDP (%)	Proportion in fiscal expenditure (%)
1996	182.68	0.26	2.30
1997	328.42	0.42	3.56
1998	595.63	0.71	5.52
1999	1197.44	1.34	9.08
2000	1517.57	1.53	9.55
2001	1987.40	1.81	10.51
2002	2636.22	2.19	11.95
2003	2655.91	1.96	10.77
2004	3116.08	1.95	10.94
2005	3698.86	2.01	10.90
2006	4361.78	2.07	10.79
2007	5447.16	2.18	10.94
2008	6804.29	2.26	10.87

Data from "Finance Yearbook of China" of related years.

ture actually dropped. The SARS event in 2003 directly exposed the problems of the public health sector, which raised the level of attention the government placed on public health, therefore the government increased investment to health sectors to consummate construction of public health, to strengthen research in prevention and cure of serious diseases and to enforce and supervise health laws. Table 13.2 shows the proportion of government expenditure on health in fiscal expenditure slightly increased from 4.12% in 2002 to 4.4% in 2006, and the proportion in the total cost of health increased from 15.7% in 2002 to 18.1% in 2006. The proportion of government expenditure on health in fiscal expenditure was unceasingly stabilized at above 4% in 2007 and 2008.

D. *Negative Situation where the Proportion of Educational Expenses in Fiscal Expenditure is Under Control, and the Rural Compulsory Educational Fund Security Mechanism is Comprehensively Implemented*

After the Asian financial crisis in 1997, as a result of insufficient domestic demand, the national economic growth slumped. In order to increase domestic demand in any way possible, the reform mentality

Table 13.2: Government Expenditure on Health and Its Proportion to Total Cost of Health and in Fiscal Expenditure from 1996 to 2008

Year	Government expenditure on health (hundred million Yuan)	Proportion in total cost of health (%)	Proportion in fiscal expenditure (%)
1996	461.61	17.0	5.82
1997	523.56	16.4	5.67
1998	590.06	16.0	5.46
1999	640.96	15.8	4.86
2000	709.52	15.5	4.47
2001	800.61	15.9	4.24
2002	908.51	15.7	4.12
2003	1116.94	17.0	4.53
2004	1293.58	17.0	4.54
2005	1552.53	17.9	4.58
2006	1778.86	18.1	4.40
2007	2271.7	20.4	4.56
2008	2757.04	–	4.41

Data from "Finance Yearbook of China" of related years; "Chinese Health Statistical Digest" in 2009.

of "education industrialization" was adopted in order to alleviate the
educational expenditure tension and expand domestic demand. Under
the influence of the mentality of "education industrialization," the proportion of educational expenses in fiscal expenditure started falling
starting in 1997, and dropped from 17.84% in 1996 to 13.39% in
2006. However, after 2001, the decrease in the proportion of educational expenses in the fiscal expenditure became stabilized at above
13% (See Figure 13.2). In 2007 and 2008, if calculated according to
the new specification of educational expenses, the proportion of educational expenses in the fiscal expenditure rose to 14.31% and 14.39%
respectively. The proportion of educational expenses in GDP was stabilized at about 2% from 1991 to 2006, and if calculated according to
the new specification of educational expenses, it rose in 2007 to 2.85%
and in 2008 to 2.997%.

It must be noted, the most prominent achievement in terms of educational fiscal expenditure is that in recent years compulsory educational fund security mechanism was comprehensively carried out in
rural areas, and the "sunlight" of public finance can shine in rural
areas. In 2006, according to the requirements of "Notice of the State
Council on Deepening the Reform of Rural Compulsory Educational
Fund Security Mechanism," in order to guarantee prompt and standard payment of central special fund for rural compulsory education, the Ministry of Finance formulated "Provisional Measures on

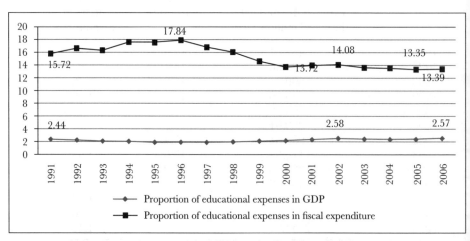

Figure 13.2: Proportion of Educational Expenses in GDP and in Fiscal Expenditure
from 1991 to 2006 (%)

the Management of the Payment of Central Special Fund for Rural Compulsory Educational Fund Security Mechanism Reform" and "Provisional Measures on the Accounting of Central Special Fund for Rural Compulsory Educational Fund Security Mechanism Reform." This policy, which exempts students of miscellaneous expenses and school fees and enhances the public expenditure security level, has been carried out throughout western regions 12 pilot counties in central regions, and 50.07 million students at the stage of rural compulsory education have enjoyed exemption of miscellaneous expenses and school fees.[4] In 2007, all students at the stage of rural compulsory education were excused of miscellaneous expenses and school fees, and were provided free textbooks; student boarders with economical burdened families were provided extra allowance for living expenses, public expenditure for elementary and middle schools and subsidy standards of school building maintenance costs were enhanced, the central financial administration disbursed 36.48 billion yuan, and local financial administrations also disbursed 32.3 billion yuan, where 150 million students and 7.8 million boarders benefited. In 2007, the central financial administration also budgeted to invest 3 billion yuan to implement rural boarding school construction projects, junior high school building modifications in central and western rural areas and modern remote education projects in rural elementary and middle schools.[5] Fiscal expenditure on education leans heavier towards rural compulsory education, which has reduced the disparity between urban and rural compulsory educational levels, and has enhanced the fair degree of education.

II. *New Changes of the Public Expenditure Structure in 2009*

In 2009, under the impact of the international financial crisis, as well as influences of domestic economic readjustments, China's economic and social development was faced with a great challenge. Under the severe international and domestic economic situation, the Central

---

[4] Data from "Finance Yearbook of China" in 2007.
[5] Data from "Finance Yearbook of China" in 2008.

Economic Working Conference determined the guidelines and over-all requirements for economic and social development in 2009. They were "to guarantee growth, to guarantee livelihood of the people, to expand domestic demand, and to readjust the structure," and the posi-tive financial policy shouldered the dual responsibility of reversing the economic downslide and guaranteeing the livelihood of the people. Under this situation, the public expenditure structure experienced new changes from January to September 2009.

A. *Characteristics of the Public Expenditure Structure from January to September 2009*

(1) *Most Vital to the Financial Policy—to Expand Government Investment*
To deal with the impact of the world financial crisis, and to realize fast steady economic development, in regards to implementation of a positive financial policy, expanding government investment was con-sidered as the means to promote domestic demand and to guarantee growth. "Key Emphasis in Work of the Ministry of Finance in 2009" placed "expanding government investment" at the top in positive financial policy measures, and pointed out need of "increasing central financial administration's investment in capital construction, mainly in agricultural infrastructure and in rural engineering constructions for people's livelihood, in the construction of security housings, and in the construction of education and medical and health etc., in post-earthquake rehabilitation and reconstruction, in energy conservation and pollutant discharge reduction and in ecological building, and to support enterprises' independent innovation, technological transforma-tion and development of a service industry, and construction of infra-structural facilities of railroad, road, airport and harbor etc." After the State Council released a 4 trillion yuan economic incentive plan, local governments of 24 provinces and municipalities proposed investment programs of nearly 18 trillion yuan, and investment projects gave priority to transportation infrastructure construction.[6] These policy measures were manifested in the fiscal expenditure structure where

---

[6] See Li Jingrui (李静睿): "Local Governments Releases the Investment Program of 18 Trillion Yuan, and Capital Source is under Attention" published in "Beijing News" on November 25, 2008.

expenditure on transportation, on environmental protection, and on agriculture, forestry and water conservancy had quickest growth speed in the previous year during the first three quarters of 2009, namely expenditure on transportation increased 98.597 billion yuan from the previous year, and grew 66.3%; expenditure on environmental protection increased 32.331 billion yuan from the previous year, and grew 56.4%; expenditure on agriculture, forestry and water conservancy increased 132.006 billion yuan from the previous year, and grew 51.2%.[7] This indicated that the government increased investments to railroad, road, airport, harbor, new energy, significant rectification projects and industries of environmental protection, as well as rural infrastructural construction, in 2009. The government expanded production scale, promoted employment, and brought about economic growth through increase in investment in infrastructure construction and other important projects.

(2) *Growth Speed of Education and Social Security Expenditures are Lower than that of Total Fiscal Expenditure*
From January to September 2009, growth speed of education and social security expenditures slowed down. Educational expenses increased 96.069 billion yuan from the previous year, and grew 17.7%, which was lower than the growth rate of 21.2% from the previous year; expenditure on social security and employment increased 77.975 billion yuan from the previous year, and grew 17.7%, which largely decreased from the previous year's growth rate of 40.4%. Taking into consideration that the annual expenditure arrangement is probably disproportioned, we also compared growth rate of expenditures on education, social security and employment from January to September 2009 with the annual growth rate in 2008. Table 13.3 shows that the growth rate of expenditures on those three items from January to September 2009 is lower than the annual ones in 2008. Because the growth rate of expenditures of these three items from January to September 2009 is lower than the growth rate of total fiscal expenditure, it is possible that the proportion of expenditures of those items in fiscal expenditure would drop in 2009.

---

[7] Data from "Financial revenue and expenditure in September 2009" at http://gks.mof.gov.cn/guokusi/zhengfuxinxi/tongjishuju/200910/t20091016_218908.html.

Table 13.3: Expenditures on Education, Social Security and Employment
from January to September 2009 and 2008

Time	Growth of educational expenses over previous years (%)	Growth of expenditure on social security and employment over previous years (%)	Growth of fiscal expenditure over previous years (%)
Jan.–Sept. 2009	17.7	17.7	24.1
Jan.–Sept. 2008	21.2	40.4	25.5
All 2008	26.5	24.9	25.7

Data from "Financial revenue and expenditure in September 2009" from the website
of the Ministry of Finance; "Financial revenue and expenditure in September 2008" at
http://finance.sina.com.cn/, http://www.drcnet.com.cn/DRCNET.Channel.Web/.

(3) *Although Growth Speed of Medical and Health Expenditure Compared to
Previous Years is Higher than that of Fiscal Expenditure from Previous Years,
Growth Speed has Slowed Down Over that of 2008*
In 2009, medical and health expenditure increased 47.749 billion yuan
from the previous year, and increased 30.5%,[8] a public service expenditure with quicker growth speed, and its swift growth was directly
caused by the "Opinions of the CPC Central Committee and the State
Council on Deepening the Reform of the Medical and Health Care
System" that was released in April 2009. The new round of medical
reform would establish and consummate the basic medical and health
care system covering urban and rural residents, and would take providing safe, effective, convenient, low-cost medical and health services
for the people as the overall objectives. Among them, the five items
of reform from 2009–2011 request the support of sufficient finance
investment,[9] and the execution of a series of policy measures, which
will lead to inevitably growth in medical and health expenditure in
2009 (See Table 13.4).

---

[8] Data from "Financial revenue and expenditure in September 2009" at http://gks
.mof.gov.cn/guokusi/zhengfuxinxi/tongjishuju/200910/t20091016_218908.html.
[9] See "Opinions of the CPC Central Committee and the State Council on Deepening the Reform of the Medical and Health Care System" (Zhong Fa (2009) No. 6).

Table 13.4: Expenditures on Medical and Health from January to September 2009 and 2008

Time	Growth of expenditure on medical and health over previous years (%)	Growth of fiscal expenditure over previous years (%)
Jan.–Sept. 2009	30.5	24.1
Jan.–Sept. 2008	35.8	25.5

Data from "Financial revenue and expenditure in September 2009" at website of the Ministry of Finance; "Financial revenue and expenditure in September 2008" at http://finance.sina.com.cn/, http://www.drcnet.com.cn/DRCNET.Channel.Web/.

For all that, the growth speed of medical and health expenditure from January to September 2009 was still lower than the growth rate in 2008 at 35.8%. At the same time, if we compare the growth rate of the expenditure on medical and health from two periods of time with that of fiscal expenditure from the previous years, we discover that, the growth rate of medical and health expenditure from January to September 2008 was 10.3 percentage points higher than that of fiscal expenditure from the previous years, but that from January to September 2009 was only 6.4 percentage points higher than that of fiscal expenditure from the previous years. This phenomenon explains that, the growth speed of the expenditure on medical and health from January to September 2009 slowed down from that of 2008.

B. *Reflections Regarding Characteristics of Public Expenditure Structure from January to September 2009*

What to think regarding changes in the public expenditure structure from January to September 2009? Our thoughts are as follows.

(1) *Emphasis on Active Government Investment Financial Policy has Intensified the Disproportion Between Investment and Consumption Growth*
In recent years, China follows the economic operation model of "high investment and low consumption;" the rate of investment always maintained steady increase, and rose from 36.4% in 2000 to 57.5% in 2008; on the contrary, the consumption rate was maintained somewhat low, and dropped from 61.1% in 2000 to 48.6% in 2008.[10] In 2009,

---

[10] "China Statistical Yearbook 2009" published by China Statistics Press in 2009.

to guarantee economic growth, emphasis from the Central Committee and other local governments of expanding government investment
certainly intensified the disproportioned situation between investment
and expansion where the economical operation was breeding huge
risk, which would have adverse effect to sustainable economic growth.
First, excessively high investment rate and excessively low consumption rate cause surplus in products, which leads to downward pressures
on product price, which then causes profit decrease for enterprises
and leads to increase in unemployment. Next, consumer demand is
the true demand, excessively low consumption rate and excessively
high investment rate often create insufficient domestic demand, and
force enterprises to seek outlets for surplus productivity and products;
they have to seek foreign demand in overseas markets which increases
export pressures, as well as the trade frictions, and the exterior risk
enhanced by the Renminbi revaluation pressure is strengthened.
Finally, excessively high investment rate and excessively low consumption rate, especially resident consumption rate, may cause investment
behavior to deviate from its consumption objective, thus cause investment to be difficult to sustain because of lacking strong support from
final consumption, which will then form major economic ups and
downs, which is disadvantageous for sustained stable healthy national
economic development. Therefore, in the coming period, the financial
policy should emphasize promotion of consumption, regard expansion
of domestic demand as the basic way of guaranteeing growth, and
regard improvement of people's livelihood as the starting point and
foothold of guaranteeing growth.

(2) *While Guaranteeing Growth, Financial Investment to Public Enterprises may
be Influenced*
For a long time, economic growth and development of public enterprises have been relatively unbalanced; "one long, another short." After
the public financial administration was officially put on the government's agenda in 1998, especially after the Third and Fourth Plenary
Session of the 11th Central Committee of the CPC, where one after
another guiding principles of "scientific development concept" and
strategic mission of "building the socialist harmonious society" were
proposed, China gradually enlarged overall investments to science &
technology, education, culture and health, where the development of
various public enterprises has made great progress. But, in 2009, to
deal with the impact of the world financial crisis, "guaranteeing an 8%

economic growth rate" became all levels of governments' most important objective, and some areas neglected the development of public enterprises in order to maintain economic growth, and the growth speed of education and social security expenditure from January to September 2009 was lower than that of total fiscal expenditure, to become two expenditures of slowest growth speed, and was lower than that of in 2008! Although it was higher than the growth rate of fiscal expenditure, the growth speed of expenditure on medical and health from January to September 2009 slowed down from that of 2008. At the same time, we must see that, expenditure on public services newly increased in 2009 was used massively in capital construction investment in the public service domain, and expenditure on public services placed emphasis on tangible capital, and not realistic human capital or social development service measures; in 2009, change in public expenditure structure seemed to return to old practices.

(3) *Increase the Proportion of Public Education Investment in Fiscal Expenditure* "China Program on Educational Reform and Development" promulgated as early as 1993 explicitly proposed that, "the proportion of financial educational appropriations in GNP will reach 4% at the end of the 20th century." This goal was originally set to reach an average level where educational expenses of developing countries accounted for 4.1% of GDP in 1991. The "10th Five-year Plan" and "11th Five-year Plan" also stressed again to "guarantee that the growth rate of financial educational appropriations is obviously higher than growth rate of ordinary financial revenue, and gradually cause the proportion of financial educational appropriations in GDP to reach 4%." But, nearly nine years passed in the new century, the "10th Five-year Plan" ended, and the "11th Five-year Plan" will expire in 2010m but, if calculated according to the new specifications of educational expenses in 2008, the proportion of public educational expenses in GDP rose merely to 2.997%; from January to September 2009, the growth speed of educational expenses slowed down, the educational expenses increased 96.069 billion yuan from the previous year, and grew 17.7%, which was not only obviously lower than the growth rate of 21.2% in 2008, but also lower than the growth rate of 24.1% in total fiscal expenditure from the previous year. Thus, it can be deduced that the proportion of educational expenses in the fiscal expenditure from January to September 2009 dropped! Education plays a vital role in the development of human resources for the entire society, and

human resource is one of most important economic development factors; simultaneously education also plays a tremendous role in promoting the advancement of science and technology and social progress. Therefore, increasing the proportion of public educational expenses in fiscal expenditure, and carrying it out relentlessly, is a difficult problem for all levels of governments.

III. *2010: Suggestions on the Policy of Consummating the Public Expenditure Structure and Expectations*

2010 is the last year for the "11th Five-year Plan" to be implemented. In order to consummate the public expenditure structure, to cause the financial policy to focus on improvement to the livelihood of the people and to strengthen the construction of public enterprises, while strengthening sustainable domestic economic growth, thus to bring about coordinated economic and social development, we give policy suggestions as follows.

A. *The Financial Policy Should go from Expansion of Investment to Expansion of Consumption*

When the Chinese economy presents steady recovery and gradual upward development trend, in order to reverse the situation of "growth depending on investment," the financial policy should shift from focus on expansion of investment into taking consumption promotion as the focus, improvement of people's livelihood as the starting point and foothold to guarantee growth, and expansion of consumption and domestic demand as the basic way to guarantee growth. Therefore, the optimization of the expenditure structure, the guarantee of and improvement to people's livelihood, and the increase of expenditures on education, medical and health, social security and employment, and housing project for low-income families etc. are one of most effective measures to expand domestic demand. At the same time, newly increased expenditure used in the public services domain should have high proportions in of investment in human capital and social development measures, which are practical and meet demand of human development; these expenditures should not be engrossed in capital construction investment, and not on public services that place emphasis on tangible capital. This way, the livelihood of the people can be improved, and domestic demand can be expanded to guarantee quality and endurance of economic growth, and a scientific development mentality can be manifested to promote coordinated economic and social development.

B. *Enhance Growth Speed of Education, Medical and Health, and Social Security Expenditures, and Guarantee Unceasing Rise of its Proportion in Fiscal Expenditure*

In 2009, although expenditures on education, medical and health, and social security maintained growth, the growth speed did not actually fulfill objectives because their proportion in the fiscal expenditure dropped from the data from January to September. With Chinese economic recovery in 2010, the people's demands of education, medical and health and social security etc. will further increase. In order to expand consumer demand, and to quicken public financial administration transformation, the growth speed of expenditures on education, medical and health and social security etc. should be enhanced, and its proportion in the fiscal expenditure should be guaranteed to rise unceasingly. Therefore, the public educational expenses should be increased, and the goal where the proportion of educational expenses in GDP reaches 4% should be realized as soon as possible; medical and health system reform should be supported, the share of government expenditure should be increased, and the government's responsibility in the medical and health domain should be strengthened to lighten residents' medical burden and to raise mid and low-income earners' welfare level; the system of basic endowment insurance for enterprise employees which integrates social unified planning with individual accounts should be advanced and consummated, the coverage of basic medical insurance for urban employees should be expanded, the new rural cooperative medical system should be comprehensively pushed as soon as possible throughout all rural areas, and the costs of fund-raising standard and of financial subsidy standard should be raised, which reduce people's worry about uncertainty in the future, and enhance consumer confidence.

C. *Build the Rural Public Service System*

In the process of building the socialist new countryside, providing public services and public products, which meet primary demand of rural residents, is a very important part. But, for a long time, providing rural public services was absent, and rural infrastructures of road, potable water and sewage treatment are obsolete; the rural social security system is not yet perfect, and the majority of rural population is unable to have basic social security and endowment insurance; education and medical service levels are more primitive than in the city. Weakness in rural public service investment has enlarged the gap between urban and rural public services so that rural populations have a difficult time obtaining basic education, medical services, social security etc., which has bereaved their right for individual development and right to survival. The gap is disadvantageous in comprehensively promoting the quality of the rural population, and even more disadvantageous for harmonious social development. Therefore, the rural public service system must be built as soon as possible. In 2010, Chinese economy enters the period of recovery development, under the dual background of building a harmonious society and socialist new countryside, establishing the rural public service system and realizing the integration of urban and rural public services will become an urgent task.

D. *Advance the Innovation of Financial Control System, and Effectively Resolve Basic-level Governments' Financial Difficulties*

County-level governments, China's basic organ of political power with self-contained functions, has a special position, which forms a connecting link between the city and rural areas, and communicates with "various industries or systems" ("条" Tiao) and "various administrative regions" ("块" Kuai). In terms of present intergovernmental responsibility arrangement of financial revenue and expenditure, the county-level government bears the main responsibility of providing basic public services, but its financial resources are very limited, especially rural expenses of taxation reform pushed since 2000 cancelled the butchery tax, fees for unified management of township public undertakings and tax on special agriculture, and reduced and remitted until all agricultural taxes were cancelled, which has had significant influence to rural county and township governments' financial sources, causing county-level governments, especially the ones in central and western regions to be in financial difficult situations, which has seriously hindered the equalization of local basic public services. To effectively alleviate basic-level governments' financial difficulty, to enhance the basic-level government's ability of providing public services, and to promote urban and rural integration, pilot reform of financial control of county directly under the provincial government should be advanced unceasingly in 2010, and simultaneously the strength of general transfer payment should be increased, and the county-level basic financial resource security mechanism should be gradually established to effectively resolve basic-level governments' financial difficulties, and to enhance basic-level government's ability to provide public services.

CHINESE WORKER SITUATION AND
LABOR RELATIONS IN 2009

Qiao Jian

I. *Present Situation of the Labor Stratum*

A. *Worker's Employment Pressure has been Alleviated to a Certain Extent*

After experiencing the deceleration of GDP growth at the beginning of 2009, the Chinese economy is gradually recovering. GDP was 21,781.7 billion yuan in the first three quarters of 2009, which grew 7.7% from the previous year if calculated according to comparable price, and sped up 0.6 percentage points from the first half year. In terms of various quarters, it grew 6.1% in the first quarter, 7.9% in the second quarter, and 8.9% in the third quarter. With the push in economic growth speed, workers' employment pressure has been slightly alleviated. In February 2009, Chen Xiwen, Director of the Office of Central Rural Work Leading Group said at the State Council Press Conference that according to findings of sampling investigation of the Ministry of Agriculture in 15 migrant worker export provinces, out of 130 million Chinese migrant workers, 15.3% of people lost their jobs or could not a job. According to the above proportion, it can be calculated that about 20 million migrant workers lost their job or could not find one and returned to their native villages because of economic distress.[1] According to the joint investigation and study of the Ministry of Human Resources and Social Security with the National Bureau of Statistics of China, by the end of 2008, in total 225 million off-farm workers got employment in the whole country, in which 140 million were off-farm workers who worked in other areas. Before the Spring Festival of 2009, about 50% of off-farm workers returned to their native village, 70 million people, where 18 million people needed

---

[1] Chen Xiwen (陈锡文): Off-farm worker who did not seek a job and have returned to their native village are about 20 million, and the government deals it with positively at http://news.xinhuanet.com/politics/2009-02/02/content_10750425.htm.

to solve the problem of employment. After the Spring Festival, 95%
of off-farm workers returned to the city to get employment, and the
other 5% (3.5 million people) got employment in rural areas or nearby
and returned to their native village to establish a business.[2] By the
beginning of July 2009, the employment rate of graduates was 68%
(4.15 million people), 30% of graduates needed to get employment,
and including those graduates without a job since the previous year,
in total there were about 3 million people. At the same time, because
of industrial restructuring and excessively low labor cost or off-farm
workers' vocational skill not being up to job level, some coastal cities
even had a phenomenon of "labor shortage" ("民工荒" Min Gong
Huang).

B. *The Labor Relation is still Unstable, and Labor Disputes still Occur
Frequently*

Since the second half of 2008, under the implementation of the "Labor
Contract Law," "Employment Promotion Law," and "Law on Mediation and Arbitration of Labor Disputes" and exacerbation of the economic crisis, the contradictions and disputes where enterprises reduced
staff, went bankrupt and had labor disputes etc. increased. All levels of
labor dispute arbitration institutions altogether accepted 693,000 cases
of labor dispute in 2008, and mediated 237,000 cases in the current
period. The registered cases of labor dispute grew 98.0% from the previous year, and involved 1,214,000 workers. Among them, there were
22,000 cases of collective labor dispute, and involved 503,000 workers.
In the first three quarters of 2009, all levels of labor dispute arbitration institutions altogether registered 519,000 cases of labor dispute,
which dropped 0.2% from the previous year, but was still a lot. In
total, 496,000 cases were concluded in current period, a 14% increase
from the previous year, and the case settlement rate was 95.6% in the
current period.[3]

Under the present situation of unstable enterprise labor relations,
social security departments of various regions implemented the Labor
Contract Law and dealt with the financial crisis to strengthen instruc-

---

[2] Progress of Chinese employment and social security work in the first half of 2009
at websites of the Chinese government on August 4, 2009.
[3] The press conference of the Ministry of Human Resources and Social Security in
the third quarter of 2009 at www.people.com.cn on October 23, 2009.

tion and services to enterprise recruitment and use, studied and drafted the supporting regulations and rules, such as the provisions on enterprise staff reduction for economical efficiency and special provisions on service dispatch etc. The Ministry of Human Resources and Social Security along with departments concerned formulated, printed and distributed "Guiding Opinions on Further Normalize National Enterprise Chiefs Salary Management." Various regions promptly issued salary guidelines and the labor market wage price in 2009 to prevent and resolve problems of enterprises owing workers money. In the coordination of collective labor relations, after the financial crisis broke out, all-China Federation of Trade Unions vigorously launched "joint promissory action" among with trade unions, staff and enterprises, which urged enterprises not to reduce salaries and not to reduce staff, and emphasized jointly overcoming the hardship and joint development.

C. *Smooth Progress in Workers' Social Security*

Because of distress in the international market, the advancement of social security became essential to push domestic demand, thus it was valued by governments of various regions. Its characteristics: First, the overall situation of coverage expansion and premium collection was good. By the end of September 2009, the insured population in basic endowment insurance and in insurance of basic medical, unemployment, industrial injury and maternity was 228.57 million, 362.95 million, 124.92 million, 144.84 million and 103.14 million respectively, which increased 9.66 million, 44.73 million, 920,000 and 6.97 million and 10.6 million persons respectively over that from the end of the previous year. From January to September, collection income of five social insurance funds reached 953.4 billion Yuan, which increased 15.4% from the previous year. By the end of September, national off-farm workers that participated in basic endowment insurance and in insurance of basic medical, industrial injury and unemployment were respectively 24.64 million, 42.92 million, 52.81 million and 15.63 million persons, which respectively increased 480,000 persons, 260,000 persons, 3,390,000 persons and 140,000 persons from that at the end of the previous year.[4]

---

[4] Ditto.

258   QIAO JIAN

Second, social security is paid in full amount on time. From January to September 2009, basic pension of 581.5 billion yuan were provided in full amount to enterprise retirees on time, which grew 16.4% from the previous year, and basic pension of enterprise retirees was provided in full amount on time for 69 months continuously. At the end of September, in total 2,484,000 persons drew out unemployment insurance, the unemployment insurance fund disbursed 21.91 billion yuan, which grew 31% from the previous year; medical, industrial injury and maternity insurance can be paid according to the provisions, and the three items of social insurance altogether paid 208.4 million yuan from January to September, which grew 29.9% from the previous year.

Third, the social insurance system is further consummated. The study and revision of "Law of Social Insurance (Draft)" and the open opinion solicitation work of "Regulations on Employment Injury Insurance (Revision Draft)" were supported, and "Provisions on Social Insurance File Management (trial)" was formulated and issued. The advancement of provincial-level unified planning of basic endowment insurance has been quickened, at present 28 provinces have established provincial-level unified planning systems; departments concerned along with the Ministry of Finance study the plan on readjusting basic pension of enterprise retirees in 2010. The serviceable range of unemployment insurance fund should be expanded; the work of unemployment insurance in aiding enterprises to stabilize operating post has made positive progress, 7 eastern provinces and cities continue the pilot program. The system of medical insurance for town dwellers has been spread comprehensively, and policies allowing retirees from bankrupt enterprises to participate in medical insurance has been smoothly advanced. The State Council continued the pilot work of the new rural social endowment insurance, and the pilot work of new rural endowment insurance has been officially started throughout the whole country.

In addition, carrying out the measures of "five kinds of postponed payment and four kinds of reduction in premium rate" to enterprises has made preliminary progress, which has lightened the burden for enterprises, but simultaneously brings hidden troubles for the future.

D. *Workers' Vocational Safety Improves*

In the first half of 2009, as a result of a need to further safety in production, as well as due to the impact of the economic crisis to enterprise production operations, national safety in production maintained a development trend of overall stabilization and improvement. In the first half of the year, in total 186,775 accidents occurred and 36,370 people died, which was a decrease of 32,787 accidents and 5,115 people from the previous year, and dropped 14.9% and 12.3% respectively. Among them, in coal mines, there were 749 accidents, where 1,175 people died, a 204 accident and 265 people decrease from the previous year, and dropped 21.4% and 18.4% respectively. Among them, the number of major accidents and casualties assumed a declining trend.[5]

II. *The Impact of the Economic Crisis to China's Labor Relation and its Characteristics*

According to viewpoints from American scholars, the primary cause of the international financial crisis is the surplus capital that flowed into the United States from Asia and the low-interest rate policy pushed by the Federal Reserve, as well as the real estate bubble along with low-interest rate, the positive mortgage loan marketing and lax supervision, the financial organs' short-term profit goals and high-risk loan policies, as well as American low-savings ratio and banks' high asset-liability ratio.[6] But the impact it has had to China is mainly in its entity economy, and greatly has influenced industrial production, and therefore the economic crisis in China is manifested in the influence of surplus capacity to the enterprise labor relations as follows.

First, the financial crisis causes all kinds of Chinese enterprises to encounter unprecedented difficulty in operation. In terms of state-owned enterprises, the national enterprises' business income grew 17.9% from the fourth quarter of 2008, and the profit dropped 34.1%. From January to April 2009, the national enterprises' business income dropped 9.2%, and profit dropped 36%. In 2008 the local state-owned holding enterprises' business income grew 18.9%, and gross profit dropped 24%. From January to April 2009, the local

---

[5] See the national basic situation on safety in production in the first half of 2009 and the analysis on the situation and key work in the second half of 2009 at www .chinasafety.gov.cn on July 20, 2009.

[6] Richard A. Posner: Pages 13–15 of "*A Failure of Capitalism—the Crisis of '08 and the Descent into Depression*" published by Peking University Press in August, 2009.

state-owned holding enterprises' business income dropped 8.4%, and
profit dropped 58.1%. Under the influence of industrial monopoliza-
tion, some areas and industries presented the effect where the privately
operated economy was extruded. Besides the large-scale private enterprises, most middle and small-scale private enterprises lacked the core
technologies and independent brand, and competitive power in the
market environment of fierce fluctuation. The impact of the financial
crisis is especially remarkable to foreign-funded enterprises, and it is
mainly manifested as follows: the foreign merchant investment ability dropped, export-oriented enterprises' order forms greatly reduced,
enterprises had financial strain, enterprise operation cost rose, and
market demand shrank, and so on.[7]

Second, export-processing enterprises' production and operation are
insufficient or production is stopped which causes reduction in staff,
or disguised reduction in staff. According to Guangdong Province's
investigation, in the Zhujiang Delta area, approximately 20% of total
number of enterprises investigated shut down, gave staff a long vacation, or went bankrupt. Manufacture enterprises accounted for 72.2%,
and under 300-person small and medium-sized enterprises accounted
for 75.2%; in Guangdong Province, from October 2008 to the end
of May 2009, more than 10,300 large-scale enterprises reduced staff
by 722,500 people. Although some enterprises had order forms, they
would rather lose money than continue with production after they
discovered the circumstance was bad.[8]

Third, enterprise recruitment is cautious, and the proportion of
flexible recruitment such as service dispatch etc. has increased. Investigation from the Enterprise Confederation showed that, under the
impact of the financial crisis, sales revenue dropped, the proportion
of many enterprises' recruitment cost increased, and the personal cost
ratio of some enterprises reached above 25%. Therefore, the overwhelming majority of enterprise recruitment demand reduced, and
recruitment was cautious. Under this background, many enterprises
did everything possible to replace the use of casual labor to reduce the

---

[7] Wang Yijie (王亦捷): The analysis on labor relations of enterprises of various
ownerships and countermeasure suggested under the financial crisis, and the paper of
international academic seminar for labor relations and laborers' rights and interests
under global economic crisis in Guangzhou in November 2009.
[8] The record of the forum for new changes of labor relations under the situation of
financial crisis and the countermeasure research in Beijing on June 18, 2009.

pressure on labor cost through the control or reduction of official staff, which increased the complexity and instability of labor relations. It is estimated by All-China Federation of Trade Unions that, there were about 27 million laborers of service dispatch; the Ministry of Human Resources and Social Security estimated about 15 million, and they have become the mainstream recruitment pattern in some industries.

Fourth, some enterprises reduce salaries or do it in disguised form, the situation of being in arrears increases, and delay in paying salary as well as 'escape' situations occur. Some enterprises directly reduced the wage standard, some enterprises reduced the staff's income in disguised form through enhancement of standard of production quota or by reducing related welfare, and some enterprises reduced the labor costs indirectly through methods such as extension of time for rest, vacations and on-the-job training etc. For example, foreign-funded enterprises in Dalian Development Zone took the means of staff's mutual adjustment between teams and groups, workshops, even factories, limited overtime work or did not arrange overtime work, or implemented policies such as "work for four days, rest for three days," "work for three days, rest for four days" and "half month or a month-long vacation," and during rest period, staff were paid 60–80% of normal wages.

Fifth, the working system of integrated computing work hours is implemented. The working system of integrated computing work hours has broken the fixed work hours of 8 hours per day and 40 hour per week, which is advantageous for enterprises to quickly arrange staff's work and off time. Under the situation of the financial crisis, after the enterprise's reduction of order form and of expectation, the compatibility of normal work hours working system was challenged seriously, and the number of enterprises that applied to implement the working system of integrated computing work hours increased massively. Some local governments have carried out investigations to the examination system of special work hours according to the actual demand of economic development, which have solved the problem of unbalanced, unstable operating time, and have guaranteed enterprises' ordered production operations.

Sixth, lack of social security for personnel has increased, and disputes involved with payment of social security premium have increased. Difficult enterprise operation and the decrease in paying capacity, along with discontentment of some enterprises with the progress of social insurance system construction, led to the situation of lag in social insurance premium payment or intermitted payment. According to investigations from the Enterprise Confederation, most enterprises reflected that the burden of social security was too great. At present, the sum total expense rate of social security and public accumulation fund for housing construction paid by enterprises for staff in average accounts for 40–50% of staff's total wages. If staff's individual payment expense rate and individual income tax is included, some enterprises have paid more than 70%, and this proportion has even surpassed levels of some developed countries. At present the urban and rural binary system and the regional division of social security are serious, migrant workers, especially off-farm workers, find it difficult to enjoy local social security, especially endowment insurance, unemployment insurance and public accumulation fund for housing construction because they do not have the local household register. When these migrant workers return to their native village or get inter-provincial employment, the social security premium paid by the enterprise for them not only cannot be transferred along with the worker, but also cannot be returned to the enterprise, but is swallowed up by the social insurance fund. This is a wasted expenditure for enterprises, moreover the staff is not willing to pay, therefore the insured enthusiasm of enterprise and staff is dampened greatly.[9]

Seventh, difficultly in employment and protection of rights and interests of off-farm workers has increased. On one hand, after the financial crisis, provinces that originally took in a big inflow of laborers release a massive number of external off-farm workers, for example, 439,600 employees reduced by the enterprises of Guangdong Province came from other provinces, which accounted for 60.8% of all staff reduced, where off-farm workers who were engaged in the low-end industry and simple work were most impacted; On the other hand, some labor output provinces presented the situation where off-farm workers returned to their native village and stayed there, which brought pressure of structural supply exceeding demand for the local labor market. Under the background of unemployment and difficulty finding employment,

---

[9] Wang Yijie: The analysis on labor relations of enterprises of various ownerships and countermeasure suggested under the financial crisis, from the paper of international academic seminar for labor relations and laborers' rights and interests under global economic crisis in Guangzhou in November, 2009.

it is difficult for off-farm workers to obtain effective protection for their rights and interests.[10]

Eighth, covert illegal acts, which dodge labor laws, have increased. After encountering the crisis, many enterprises chose the means of "soft reduction in staff," such as salary reduction, change of operating post, and reassignment of working place etc., without consultation between labor and management, which led to resignation by the worker at his own initiative; some enterprises took the massive use of service dispatch labors to dodge the use of labor contract workers, even for the purpose of paying less social insurance premium and of avoiding labor supervision through dispatch to foreign lands and buying insurance in strange areas; staff who wanted to take leave also tried to let the enterprise propose termination of labor contract by working slowly or sabotaging production tools etc.[11]

Ninth, labor dispute cases have increased largely, the proportion of group dispute cases has increased, the degree of conflict between labor and capital has intensified, and violence and non-rational ingredients in group events have increased. Under the superimposition of the implementation of new "Labor Contract Law," "Employment Promotion Law" and "Law on Mediation and Arbitration of Labor Disputes" and of economic crisis exacerbation, the contradictions and disputes where enterprises reduce staff, go bankrupt, and have the labor disputes etc. have increased. For example, in 2008, gross labor dispute cases accepted by the Zhejiang Province Labor Dispute Arbitration Institutions grew 76% from the previous year, in which the cases of payment for labor dispute accounted for 46.3%. Sichuan labor dispute arbitration institutions accepted 5,869 cases in the first quarter of 2009, which grew nearly 23% from the previous year. The labor disputes of Sichuan state-owned enterprises doubled from the previous year. Meanwhile, conflict between contending parties has enhanced greatly, and some areas presented extreme behaviors such as workers jumping off the building and murder etc., for example, the malignant case where Dongguan staff Liu Hanhuang (刘汉黄) killed two

---

[10] Sun Qunyi (孙群义): Thoughts about China's economic crisis and changes of labor relations, from the paper of international academic seminar for labor relations and laborers' rights and interests under global economic crisis in Guangzhou in November 2009.

[11] The record of the forum for new changes of labor relations under the situation of financial crisis and the countermeasure research in Beijing on June 18, 2009.

senior managers of Taiwan-owned enterprise as a result of wanting a raise, the event of off-farm worker Zhang Haichao (张海超) where he "opened his chest to examine the lung" to prove he had suffered from occupational disease, the event that Jilin Tonghua Iron & Steel Group Co. Ltd. staff ganged up on General Manager, Chen Guojun (陈国君), and killed him because of stockholder's rights adjustment, the event where more than 30 people of Hainan threw incendiary bombs, which caused injury to 12 persons, in asking for salaries, the event where Fuji Kang, a 25 year-old staff, jumped off a building to commit suicide, and the event where a worker of Gou Street Liao Shikai (廖世锴) who was discontented with long-term overtime work in the factory jumped off a building and died, and so on. These all indicated the opposition to labor-capital contradictions and labor-administration contradictions have enhanced.

Tenth, the short-term policy "postponed payment of five kinds of social insurance premium, reduction of four kinds of social insurance premium rate, three subsidies, and two consultations" etc. released by the labor security department to alleviate burdens for the enterprises during crisis may leave behind hidden troubles for the coordination of labor relations after economic resurgence. "Postponed payment of five kinds of social insurance premium" refers to enterprises in difficulty that are incapable of paying the social insurance premium temporarily are allowed to postpone the payment of five social insurance premiums, retirement, medical service, unemployment, industrial injury and child-bearing, under certain conditions; "reduction of four kinds of social insurance premium rate" refers to the reduction of four kinds of social insurance premium rate except endowment insurance at specific stages; "three subsidies" refers to using social insurance subsidy, post subsidy and unemployment insurance fund for the enterprises in difficulty to stabilize jobs, as well as to give subsidy using special employment fund for enterprises in difficulty to launch on-the-job training for employees; "two consultations" refer to, when enterprises in difficulty have to lay off staff because of economic hardship, for those who are truly incapable to pay economic considerations, on basis of the legal equal consensus between the enterprise and the trade union or the staff, the agreement for payments by installments or payment of economic considerations by other ways may be signed. These policies may help maintain enterprises' survival and development during times of crisis, but possibly also initiate inflation and reduction of social security paying ability etc., which will bring hidden troubles in terms of labor disputes in the future.

Generally speaking, the economic crisis has increased difficulties in mediating and handling labor relations. Because of the superimposed effect of the crisis and of the implementation of new labor law, labor-capital benefit are obviously opposed, the labor-administration contradiction becomes increasingly prominent, the means where workers and management dodge the laws becomes increasingly covert, and cases of labor dispute and illegal cases largely increase, which increased the work and difficulty of mediating and handling labor relations. In addition, means to handle labor dispute and labor supervision organizations lack strength, thus the pressure on mediation of labor relations and of stability maintenance sharply increased. On the other hand, the financial crisis did not transform into a serious crisis for labor-capital relationship or cause a huge labor movement.[12] From China's experiences, it is acts where the government and all-China Federation of Trade Unions impelled and urged mutual tolerance, understanding, concession and compromise between labor and management, which helped to overcome the times of hardship. Facing the financial crisis, various regions created and accumulated experiences from mutual understanding and concession between labor and management, and jointly pulled through the difficulty; for example, the trade union widely launched "joint promissory action" amongst enterprises and staff to guarantee that operating posts were not reduced, wage income did not decrease, and staff understood and supported the flexible work hours, flexible wage and flexible recruitment measures taken by the enterprises temporarily.

III. *Labor Legal System and Protection of Laborer's Rights and Interests Face a New Test*

A. *Labor Relation Policies to Deal with the Crisis*

Since the end of 2008, to deal with the financial crisis, the State Council and various ministries and commissions released a series of policy documents, policies of finance and currency to increase investment for expansion of domestic demands, measures on stabilizing employment posts and labor relations, which mainly strengthened the flexibility

---

[12] In November, 2009, US Cornell University School of Industrial and Labor Relations Dean Professor Harry Katz also expressed similar viewpoint when he visited China.

of social insurance system and of labor standard readjustment, and helped enterprises stabilize employment and to lessen reducing staff. These policies include "Notice of the State Council on Doing a Good Job in Employment under the Current Economic Situation,"[13] "Notice of the State Council General Office on Strengthening Graduates' Employment Work," "Notice on the Issues concerning Doing a Good Job in Off-farm workers' Employment After Spring Festival" of the Ministry of Human Resources and Social Security, "Notice on Taking Positive Measures to Reduce the Enterprise Burden and to Stabilize the Employment Situation" of the Ministry of Human Resources and Social Security, the Ministry of Finance and the State Administration of Taxation, "Guiding Opinions on Dealing with Current Economic Situation and Stabilizing the Labor Relations" of the Ministry of Human Resources and Social Security, All-China Federation of Trade Unions and the China Enterprise Confederation, and "Opinions on Thorough Advancing 'Joint promissory action'" of All-China Federation of Trade Unions, and so on. The main contents of these policies are as follows.

First, within 2009, social insurance premiums in retirement, medical service, unemployment, industrial injury and child-bearing are to be reduced in stages to lighten the payment burden of enterprises in difficulty and the insured persons' premium burden.

Second, enterprises in difficulty that are incapable of paying the social insurance premium temporarily are allowed to postpone the payment of five social insurance premiums within 2009 and less than 6 month-long deadlines.

Third, regulation and early-warning signs of unemployment; state-owned enterprises are encouraged to lessen staff reduction.

Fourth, the unemployment insurance fund and the special fund of employment are used; enterprises in difficulty are supported and encouraged to launch staff's on-the-job training, shift-work and consultative salary etc. to stabilize staff, and to guarantee that they do not reduce staff. The unemployment insurance fund may be used in paying the subsidy for social insurance and post subsidy.

---

[13] See Notice of the State Council on Doing a Good Job in Employment under the Current Economic Situation, at http://www.lawinfochina.com/law/display.asp?db=1&id=7473.

Fifth, readjustment of enterprise minimum wage standard is postponed temporarily. Enterprises with the right conditions and advanced-technology service outsourcing enterprises are guided to implement the integrated computing work hours and the indefinite work hour system.

Sixth, government investment is increased massively, and a 4 trillion yuan two-year investment plan is implemented. Among them, the Central government planned to increase investment of 1.18 trillion yuan to implement structural tax reduction, and to expand domestic demand; industrial readjustment and promotion plan is implemented widely to enhance overall competitive power of national economy; independent innovation is advanced vigorously, and technical support is strengthened to enhance stamina of development; social security level is increased, urban and rural employment is expanded, and development of public enterprises is promoted.

Seventh, labor and management are actively supported and encouraged to work together to stabilize the employment situation. All levels of Enterprise Confederations should jointly with related enterprise organizations guide and encourage enterprises to earnestly undertake social responsibility, and make efforts not to reduce staff. All levels of trade union organizations should vigorously launch the "joint promissory action" among trade union, staff and enterprise, and guide the staff to understand and support the enterprises on measures of flexible work hours, on-the-job training and consultative salary etc., mobilize the staff to offer opinion on enterprise development, to diligently raise labor productivity, to reduce the production and operation costs, and to jointly overcome the times of hardship and to help design development along with the enterprise.

Eighth, enterprises are impelled to speed up the establishment of a collective negotiation mechanism. Difficult enterprises in production operations may take measures on flexible work hours, on-the-job training and consultative salary etc. through collective negotiation with staff, including off-farm worker, to deal with the current economic hardship, and to stabilize employment posts and labor relations.

Ninth, instruction and management of staff reduction for enterprises in difficult with economical efficiency is strengthened, and the enterprise behavior of staff reduction is normalized to maintain staff's legitimate rights and interests. Enterprises may sign agreements on payments of economic considerations by installments or by other methods when implementing staff reduction for economical efficiency.

Tenth, the problem of delay in wage payment amongst enterprises is actively prevented and handled properly. The wage security money system is further established, and the implementation scope of wage security money system is gradually expanded.

Eleventh, the communication and mediation system of settling major issues concerning labor relations is established and consummated. The emergency mechanism for mediation and handling of labor relations should be established and consummated, experiences from handling group events initiated by labor relations in recent years should be earnestly summarized, and serious group events initiated because enterprises are incapable of paying wages or abscond after back pay etc. should be handled properly.

In addition, the government implements a series of policy measures for off-farm workers who return to their native village, for example, guarantee the land contracting rights and interests of off-farm workers who return to their native village, and strengthen off-farm workers' skill training and vocational education. Some labor export areas stipulated that off-farm workers who return to native village and fail to get employment for over 3 months will be supported by the local governments for no longer than half a year; the local governments may give the unemployment benefit according to 70% of minimum wage standard.

The Ministry of Human Resources and Social Security emphasized that, under the situation of the financial crisis, there must be focus around the objectives of the Central Committee, "to guarantee growth, to guarantee livelihood of the people, to guarantee social stability," transform the habitual work mentality of labor security supervision and rights protection at the swift economic growth time from "one emphasis" into "two equal attentions," namely transform from emphatically maintaining workers' rights and interests into paying equal attention to maintenance of workers' rights and interests and promotion of enterprise development, and paying equal attention to maintenance of workers' basic rights and interests and long-term benefits, and proposed the slogan of "flexible law enforcement."[14]

---

[14] An official interpretation of "flexible law enforcement" is that it emphatically establishes multi-channel open mediation net, and settles disputes with the flexible way in the basic units.

B. *Influence to the Labor Legal System and Protection of Laborers' Rights and Interests*

The guiding principle and policy spirit of competent administrative department has had enormous influence to the law-enforcement environment of the labor legal system. The questions are brought, namely whether the labor law formulated during the upward period of economic growth can apply to the downward period of economic crisis? Under the background of crisis, are the labor administration departments and the local governments authorized to change the standards and criterion for labor security law-enforcement supervision, even violate the "interpretations" of law and implementation? From the practical situation, some areas released "authority files," which interprets the labor law beyond their authority, and some were trying to suppress the workers' behaviors to legally maintain their rights, where the protection of laborers' rights and interests faced new problems.

First, "Labor Contract Law" is beyond their authority. In order to adjust to the economic crisis, the implementation of this law encountered unprecedented resistance; many people were formerly discontented with the concerned provisions of "Labor Contract Law," and then all sorts of adverse effects brought by the economic crisis were blamed for the implementation of this law. This time, not only did entrepreneur representatives and some representatives of educational circles "not think highly of" ("唱衰" Chang Shuai) the new law, but some heads of local governments and leaders of labor administration departments and judges did as well.

Next, some areas did not consider the change of resident consumer price index, and were forced to suspend the readjustment of minimum wage standard. The Ministry of Human Resources and Social Security issued a notice on November 17, 2008 after the financial crisis broke out, and proposed to postpone the readjustment of enterprise minimum wage standard according to the economic situation and the enterprises' practical considerations, and various regions also suspended readjustment of the minimum wage.

Third, "Law on Mediation and Arbitration of Labor Disputes" is interpreted and executed in such a way that workers' rights and interests are damaged. For example, Guangdong Provincial Higher People's Court and Guangdong Province Labor Dispute Arbitration Committee printed and distributed "Guiding Opinions on Certain Issues that Apply to 'Law on Mediation and Arbitration of Labor Disputes' and 'Labor Contract Law'," and Articles 1 & 2 of the Guiding Opinions have reduced the acceptance scope of labor dispute case stipulated in "Law on Mediation and Arbitration of Labor Disputes;" for example, it thought that not paying the social security belonged to labor dispute, which removed the circumstance of "not paying the full amount." In regards to the time limit of arbitral procedure of case closing within 45 days stipulated in "Law on Mediation and Arbitration of Labor Disputes," Article 6 ranks "case listing" as the cause of ceasing, and stipulates that, when worker brings a complaint to court, the worker must submit "the voucher issued by the Labor Dispute Arbitration Committee that has accepted his/her application and the certificate that states the case has not been heard," and "the certificate that states the complaint has not been ruled," which shows a discrepancy in the legislation spirit of the "Law on Mediation and Arbitration of Labor Disputes." Similarly, Article 7 stipulates that " 'three days' and 'five days' stipulated in "Law on Mediation and Arbitration of Labor Disputes" all refer to working days," which also violated the provisions of "Law of Civil Procedure," which creates a situation where labor dispute cases are delayed in being handled.

Moreover, the pre-mediation procedure is man-made, to lengthen the time for workers to maintain their rights and interests, and mediation is done based on worker' concessions. "Law on Mediation and Arbitration of Labor Disputes" and the law of civil procedure etc. stipulate voluntary mediation, and "where parties are not willing to mediate, mediation fails, or the mediation agreement is reached but not fulfilled, an application for arbitration may be made to the labor dispute arbitration commission." But, to delay the peak of "blowout" of labor dispute cases and to reduce the workload of labor dispute arbitration, some areas forced pre-mediation "fast dispute settlement, convenient for parties" procedures, and the Arbitration Committee did not register labor dispute without the mediation procedure. Besides some cases where the parties wish for mediation to be settled through this procedure, other parties must follow the long procedure of "mediation" of "arbitration, first instance and second instance." Moreover, facing the statistical high mediation rate, according to related investigations, besides a few special cases, especially collective dispute cases, the overwhelming majority of labor dispute cases are mediated based on laborers' concession.[15]

---

[15] Duan Yi (段毅): The exploration and analysis on the present situation of labor rule of law under the economic crisis, from the paper of international academic semi-

Fourth, service dispatch is prevalent, and various regions' use of dispatch laborers beyond "temporary, auxiliary and replaceable" increased. In regards to applicability, Article 66 of "Labor Contract Law" stipulates that service dispatch should be generally restricted in temporary, auxiliary or replaceable operating posts. After the law was released, there were a variety of interpretations regarding this clause. But analyzed from legal terms, this clause belongs to the initiative provision because it does not use words such as "should" and "must" that represent peremptory norm. Investigations by the Institute of Labor Sciences of the Ministry of Human Resources and Social Security have confirmed that, the phenomenon where various regions used dispatch laborers beyond "temporary, auxiliary and replaceable" not only had widely existed before "Labor Contract Law" was promulgated, but also has further increased after "Labor Contract Law" came into force.

The "Labor Contract Law" position on service dispatch is to provide flexibility of recruitment quantity, reduce unemployment due to friction, but at present, the function of service dispatch is very limited in this aspect. Most dispatch enterprises do not accept temporary and replaceable dispatch businesses; moreover do not accept labor return due to fluctuation of employer's production or due to the season factor. Because "Labor Contract Law" stipulates that the service dispatch company must sign an above two-year fixed-term contract with the dispatched worker, practically, the dispatch company is incapable of undertaking this labor contract term, and the labor contract term is basically transferred to the employer. Therefore, for the employer, service dispatch value is more manifested in dodging dispatch without fixed-term labor contract and probative dispatch, and this is also why it is favored during times of crisis.

The protection of service dispatch worker's rights and interests is unsatisfactory. First, the problem of unequal pay for equal work is quite prominent in state-owned enterprises. Compared with regular staff of state-owned enterprises, they have a somewhat lower salary (compared with external general enterprises, they have a slightly higher salary), and the gap between the two salaries is above 50% in some sectors. Second, although the payment ratio of social insurance is quite high, the payment base is somewhat low and the problem

---

nar for labor relations and laborers' rights and interests under global economic crisis in Guangzhou in November 2009.

of buying social insurance is prominent in relatively primitive areas. Third, although there are no statistics regarding the national situation, considerable amounts of service dispatch workers have not yet joined the trade union. According to investigations by the Shanghai Federation on Trade Unions, 44.9% of service dispatch workers have joined the trade union organization of their work unit, 17.2% have joined the trade union organizations of the service dispatch organization, 2.8% have joined the trade union organizations of their household register locale, but 35.1% have not yet joined a trade union organization.[16]

In view of the fact where various regions widely violate the law to execute the law and decide a case, "Certain Opinions on Doing a Good Job in Administrative Trial Under the Current Situation"[17] promulgated by the Supreme People's Court in July 2009 requested that, all levels of courts insist on the uniform principles of the legal system, not to sacrifice the law by acquiescing obviously illegal mandatory provisions and acts of infringing parties' legitimate rights and interests. Illegal acts that arbitrarily break legal rules to form new local protection and trade monopolies and infringe upon the legitimate rights and interests of citizen, legal person and other organizations under the veil of dealing with the crisis, must be legally corrected. Simultaneously, "Opinion" also proposed this plausible proposition which "must insist in the integration of the principle of legal system and flexibility, the integration of the legal criterion and policy consideration," which explained that, under the background of economic crisis, how relations between labor legal system and labor policy ought to be handled needs to be further explored and implemented.

In addition, today when labor relation in China increasingly becomes marketized, globalized, diversified and flexible, it is difficult to purely depend upon the regulation of the national labor legal system to adapt complex labor relations of various regions; especially when the economy enters a downward period, the function of independent gambling between labor and capital should be more displayed to realistically deal with issues of the labor-capital relationship. Up to now, the trade union has initiated "joint promissory action" to urge

---

[16] Li Tianguo (李天国): Present situation, issues and challenge of service dispatch legislation regulation of China from international seminar for "service dispatch and legislative regulation" in Beijing in October 2009.

[17] Yang Weihan (杨维汉): The Supreme People's Court: Forbid breaching the law to infringe the rights under the veil of crisis at www.xinhuanet.com on July 5, 2009.

enterprise not to reduce salaries and staff, and is the strongest support strength of the labor legal system; it specially issued the Guiding
Opinions on Launching Trade Wage Collective Negotiation Work[18] in
2009, to strengthen the construction of trade union organizations, to
expand the coverage of wage collective negotiation, to enhance effectiveness, and to cause the trade wage collective negotiation system to
play the major role in maintaining staff's rights and interests and in
promoting harmonious labor relations. In some coastal areas where
group events frequently occur, the trade union organizations started
to explore the subject of organizing a strike.[19] But, generally speaking,
advancing the democratic, mass and social transformation of trade
union organization system, strengthening the inner link between the
trade union and members, seeking "resources and methods" from
members and staff, promoting consciousness of labor right protection,
and strengthening the construction of representative and of consultative, negotiation, organizing and mobilization ability, all are still the
intrinsic requirement of the market economy in regards to the function
of the trade union, and are urgently needed of the trade union to deal
with the crisis.

---

[18] Guiding Opinions of All-China Federation of Trade Unions on Launching Trade
Wage Collective Negotiation Work published in "Workers Daily" on July 21, 2009.
[19] For example, it determined four conditions to initiate and organize a strike:
Capital's vicious right infringement; conclusive evidence; limitation of strike within
the factory zone; protection of production equipment, and so on.

REPORT ON FARMER DEVELOPMENT IN 2009

Fan Ping

I. *Formation and Characteristics of Farmer Group*

According to data from the "China Statistical Yearbook 2009," at the end of 2008, the basic condition of farmers was that, the rural population was 721.35 million persons, and the urbanization level was 45.68%; employed persons in the first industry were 306.54 million persons, which accounted for 39.6% of all employed populations; and the proportion of first industry in GDP was 11.3%. China's urbanization level was lower than that of similar developing countries, and the change of employment structure obviously lagged behind that of industrial structure and urbanization advancement.

A. *About Various Groups Within the Farmer Stratum*

According to the relations between farmer and land, the present rural populations may be divided into three parts; personnel that enter the city for work, deprived of land farmers and professional farmers. To promote urbanization and economic and social development, China needs to resolve the issues concerning these three types of farmer.

Personnel that enter the city for work are so-called off-farm worker. Amongst these people, some work in the city for a long time, and 70% are young people at 30 year-old below. Although they do not necessarily have town people's ideology and life style, most of them are not willing to return to rural areas; they are not willing to give up the land, but it is already difficult for them to resort to agricultural production; they also request to retain the land, and their goal is mainly to obtain survival security, and not for employment. The report of the National Bureau of Statistics of China indicated that, before the Spring Festival of 2009, in the 140 million off-farm workers who went out, a total of 70 million off-farm workers returned to their native village, in which about 20% namely 14 million persons returned to their native village because enterprises were under the impact; In other words, at that time, 20 million off-farm workers lost their job because of the international financial crisis. According to tracking investigation of off-farm workers' employment and mobility status from December 2008 to February 2009, at the beginning of the year, off-farm workers' unemployment exacerbated, and off-farm workers who lost job and returned to their native village had intentions of going back out for work. Under the promotion of related policies, the environment when off-farm workers got employment in their native place was better than the environment when they went to other areas for work; the employment environment in central and western areas was better than that of the eastern area. Recent data from the National Bureau of Statistics of China confirmed that, in the second quarter of 2009, newly increased off-farm workers in eastern areas was 560,000 people, which grew 1.6%; 800,000 people in central areas, which grew 1.8%; 2,420,000 people in western areas, which grew 6.5%. The contribution of increased employment of off-farm workers in central and western areas surpassed eastern area. By the end of the third quarter, in total 151.98 million rural labors went out to work, which increased 1.01 million over that at the end of second quarter, and grew 0.7%. The report of the Ministry of Human Resources and Social Security on the work status of off-farm workers from 250 administrative villages showed that, above 94% of off-farm workers returned to the cities by the end of September 2009.

Off-farm workers establishing their own business has become a new point of growth of the rural enterprise. It is calculated according to sampling investigation findings of the Ministry of Agriculture that, in total about 5.2 million off-farm workers returned to their native village to establish a business, they established 850,000 rural industry and commerce enterprises, and each enterprise in average had 7.5 people. The number of off-farm workers who returned to their native village to establish a business or to get employment has increased; on one hand, this promoted the modernization process of rural social culture, and played a role in changing farmers' cultural ideas, such as those in marriage and child-bearing etc.; on the other hand, this also brought some problems, for example, some off-farm workers who fell into a habit of city life felt they cannot adapt back to rural life after returning to their native village; disputes of land circulation increased in some areas; after returned to native village, some off-farm workers' children faced a dilemma in education because the hometown school was different than their original school in the city in terms of teaching material, teaching progress, quality of teaching and conditions etc.

About deprived of land farmers. This group is mainly comprised of urban suburb farmers, as well as villagers of other rural areas whose land has been taken up by engineering projects. They are faced with urbanization pressure of expansion and lose their land; their land was used in the distribution of huge value-added income production by urban development, and has become one of the important roots of the interest contradiction in Chinese society. Some of them have integrated with the city, and separated from farmer status; some no longer have land resource, and cannot be covered effectively by the urban social security system, therefore they have become an unemployed farmer group without social security and land. They are not generally willing to give up their land, thus their contention and guard over their land often became the focus of social conflict, and they are the focal group in rural social contradictions and urban and rural social conflicts in 2009.

About professional farmer. This is a farmer group that has farmer status and contracts land to be engaged in agricultural production, and they mainly plant crops. They direct affect and bear the responsibility of grain security. They depend on the land and farming to make a living, and besides leaving rural areas to become off-farm worker, it is impossible for these people give up their land; when the average return of crops is too low, they do not have the motive force to protect the cultivated land after maintaining a self-sufficient life.

B. *Farmer's Incomes and Expenses in 2009*

According to data of the National Bureau of Statistics of China, in the first three quarters of 2009, average income per rural resident was 4307 Yuan, which grew 8.5% from the previous year, and the increased range fell 11.1 percentage points from the previous year, but was 0.4 percentage points higher than that of the first half of the year. With no view of price factor, it actually grew 9.2%, and the increased range fell 1.8 percentage points from that of 2008. Farmers' increase in speed of income in the third quarter was obviously quicker than that in the second quarter. In the first three quarters, wage income in rural residents' income grew 9.9%, income from selling agricultural products grew 4%, income from production operations in the second and third industries grew 10.5%, property income grew 11.7%, and transfer income grew 26.4%. The increase of transfer income was obviously quicker, and the increased range reached 26.4% over that of the previous year. At present, farmer's transfer income is composed of three major parts. First is various subsidies, such as agricultural material subsidy which has been implemented for several years and subsidy for purchasing large-scale machines and tools, they belong to transfer income; Second is various social security funds; Third is relief funds. In 2009, the central government increased transfer payment under the situation of economic hardship, and the central financing expenditure for "agriculture, farmers and rural areas" arranged 716.14 billion Yuan, which grew 20.2%. "Promoting automobiles in the countryside," ("汽车下乡" Qi Che Xia Xiang) "Promoting home appliances in the countryside" ("家电下乡" Jia Dian Xia Xiang), promotion of various measures to stimulate rural expense has quickened the increase of transfer income while farmers make purchases and obtain material benefit. Income from outside work for farmers has also increased. Investigation by the National Bureau of Statistics of China showed that, by the end of the third quarter in 2009, the average monthly income of labors who go out to work was 1444 Yuan, which increased 40 Yuan from that at the end of the second quarter, and grew 2.8%.

While farmers' income generally increased, within rural areas, the income gap among farmers from various areas increased. The proportion of farmers' income growth in Zhujiang Delta, the Changjiang Delta and Beijing is high. In the first half of 2009, in the Shanghai suburb rural family, average disposable income per person grew 7.6% from the previous year.

In 2009, the growth of rural expenses exceeded that of the cities. During the first three quarters, urban consumable retail rates were 6,101.3 billion Yuan, which grew 14.8%; consumable retail rates at county-level and below were 2,866.3 billion Yuan, and grew 16.0%, where the growth of rural market expenses was quicker than that of the city.

C. *Farmers' Social Security in 2009*

Besides growth in farmers' income, coverage of various rural social security systems and policies has also expanded. The central government has enhanced public expenditure for rural schools and the subsidy standard for boarders from families with economic hardship, has consolidated and developed the new rural cooperative medical system, and has gradually expanded the scope of rural minimum social security. By the end of June 2009, more than 44.7 million farmers were integrated into the minimum social security system. According to the spokesperson of the Ministry of Human Resources and Social Security, by the end of June 2009, the number of off-farm workers that bought basic endowment insurance, basic medical, industrial injury and unemployment insurance reached 23.8 million persons, 41.53 million persons, 50.54 million persons and 15.18 million persons, respectively. At the same time, the national generalized system of pension preferences that farmers were allowed to enjoy after reaching 60 years old was being arranged. The State Council executive meeting examined and approved the guiding opinions on the pilot work of the new rural endowment insurance system, suggestions of local governments was being solicited for this guiding opinions, the department concerned prepared it to be officially issued after further revision and consummation, and then began the pilot program. Old rural social security in the past was self-deposit. The new rural endowment insurance is an integration of individual payment, collective subsidy and government subsidy, and has three channels for fund-raising. The central financial administration gives subsidy to the local financial administration, and this subsidy is directly given to farmers. This is another significant policy that benefits farmers, after a series of policies, including abolition of the agricultural tax, direct subsidy for agriculture and the new rural cooperative medical system etc. The payment structure of the new rural endowment insurance is designed into two parts. One part is the foundation pension, and the other is the pension of individual account. The foundation pension is guaranteed be paid by the national financial institution.

II. *Agricultural Modernization has Obvious Progress*

Agricultural modernization had obvious progress in 2009. First, the central government took it seriously, and released a series of guiding documents, and eliminated the shortcomings and tried to be practical; Second, agricultural investment increased; in 2009, the investment on "agriculture, farmers and rural areas" amounted to 716.1 billion Yuan; Third, innovation of agricultural modernization mechanism and socialized services had important breakthrough. Under these three conditions, plus the enhancement of farmers' production enthusiasm and innovative ideology, some off-farm workers who returned to their native village brought innovative spirit to agriculture, which led and promoted the enhancement of agricultural modernization.

Deepening the rural reform and innovation of agricultural operation system mechanism was a highlight of rural economic development in 2009. "Advancing innovation of agricultural operation system mechanism, and quickening transformation of agricultural operation" are proposed at the Third Plenary Session of the 17th CPC and insist in the stabilization and consummation of the rural basic operation system, and the key is advancement of "two transformations," namely transformation from family-run operation to enhancement of intensity level, and from unified operation to enhancement of organization degree. The core of the advancement of "two transformations" is to maintain farmers' rights to contracted land, to guide steady healthy development of land circulation, and the key is to consummate the mechanism for mediation and handling of disputes concerning land contracts.

In the process of agricultural modernization, Zhejiang's method of work is worth paying attention to. First, Zhejiang devoted to promote agricultural construction and development by means of marketing. Agricultural product marketing infused new vigor for Zhejiang agriculture, and also was a turning point for agricultural growth. The extensive operation, which gave priority to small-scale farming by individual owners, started to fade out, and modern agricultural marketability, standardization, large-scale and brand become increasingly clear. The Xianju County Bureau of Agriculture, with good ecological condition, integrates "Zhejiang green agricultural products" with supporting "green agricultural products exclusive market." Agricultural products that enter the market must have an "ID card." The market is equipped with monitoring equipment and personnel. Xianju green rice rose from 1.8 Yuan/kg to 3 Yuan/kg; the price of local farmhouse pig is 2 Yuan/Jin higher than the original price. Xianju's ecological dominance has transformed into economic superiority, and the proportion of sale of Xianju agricultural production has had remarkable promotion. Shengzhou made a special plan on tea brand construction; First, the quality is improved through the revision of production technical standards, and a quality security system and of quality tracing system is established; then it is expanded into the market, "Shaoxing opera" is integrated with "Longjing tea of Hangzhou," teahouses and the specialty shops are established in Beijing and Hangzhou etc. In the past, Huangyan mainly sold agricultural products to large-scale free wholesale agricultural products markets in Shanghai and Hangzhou etc. through the pattern of "Leading enterprises + cooperative shop + peasant households," and its characteristics were big quantity, less variety, low price and bad guarantee; but now, through the coordination of marketing management center, the local agricultural products have established a supply-demand alliance with the supermarket and specialty shop etc; although quantity is few, variety is more, appearance is nice, work load and cost have increased, the price is high, and sales are stable, therefore farmers obtain more benefit. The establishment of the marketing management center not only has resolved the difficult problem in the sale of agricultural products, what is more important is that it has strengthened the importance of marketing in the entire process of agricultural production, which has created the condition for productive agriculture to transform into operational agriculture.

Next, strength of land circulation advancement increased. Modernization of agricultural operation and management enhanced the value of land, increased farmers' income, and also promoted large-scale land operation. The average circulation rate of land was less than 20% in the whole country, and it was 28% in Zhejiang, which was 8 percentage points higher than the total, and it reached as high as 58.3% in some areas such as Cixi County. This change indicated that, the marketing function has increased, which has caused Zhejiang rural petty-farmer management to experience upgrading, and to move toward modern agriculture where standardization, large-scale operation and brand management are the characteristic.

Third, informatization of agricultural production operations advanced. Zhejiang Province's Internet "farmer mailbox" has had good results. This province registers and develops the Internet farmer mailbox using real name system, and allows the farmer mailbox to be networked with their cell phone. Because the information is real and reliable, usage is quick and convenient, registered users of farmer mailbox have in 4 years registered 1.9 million households, and many farmers use this mailbox to successfully trade. At the beginning of 2008, Zhejiang Province specially held the first on-line agricultural expo using "farmer mailbox," trade of 270 million Yuan was achieved within a week, and average trading volume per day reached more than 30 million Yuan. In 2009, "help every day" activity of farmer mailbox had a remarkable effect; registered farmers only needed to issue a message through the farmer mailbox if they needed help in the sale of agricultural products, and all registered users' receive the message of help. Statistics indicated that, by the end of 2008, Zhejiang carried out 22 activities concerning production and marketing of red bayberry and grape etc. successively used the farmer mailbox, the volume of business amounted to above 5.1 billion Yuan, which reduced the marketing cost by 230 million Yuan. The successful operation of farmer mailbox had profound influence to Zhejiang's change in marketing of agricultural products, and agricultural product on-line marketing is more and more so universally applied in Zhejiang.

Moreover, under the vigorous support of central financing and local finance, agricultural insurance has had considerable development. In the first half of 2009, agricultural insurance maintained fast development; by the end of June, income of agricultural insurance premium reached 7 billion Yuan, 143.65 billion Yuan in risk security was provided, the insured peasant households were 61.52 million householdtimes, 350 million Chinese acres of crops and 360 million domestic animals were insured, and 3.41 billion Yuan in compensation was paid to 5 million disaster-stricken peasant households, which effectively supported the rehabilitation of post-disaster agricultural production.

III. *The Scope of Rural Land Circulation is Enhanced*

Under the condition of household-based contract system, land property right relation is beneficial in mobilizing farmers' enthusiasm in family-run operation, but the flaw is dispersed management rights, which is disadvantageous for large-scale operations and modernized development of agriculture, thus this is the primal problem that needs to be resolve in order to deepen the reform of land property authority relation. The "Decision" at the Third Plenary Session of the 17th CPC proposed to impel and consummate the circulation of land contracting managerial authority, namely based on the household-based contract system, on one hand, the powers and functions of farmer' land contracting managerial authority should be fully realized to cause the land contracting management managerial authority to truly become farmer's property right; On the other hand, the land property system has guaranteed the realization of land managerial authority.

In 2009, in some rural areas where industry and commerce were quite developed, the circulation of rights of land usage in rural collective construction was quite universal. Economic development led to demand of rural land, and caused property value of rural collective land to gradually appear. The market behavior, which spontaneously exchanges land rights in rural collective construction through sale, transfer, lease, joint management, etc., for a long time already existed, but not it is further expanding. Many areas are exploring land contracting managerial authority circulation in different ways.

Chongqing and Chengdu have taken many forms in advancing urban and rural unified planning; for example, proprietors might become shareholders through the land contracting managerial authority, where agricultural land is placed in the hands of leading enterprises and influential families, thereby intensive land management is brought about; when agricultural land became urban land, farmers whose cultivated land was requisitioned and mobilized to move were compensated by cash compensation and stock compensation; their land was used for non-agricultural purposes such as house sites etc. Through these measures, circulated land have brought huge economic benefit, farmers' income has increased, and the phenomenon of abandoned arable land has reduced, where new life has been given to rural land.

The Standing Committee of the Fujian Provincial People's Congress considered and approved "Regulations of Fujian Province on Promoting Agricultural Cooperation between Fujian and Taiwan," and stipulated that, Taiwanese farmers who have agricultural operations in Fujian may obtain land contracting managerial authority through the way of rural collective land circulation. This provision may effectively resolve the bottle-neck problem on land that Taiwan businessmen have on agricultural development in Fujian, which is regarded and highly praised by Taiwan businessmen who operate in Fujian.

Beijing suburban farmers buy stocks of their own land to become company shareholders, on the premise that the annual income per Chinese acre is guaranteed not to be lower than 1200 Yuan, and the annual cash return rate of buying stock is not lower than 10%; they are also engaged as the plantation worker and participate in corporate profit distribution to obtain wage income of several hundred Yuan every month. It is interesting that, the most-favored-side clause also appeared in Beijing farmer's land circulation in 2009; under the premise of rent standard, the special restricted clause where the rent was not lower than that of the peripheral villages was also added, and villages and towns established the land circulation platform, issued information, and provided services. In Chongqing and Chengdu, circulated land have brought huge economic benefit, farmers' income has increased, wasted arable land has decreased and new life has been given to rural lands.

Based on insistent on the rural basic management system, Zhejiang proposed that "farmers be entrusted with more secure land contracting management right, the existing land contracting relations maintain stable and invariable for a long-time," "consummates the powers and functions of land contracting management right, guarantees legally that farmers' right of possession, usage and right to earnings from contracted land." This is another innovation in consummating the rural land production relations after the rural reform for 30 years, and means that it can bring property income for farmers. The Zhejiang Provincial Bureau of Industry and Commerce and the Zhejiang Provincial Agriculture Department jointly took the lead to release the first "Provisional Measures of Zhejiang Province on the Registration of Professional Cooperative Society Evaluating Farmer's Rural Land Contracting Management Right as Investment" to normalize land circulation. Under the investment principle of voluntary payment and equal consultation, "Provisional Measures" made concrete stipulation to the investment way, investment object, way of capital assessment and verification, business scope and gross investment. The land management right can put up capital, which not only solves the issue of farmers' fund for large-scale management, but also provides security for farmers' to "leave but not abandon the land." The property warrant of land managerial authority may resolve the problem of "leaving but not abandoning the land," and may relieve the mechanical nature in the human and land relationship, and may also guarantee the stability of ownership relation between human and land. To evaluate the rural land contracting management right as investment on the base of the principle of equal consultation and voluntary paid, has three bottom lines, namely not be allowed to change the nature of land ownership, not be allowed to change the agricultural use of land, and not be allowed to damage farmers' land contracting rights and interests. Thereby, the first 12 new peasant professional cooperative societies established by peasant households through evaluating rural land contracting management right as investment appeared in Zhejiang, and were officially issued business license for industry and commerce on March 15, 2009. This symbolized that Zhejiang farmers' land management rights might be changed into property rights and stockholder's rights from now on, but the management right and the use of land would not actually have any changes. By the end of 2008, in Zhejiang Province, the area of land circulation amounted to 5.46 mil-

lion Chinese acres, which accounted for 27.6% of total areas of contracted cultivated land; 2,765,400 peasant households were involved
with circulated land, which was 29.6% of total peasant households of
contractual management in this province, and farmers' demand of
becoming rich through land circulation was very exuberant.

To normalize land circulation, Zhejiang, Jiangsu and Sichuan etc.,
one after another, released model texts on contracts on land circulation. The State Administration of Industry and Commerce indicated
that on the base of experiments in Jiangsu and Zhejiang etc., it would
formulate the model text of contract on promoting nationwide land
circulation as soon as possible, and would emphatically normalize and
determine related contents of land contracts contracting managerial
authority circulation, such as subject, term of validity, cost, payment
method and time, parties' rights and obligations as well as liabilities for
breach of contract etc., which guaranteed that the rural land contracting management right circulation would not change the agricultural
use of land, and would maintain both parties', especially farmers',
legitimate rights and interests.

It is observed that, the household contract responsibility system with
remuneration linked to output is to solve the problem of "everyone
can his best," and the rural land employment right circulation is to
solve the problem of "all land can be used." The intensive and large-
scale operation is the inevitable requirement of modern agricultural
development, and also requires land circulation. It is to be noted that,
farmers are the vulnerable subjects in the process of land circulation, and they lack necessary knowledge about the contract law, lack
the foresight ability for land revaluation, and even lack the right to
speak. Therefore, the land circulation system should be further consummated, more ways of circulation should be provided for farmers'.
When carrying out the policies, the wishes of the farmers and their
voices must be respected, and the land value should be assessed reasonably to enhance the scientific and serious nature of the contract;
farmers ought to be guaranteed share of income, and stability over a
longer period of tine, in order to bring about good results.

IV. *Rural Basic-level Organizations*

In 2008, there were 19234 towns, 15067 townships and 604,285 villagers' committee organizations throughout the whole country. The
villagers' committee reduced yearly, and reduced by nearly half, over

119,042, in 1998. Villagers' committee members were 2,339,000 people, and besides a slight increase in 2003, since 1990 presented a declining trend as a whole. The quantity of villagers' committee reduced, but supervisory work way of rural basic-level organization was innovated, the service space expanded, and faced increasingly complex work contents, new difficult problem also appeared unceasingly.

A new problem in villagers' self-administration is the association of rights and interests between rural villager status and contracting of land. According to the current land legal system, the rural land belongs to farmer collectives, and villagers enjoy the land contracting management right. The "Law of Land Management" and "Law of Rural Land Contracting" stated that "the rural collective economic organization" is not defined explicitly in the law. The question then is, who is a member of the "rural collective economic organization" or the "village?" What qualifications are need to become a member of the organization or village? The law does not stipulate in explicit terms. Generally it is understood that, membership is defined by one's registered permanent residence. "Provisions of Guangdong Province on the Administration of Rural Collective Economic Organization," formulated in 2006, emphasized the criterion of taking registered permanent residence as the principle. But the practice, which allows a person to enjoy land contracting management right so long as he/she has registered permanent residence in some village, has become a difficult problem to initiate rural land disputes because the rural household register cannot be decided and managed by the villagers' committee and the villagers' congress. If registered permanent residence is regarded as the condition to village membership and land contracting, there is appears a question of "time difference," namely how immediate are the rights once one is registered in some village. In fact, the lands are readjusted once every several years, sometimes not within ten years, therefore the newcomer is unable to obtain land contracting rights immediately. Should some farmers lose their leasing contract immediately if their registered permanent residence is moved out this village after they lease their contracted land to other people? If it does, it is obviously unfair for the person leasing, and this will cause its investment to be invalid. At present, people's status of household register encounters many changes, and brings difficulty in definition of land rights, and creates the massive conflicts between rights and interests of village management and villagers. This urgently needs authoritative and explicit judicial interpretation.

In recent years, in regards to the tenure renewal of villagers' committee, the phenomenon of bribery at election has increased, and complaints and appeals bypassing the immediate leadership, concerning basic-level elections, have also increased. In 2008, after the election of the eighth villagers' committee of Zhejiang Province, 294 cases of law violation and discipline were ferreted out in various areas, where bribery at election was the majority. Yiwu City investigated 37 cases of fixed elections and bribery at election, 10 party members were given party disciplinary measure, and 90 people were given administrative detention. In June 2009, the General Offices of the CCP Central Committee and of the State Council printed and distributed "Notice on Strengthening and Improving the Election of Villagers' Committees,"[1] and normalized the procedure and control measures of villager self-administration election. Present-day villagers' committee are different than those in the 1990s, and the government needs to give standard and instruction in view of the changes to the rural development situation and realistic demand, which guarantees farmers' rights and interests and rural public order.

The rich administering village affairs has become a new rural phenomenon that requires attention. Comprehensive data discovered that, 1/3 of villages of advanced economic rural areas and above 2/3 of villages in Zhejiang, villagers who become rich first, such as entrepreneur of industry and commerce and culturists etc., hold positions of director of villagers' committee or secretary of village party branch. Some "boss village officials" construct the new rural areas with their own funds, and many "boss village officials" mainly plan the way for development of rural areas. They have a liberal mentality, strong organizing capacity, and modern market ideology, formed in long-term enterprise management, which is prominent in the new rural reconstruction. But, "boss village officials" concurrently hold two posts, and their energy is scattered, which has led to debates about whether village cadres ought to be full time. In Wenzhou and Taizhou, rural areas of Zhejiang Province, there is the phenomenon where cadres of two committees of some villages engage in external affairs to make money and assign someone else to handle village affairs. The villagers' committee is an

---

[1] See Notice Printed and Distributed by General Office of the CCCPC and General Office of the State Council on Strengthening and Improving the Election of Villagers' Committees, at http://www.lawinfochina.com/law/displayModeTwo.asp?id=7750&keyword=.

autonomous organization, cadres of villagers' committee do not have
financial allocation support, and their main arena of work is "not separate from production," therefore it is impossible to limit them from
engaging in other trades, like government officials are limited; however, entrusting village affairs to other people is inappropriate because
village cadres bear the trust of the villagers, and trust ought not be
transferred in such a way.

The motives of most "boss village officials" is simply out of consideration for the public welfare, and is for the purpose of benefiting the
home village, town and the common people. But there are also hidden motives which cannot be neglected; once there is conflict between
"impulsion of public welfare" and selfish "impulsion of private benefit,"
under the new situation of the rural market economic development, of
the subdivision of occupational differentiation, and of the increase in
villager non-uniformity, a difficult problem arises because the majority
of villagers' field of vision, experiences and skills are limited. Through
some investigations and interviews, we discovered that, in some village
cadre troops that are composed of the wealthy, there does exist the
phenomenon where one takes advantage of his position and power
to enter a higher platform, to develop better personal connection,
and to further seek or protect economic interests, there are even acts
that practice fraud in secret, increase benefits, and expand own and
its family influence in the village collective economy. At present, the
prominent rural problem is shortage of talent. The rich are often the
local able person, and they often chose to leave the rural areas instead
of staying and helping with the development of "agriculture, farmers
and rural areas." However, they should be encouraged to stay and
take up a post of village cadre. In terms of the long-term puzzle for
rural areas, where talent all flows out, this is a good way to impel the
backflow of talents and funds. But training and supervision also need
to keep up with and reach the designated position; otherwise abuse
of position may occur. Entrepreneurs being engaged in politics has
become a tendency, so long as the policy adjustment is appropriate,
this group of cadres can become the important force to advance village
democracy. To avoid the negative problem where "the rich administer
village affairs," the key is to consummate the supervision mechanism,
and to resolve the problem with an open transparent system. Open
village affairs should be deepened, and matters concerning people's
vital interest should be unfurled promptly, which guarantees villagers'
rights to know, to participate and to supervise; objective management
should be quantified, personnel mechanism, which rewards excellent

talents and eliminates the inferior should be formed, and village cadres who only seek the position and do not administer village affairs must be promptly readjusted and investigated.

Moreover, in 2009, founding and using the local area network of rural information service platform to popularize scientific knowledge and to spread science and culture became one new form of rural basic-level organizations serving villagers. The Lantian Village Party Branch of Nanan City, Fujian founded "century village" rural information service platform. This information service platform has two modules and eight functions; the first module is the module of management and open village affairs, and has four functions including government supervision, management of village affairs, village accounting comput-erization and rural community services etc.; The second module is the module of rural market service, and has four functions including peas-ant family shop, service demand, Xinghuo Science and Technology training, enterprise exhibits etc. The village also switched the infor-mation of network platform to cable TV video to allow villagers who are computer illiterate to know about village affairs. More than ten information sites were established in the village to serve the villagers. This platform has good results since being implemented the previous year. The villagers can not be informed of village affairs and supervise the village financial management etc., but also may issue information about supply and demand to become "net shop" boss, and can be trained in science and technology on "the net school." Before, village affairs were not public, and misunderstanding and mistrust between mass and cadres frequently occurred, thus the work of the village lacked cohesive force. The construction of "century village" network platform has resolved the former problem of unclear communication and unclear understanding between the cadres and the public, has raised the efficiency of village-level government affair management, has increased the strength of mass participation and supervision of village affair management, and has strengthened the cohesive force of village-level work.

V. *Rural Public Services*

Because debt was so great, rural public services lagged, and there was big disparity between rural and urban areas in social enterprises and infrastructures. In 2009, as a result of national investment and local finance support, rural public services made remarkable progress. In standardized kindergarten of suburb rural areas of Chengdu, rural children enjoyed similar teaching staff and facilities as those in the city. Measures on the standardized project to bring about equal distribution in urban and rural education and health resources have begun to be implemented in trials. Establishing the urban and rural unified public service system needs first to formation of a public finance system, which covers urban and rural areas, and thus needs to readjust the national income distribution pattern. The government's functions of social management and public service should be further extend from the cities into the rural areas, and public services should be explored, for example, government gives out a contract to purchase services for the convenience of farmers, and so on.

The construction of village-level health system is weak in the construction of the rural health service system. In Luohe City, to promote construction of the rural medical service system and "trade of funds by means of resources," above 80% of farmers participated in the new rural cooperative medical system, the insured population reached more than 1.4 million, and the total amount of funds of the rural basic cooperative medical account reached nearly 17 million Yuan. If calculated according to a standard of 40 Yuan per person every year average of medical expenses, this city would have medical market resources of more than 56 million Yuan. Regarding resources under the control of the government, Luohe City adopted the method of work inclining towards rural cooperative medical fixed health center, and let rural cooperative medical fixed health center provide high-quality medical and health care services for farmers while using these resources. Adopting this method, they built up 177 high-standard rural cooperative medical fixed health centers in 177 administrative villages of Yancheng area within several months, where the medical market resources under the control of the government were transferred effectively into the rural medical and health care construction funds, which the government may spend and use. This method of trading the funds by resources is worth using for reference in construction of rural medical and health service system.

VI. *Conclusions and Suggestions*

In 2010, steady rural agricultural economic development will face new challenges and difficulties. Unified planning of urban and rural development is in an important period, the unified planning task of regional development is arduous, and the international trade environment is still stern, which makes it more difficult to maintain positive rural agricultural development. Maintaining steady agricultural development and stable rural society, and promoting rural labor transfer employment and sustained increase of farmers' income are still the basic objectives of coordinated rural economy and social development. Generally speaking, various contradictions including somewhat low farmers' income levels, the weak rural industry, the unbalanced rural economic and social development, primitive social security construction and gap between urban and rural areas, etc., are still prominent.

Rural land circulation should be further consummated. From the situation and effect of development in 2009, rural land circulation may become a new pivot that is established in rural areas and leads unified planning of urban and rural development, to become a significant breakthrough that enhances farmer's property income proportion, to become a significant economic policy that integrally impels sustained economic growth, and to be the continuation and consummation of the household contract responsibility system with remuneration linked to output. The significance of land circulation (trade of the market principle) rests with that, when the land becomes an exchangeable commodity, on one hand, generally the buyer can create more profit than the seller with the land; on the other hand, the land transaction or mortgage etc. can provide direct monetary value for the land owner. Rural land circulation includes farmland circulation and rural reconstruction land circulation, and this will readjust the pattern of rural economic and social development, and will activate all kinds of factors, therefore on the premise of practice, investigation and study should be actively pursued to find out problems, and then corresponding measures need to be formulated to solve them, and promote its development. It is to be noted that, the land may be revalued under circulation, rural labors and reselection of employment direction in land circulation may be reorganized, all are inevitable trends, but will also change and restructure villagers' development expectation, thus will be possible to cause new social cooperation and new social conflicts. We must have foresight and corresponding preparation for this in terms of villager self-administration, rural social management and rural public services, and must have the foresight and security in direction, technology and procedure. Collective ownership and state-owned land should have equal price for equal land, and it is not suitable to unceasingly implement low-price expropriation compensation when transferring land usage. The distribution of differential land rent income by the market principle produced in land transaction should be readjusted through tax revenue. On the premise of conforming to the land use plan, peasant households may transfer, lease, mortgage and sell the long-term use right of land or buy stock in various usages, thus increasing their property income.

Training of farmers is not only important, but also urgent. The increase in farmer's skill is helpful for off-farm workers to get employment. Along with the development of modern agriculture, more rural surplus laborers who are separated from the land go out to work, but their skill level will decide their income level. Farmers without skill have less human capital investment, and most of them are engaged in physical labor; on the contrary, most skilled off-farm worker are engaged in semi-physical labor and non-physical labor, the former has low income, and the latter may have higher income. In addition, labor market competition provides low-skill off-farm workers' work that is often provisional, seasonal and instable. Along with market economic development, they will be replaced by skilled workers, thus the phenomenon of off-farm worker backflow may emerge. Therefore, the enhancement of farmers' skill is significant to promote off-farm workers' steady employment. Goals in training should be realized, newly grown labors should be emphasized, medium and long-term training should be given priority, and skill and educational qualifications are focused on, and training workers in accordance with their demands.

The modern agricultural industrial system should be built, and the transformation of agricultural production way should be quickened. At present, agriculture has surpassed farmers' accumulation of traditional knowledge, the binding force to remuneration linked to output in system for contracted responsibility has been relatively weakened. At present, in terms of agriculture, what to plant or how to plant are increasingly decided by the market and by input-output efficiency, and not by the farmer. Therefore, they urgently need the government to provide effective guidance and services. Guiding and building modern agriculture should be put on the agenda, advancement of agricultural management system innovation, enhancement of farmer organization degree, increase of agricultural production efficiency, and enhancement of agricultural product standardization and marketability level, all need the model to lead the way, and need further spread and innovation. Rural public services also need to serve this goal, and the government's intervention and promotion are indispensable.

The construction of rural basic-level organization should be strengthened. Rotational training of new knowledge and new skill, post qualification training and training of public government affairs etc. to rural cadres should be strengthened to improve quality of rural cadres. For new problems that arise in rural areas, the government departments concerned should give prompt instruction.

STATISTICAL CHARTS ON SOCIAL DEVELOPMENT
(2009)

Zhang Liping

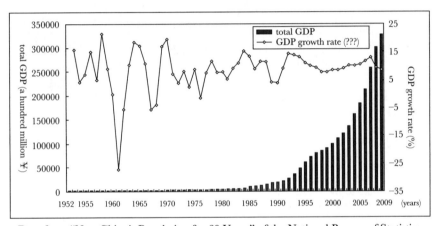

Data from "New China's Population for 60 Years" of the National Bureau of Statistics of China, published by China Statistics Press in 2009.

Figure 16.1: Changes in GDP from 1952–2009

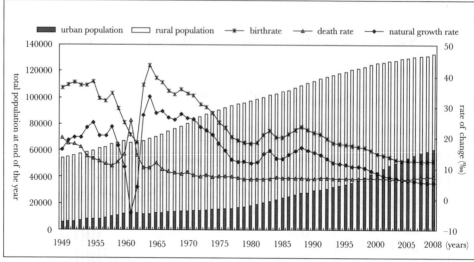

Note: 1. Data before 1981 is the statistical data of household register; data in 1982, 1990 and 2000 is census data; data in 1987, 1995 and 2005 is calculated according to data of 1% population sampling investigation, data of other years is calculated according to population change sampling investigation; data from 1982–1989 is readjusted according to the census data in 1990; data from 1990–2000 is readjusted according to the census data in 2000. 2. In the population by the urban and rural areas, soldiers in active service are included in the urban population.
Data from "New China's Population for 60 Years" of the National Bureau of Statistics of China, published by China Statistics Press in 2009.

Figure 16.2: Changes of Population from 1949–2008

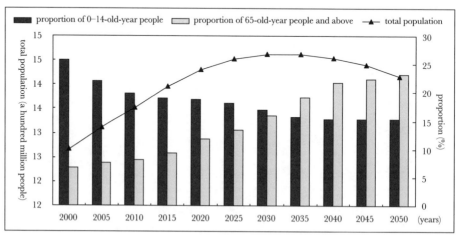

Data from "World Population Prospect: The 2008 Revision" of the Population Division of the Department of Economic and Social Affairs of the United Nations Secretariat.

Figure 16.3: Forecast of United Nations on China's Population (China)

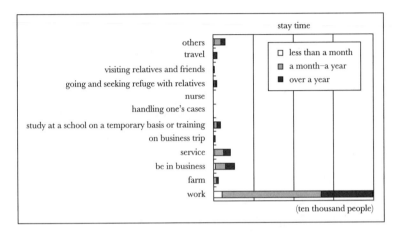

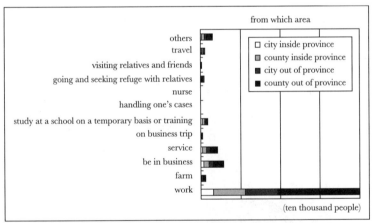

Note: the time of data statistics is at 24:00 on June 30, 2008 in the Table.
Data from "National Collection of Statistical Data on Floating Population 2008" of the Public Security Bureau, Ministry of Public Security, published by Qun Zhong Press in 2008.

Figure 16.4: Temporary Populations by Time of Temporary Residence and Place of Origin in mid-2008

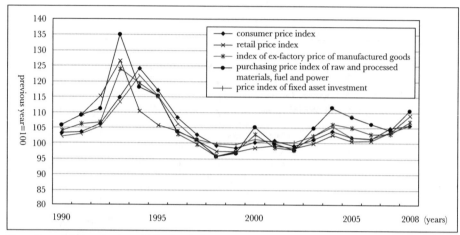

Data from "China Statistical Yearbook (2009)" of the National Bureau of Statistics of China, published by China Statistics Press in 2009.

Figure 16.5: Changes of Price Indexes from 1990–2008

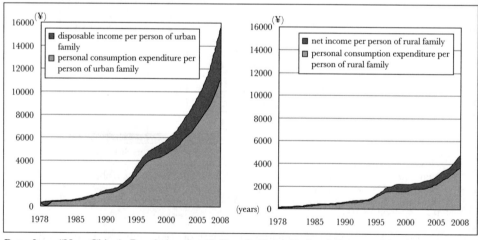

Data from "New China's Population for 60 Years" of the National Bureau of Statistics of China, published by China Statistics Press in 2009.

Figure 16.6: Average Income and Expenses Per Person of Urban and Rural Resident Families from 1978–2008

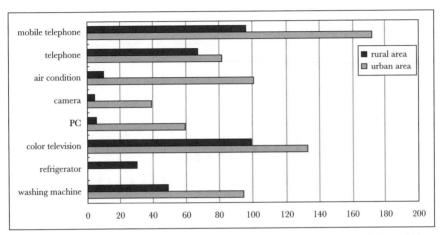

Data from "China Statistical Yearbook (2009)" of the National Bureau of Statistics of China, published by China Statistics Press in 2009.

Figure 16.7: Possession of Durable Consumer Goods of Every Hundred Urban and Rural Households in 2008

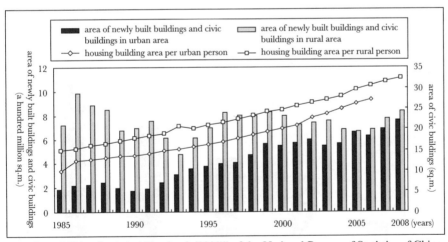

Data from "China Statistical Yearbook (2009)" of the National Bureau of Statistics of China, published by China Statistics Press in 2009.

Figure 16.8: Newly Built Buildings and Civic Buildings in Urban and Rural Areas from 1978–2008

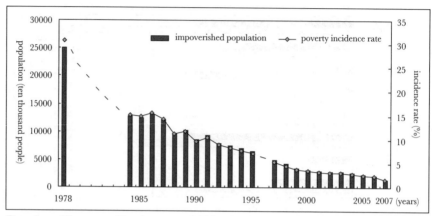

Data from "Report on Development of China 2008" of the National Bureau of Statistics of China, and "Chinese Rural areas Impoverished Monitor Reports 2000" of the Rural Economic Survey Team, National Bureau of Statistics of China.

Figure 16.9: National Changes of Rural Impoverished Population and Falling into Poverty Rate

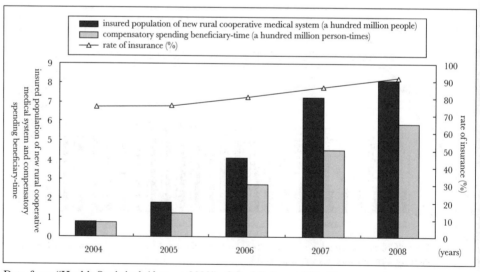

Data from "Health Statistical Abstract 2009" of the Ministry of Health.

Figure 16.10: National New Rural Cooperative Medical System from 2004–2007

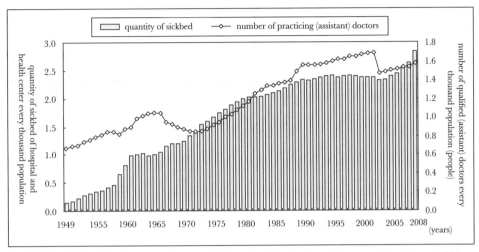

Data from "New China's Population for 60 Years" of the National Bureau of Statistics of China, published by China Statistics Press in 2009.

Figure 16.11: Number of Beds and Qualified (Assistant) Doctors of Every Thousand Population in Various Health Institutions

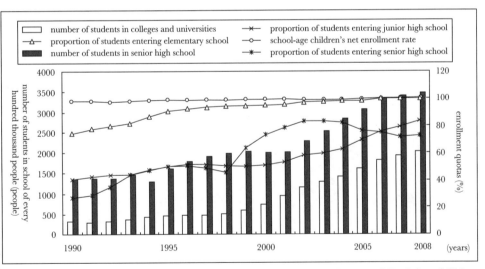

Data from "New China's Population for 60 Years" of the National Bureau of Statistics of China, published by China Statistics Press in 2009.

Figure 16.12: Average Number of Enrolled Students, Enrollment Rate and Enrollment Quotas in All Schools

INDEX

Langfang, 90
late stage of industrialization, 211–212
Law of Land Management, 286
Law of Rural Land Contracting, 286
Law on Compulsory Education, 99
lead pollution, 143
leisure activity, 32
lodging, 27, 45–46, 101, 190
low-end processed products, 57
low-income group, 25, 39–40, 71, 133

Macao, 46
manager stratum, 210
manufacturing industry, 2, 45–46, 52,
 127, 129, 131, 157–158, 224 n. 2,
 226, 235
marriage and blood relationship, 162
mass consumption, 14, 21
mathematics contest, 98–99, 103
medical and health expenditure,
 246–247
medical insurance, 5, 15, 41, 71–76, 85,
 106–113, 189, 239, 251, 258
medical insurance system, 5, 74
medical reform, 71–73, 105–107, 109,
 111–112, 114, 116, 246
medical security system, 15, 19, 74,
 106–110, 112–113, 239
medicine as income, 117, 119
medicine bid, 118–120
medium stage of industrialization, 199,
 211–212
migrant workers, 49, 255, 262
miniaturization of the family,
 175, 202
Ministry of Education, 4, 87, 91, 94, 97,
 100, 102–103, 152
Ministry of Finance, 73, 109, 144–145,
 242, 244, 258, 266
mobs, 123, 126
murder, 122, 132, 136, 198, 263

National energy conservation
 propaganda week, 153
national investment, 153
National Program for Medium- and
 Long-term Educational Reform and
 Development, 90, 102
National security, 12
negotiation mechanism, 113, 267
Netizens, 70, 103
New Medical Reform, 105–109,
 111–116, 119

New Medical Reform Plan, 71–72,
 105–109, 112–116, 119–120
new rural endowment insurance system,
 6, 76, 78, 80, 279
NGO, 191
non-agricultural family-run operations,
 185–186
non-governmental education, 89–90
nuclear electricity, 157

off-farm worker, 82, 104, 206, 210, 214,
 216, 223, 224 n. 2, 225–226, 228,
 230, 233–236, 255–256, 262–264,
 267–268, 275–277, 279, 292
one child policy, 174, 219
organized crime, 6–7, 122, 136
outside social support, 191

patriotism, 177
Payment for medical security, 114
Peasant, 4, 31, 185–186, 281–282,
 284–285, 292
peasant workers, 4, 6, 10, 52, 54–55,
 59, 61, 65–66, 74, 80–82, 125–127
peasant workers endowment insurance,
 80
Personal consumption pattern, 27
personal savings, 3, 38
pharmaceutical policy, 116
pharmaceutical production, 117
planned economic system, 206
planned economy, 118, 203, 205, 211,
 217, 237
pollutant discharge reduction, 139–142,
 149, 152–153, 157–158, 244
pollution, 11, 139–140, 142–149,
 151–156, 158–159
pollution liability insurance, 147
population birth peak, 219–220
population bonus, 221
Pornography, 123, 136
preferential policy in taxes, 186
President Obama, 71
private businessmen stratum, 210
productivity level, 197
Promoting the livelihood of the
 people, 106
propaganda, 74, 84, 151, 153, 160
propensity for consumption, 35–36,
 39–41
public expenditure for rural schools, 278
public finance, 75, 237, 242, 290
public medical insurance fund, 112